# THE

# WIDOW

# WAVE

# THE
# WIDOW
# WAVE

*A True Courtroom Drama*
*of Tragedy at Sea*

## Jay W. Jacobs

QUID PRO BOOKS

New Orleans, Louisiana

35/0577

Published in 2014 by Quid Pro Books.

ISBN  978-1-61027-262-9  (pbk)
ISBN  978-1-61027-273-5  (hbk)
ISBN  978-1-61027-263-6  (ebk)

QUID PRO BOOKS
Quid Pro, LLC
5860 Citrus Blvd., suite D-101
New Orleans, Louisiana 70123
*www.quidprobooks.com*

𝐪𝐩

Publisher's Cataloging-in-Publication

Jacobs, Jay W.
    The widow wave : a true courtroom drama of tragedy at sea / Jay W. Jacobs.
        p. cm.
    ISBN 978-1-61027-262-9 (pbk)

1. Jacobs, Jay W.—Trials, litigation, etc. 2. California—Trials, litigation, etc. 3. Boating accidents—Trials, litigation, etc. I. Title.

KD378.C45.J82 2014                                      812'.31.5—dc22
                                                        2014431789
                                                        CIP

Front cover image adapted from photograph © by Mana Photo, used by permission. Author photograph provided courtesy of Marsha Jacobs.

*For*

*Three strong women in my life*

My wife Marsha

My mother Elizabeth

Janet Dowd


*I Owe You All So Much*

"There are no roses

on a sailor's grave,

no lilies

on an ocean wave.

The only tributes

are the seagulls sweep,

and the teardrops that

the sweetheart

weeps."

— *Anonymous*

# A Note to the Reader

A number of years have passed since the events in this true story occurred concerning the worst recreational fishing boat accident that ever happened in San Francisco, and the subsequent trial. When I decided to write this story, the trial transcript was no longer available. In preparation for writing, I reviewed the court clerk's file, interviewed some of the people involved, revisited many of the locations, and conducted research. The following reference works were referred to: the United States Coast Pilot, various charts, tide and current logs, the Coast Guard report concerning the disappearance of the *Aloha*, documents from the National Weather Service, the Coroner's office autopsy report, and what remained of my case file, memoranda and notes.

Much of the book is in dialogue form. Words stated within quotation marks are reconstructed from my memory. While not word for word, they are the substance of what was said, and I believe them to be a true and accurate reconstruction.

The feelings and emotions I describe in others are as I remember and interpret them. While I make no claim of omniscience, I believe that feelings such as joy, fear, anger, love and frustration are capable of almost universal understanding. Where such feelings and reactions in others are stated, they are my interpretations, unless otherwise noted.

The parts of the story where I attempt to portray what may have happened to the boat, and what the men onboard may have done, are based on my conversations with boat operators, experts in the fields of oceanography, meteorology, and navigation, and my own experiences at sea.

# THE

# WIDOW

# WAVE

# 1

In the entire case, the only fact that everyone involved agreed on was this: at some point during his long flight from Manila to San Francisco, H. Tho Ang flew right over the beginnings of the storm that, a few days later, would take his life. It would be the worst recreational fishing boat accident ever to happen in San Francisco's long maritime history.

If Mr. Ang had looked out through his window to the ocean below, nothing would have aroused a premonition of danger. The winds churning the ocean's surface into a mass of white-capped waves scarcely seem ominous when viewed from 39,000 feet.

As the plane flew eastward across the Pacific, a meteorological reaction of major proportion was rapidly evolving. Two different and very dangerous air masses had converged and were interacting. A fast moving accumulation of frigid air, which originated in the Siberian Arctic, was hurtling toward a swirling mass of unusually warm tropical air that had been hovering over the Central Pacific for weeks. The two weather fronts collided 1,500 miles northeast of Hawaii . . . a ticking meteorological time bomb that would explode a few days later.

Acting like David's sling, the storm's violently spinning epicenter would hurl the thirty and forty foot waves it created toward the California coast, two thousand miles away.

Cruising in the calm air of the upper atmosphere, the airliner was completely unaffected by the events taking place on the ocean's surface. For all the effect it had on the plane, the storm brewing below could just as easily have been occurring on another planet.

**2**

Omiyakon is a remote village located in the vast drainage basin of the Lena River in far eastern Siberia. Winter begins in September, and does not relinquish its icy grip until May, nine long months later. The brief summer is from June to August. There is no spring or fall.

Despite its tiny size and isolated location near the Arctic Circle, Omiyakon has a unique characteristic differentiating it from any other place: it is the coldest inhabited place on earth. One year the thermometer dropped to a world record low temperature of minus 90 degrees below zero.

The extreme cold makes the Lena basin one of the most inhospitable places on the planet. In the dead of winter, the words 'below' and 'zero' always seem to be used together.

Omiyakon's residents seldom venture out alone; a breakdown on a deserted track could be fatal. At zero degrees Fahrenheit, frostbite attacks exposed skin in fifteen minutes. At minus 40, water begins to freeze in a matter of seconds, and at minus 60, steel can shatter like glass.

In this brutally cold environment there is one unexpected element of beauty: at exceptionally low temperatures a deep breath expelled into the bone dry arctic air freezes instantly, forming miniature ice crystals that make a tinkling sound as they float downwards.

The Lena basin has one other distinction not noted in any record book. Despite its unbelievable frigidness, the basin is the birthplace of some of the earth's most catastrophic storms; not the arctic blizzards one would expect . . . but major tropical storms.

Every winter the mountain ranges surrounding the basin trap huge masses of bitterly cold arctic air. The impounded air builds to a point where the mountains can no longer contain it. Propelled by the arctic jet stream, the massed air begins to flow over the mountain crests, taking it thousands of miles southeastwards toward the tropical air in the mid-Pacific. This phenomenon of fast moving arctic air is referred to by meteorologists as the 'Siberian Express.'

When a significant drop in temperature occurs in an area the size of the Lena basin, the collected weight of billions of compacted air molecules results in a substantial increase in barometric pressure.

Two weeks before Mr. Ang's flight, masses of cold arctic air had blanketed the Lena basin, raising the barometric pressure to an unusually high 30.59 pounds per square inch. North of Hawaii, just the opposite effect was taking place. The heat of the sun expanded the air molecules, dropping the barometric pressure to 28.99 psi. When the icy arctic air converged with the mass of swirling tropical air, its warmth pulled the cold air into its vortex like a spider's mating dance.

The seemingly insignificant difference between the 30.59 barometric pressure in the Lena basin, and the 28.99 pressure north of Hawaii, was a textbook example of a major tropical storm being born.

It was over these beginnings that Mr. Ang flew.

# 3

When the incident occurred, I was defending a client in a month-long trial in San Francisco. The pressure of preparing for each day in court interrupted my usual routine of reading the morning paper, but I heard on the evening news about a fishing boat named the *Aloha,* with five men onboard, that had disappeared outside the Golden Gate. Later broadcasts indicated an extensive sea and air search had been conducted by the Coast Guard, but no survivors were found.

A week later, I read in Sunday's *San Francisco Chronicle* an article with the lead line "The Graveyard of Ships." The story caught my attention because of my interest in maritime matters. Fifteen years earlier I had been a sailor in the merchant marine. Over a two and a half year period, I had sailed many of the world's trade routes on cargo ships, ore carriers and tankers, mostly old tramp ships bound for unexotic ports in the Far East, or voyages nobody else wanted like crossing the North Atlantic in mid-winter.

The "Graveyard" story focused on the hazards created by the seven-mile-long sand bar that surrounds the entrance to the Golden Gate. The article recounted the grim history of the number of vessels that had come to grief, and the hundreds of lives lost, in the treacherous waters around the San Francisco Bar since the Gold Rush era. The reporter theorized the *Aloha* may have been steered too close to the edge of the Bar, similar to an event that occurred a year earlier when three men were swept overboard by an unexpected rogue wave.

In the succeeding days, there were news reports of other incidents involving large waves which caught a lot of people off guard, resulting in a total of eleven deaths.

Due to the press of the trial, I had not followed the stories closely, but it seemed odd that so many incidents occurred at a time when the weather was not particularly stormy. It was early March with its usual quota of rainy days, but there had been no high winds. After a few days, the incidents involving the storm waves were replaced by other news stories.

The interest I had in the sea was a mystery to my family. I was born in Chicago, a long way from the ocean, and no one on either side of the family had any involvement in the shipping industry. Both grandfathers were railroad men, and my father was a lawyer. In high school I watched him try a number of cases. Although I found them interesting, they sparked no desire in me to follow in his footsteps. I wanted to be in the shipping business. After obtaining my seamen's papers, I worked during college summer breaks in the merchant marine. Upon graduation, I continued sailing for a short while. Tiring of long voyages at sea, I obtained a job in the operations section of a shipping company in New York, and later was promoted to the chartering department. I liked the shipping industry, but the opportunities for advancement were few, eventually leading to my decision to attend law school in San Francisco. This decision pleased my father, but when I told him in my final year that I would not join him in Chicago where he had built up a substantial practice, he was disappointed. I felt I would be standing in the long shadow of his reputation as an excellent trial lawyer and never know if I was making it on my own merits.

After passing the California Bar examination, I went into practice on my own in San Francisco. Dad warned me that getting established would be a slow process, but I gradually built my practice to the point where I had two associates, mostly defending people who had been sued in civil actions. I made a specialty of maritime matters and found my experience at sea very helpful in handling boat cases. I also discovered admiralty and maritime law was a difficult area to master, and it had taken a number of years to gain a sound understanding of its intricacies.

My first office was in an old building downtown. When the practice expanded enough to hire an associate, I moved to the brand new Embarcadero Center with a view overlooking the harbor. This was where I met Marsha, my future wife. One afternoon after returning from court, I stepped into the elevator. A moment later, a tall blonde dressed in a knee length skirt entered. I've always loved freckles, and immediately noticed her legs were sprinkled with them. I was busy staring when the legs started moving, and she was off the elevator. Before I gathered my wits to notice which floor we were on, the doors closed and the elevator continued upwards.

A month passed before I saw her again. Deciding to act quickly before she once again disappeared, I stoked up my courage and introduced myself. We chatted briefly and, to my astonishment, I learned she was a private investigator. Not long afterwards we began dating, and eventually we married.

Halfway through the long trial I was in, the judge ended one of the sessions early and I was back in the office by midafternoon. I hadn't been at my desk long before Lee Carlson from Allstate Insurance Company called. In the past, Lee asked me to defend a few of the boat owners they insured who had been sued.

He asked how the trial was going, and then got into the reason for his call.

"Jay, we issued a boat owner's liability policy on a thirty-four foot cabin cruiser. The boat was out salmon fishing a little more than a week ago, and disappeared. The owner, his son, and three other men were onboard. The Coast Guard conducted an extensive sea and air search, but found no trace of the boat. There are no survivors, and no witnesses have been located. No bodies have been recovered. All the men are presumed to have drowned. There may be litigation concerning this matter and I'd like your thoughts concerning liability."

As Lee was talking, the similarity between what he was describing and the "Graveyard of Ships" article came to mind.

"Are you talking about the boat that was mentioned in last Sunday's paper?" I asked.

"Yes. Francis Dowd, the man who owned the *Aloha*, was our policy-holder. There is a total of $1,100,000 coverage on the boat." He then added the *Aloha* had been burglarized a few months earlier and some of the navigation equipment had been stolen.

I heaved a sigh. "Lee, that could be real trouble. I suggest you follow up on this right away. Certain safety equipment such as life jackets, fire extinguishers, and signaling devices are mandated by law to be on a boat. If your man sailed without the legally required equipment, it would clearly be negligent."

I thought for a moment. "The owner's wife is probably too upset to talk with you right now. Is there anyone else you can speak with to find out about the safety equipment?"

He said he would look into it.

I told him with five men missing, the Coast Guard would thoroughly investigate the incident, and suggested he call the Marine Safety Office at

Coast Guard headquarters in Alameda to confirm an investigation had been started.

"All right, I'll call them. When your trial is over, think about any potential liability issues that might come up and get back to me when you can."

I said there might be some special rules in admiralty law that apply, and I would do some legal research work before I called him back.

The following week, before my trial was over, Lee called again. He told me the Coast Guard was investigating the disappearance, but so far no witnesses had been found who had seen the *Aloha* that morning.

I asked him to tell me about the men onboard the boat.

"The boat owner, Francis Dowd, was a senior executive with Raytheon. His son, Gerald, was also onboard. He was a nineteen year old college freshman, apparently home for spring break. The other men were John Kennedy, who was Francis Dowd's brother in law, Werner Buntmann, an executive at Raytheon, and a man named H. Tho Ang, also known as Andy Ang. He was visiting from Manila and had a business relationship with Raytheon. Ang and Dowd were friends as well as business acquaintances. The men were going to the Duxbury Reef area for salmon fishing." Lee asked if I knew where that was.

I said Duxbury was a popular spot for salmon, and I had been there a number of times myself.

Then I asked whether he'd learned anything about the missing safety equipment.

"The boat was kept at the Sausalito marina, and I've ordered a copy of the Sausalito Police Department burglary report to see exactly what was taken. I've been in touch with Mrs. Dowd, the widow of the boat owner. She told me replacements for some of the stolen items had been purchased. She is going to search through the credit card receipts and checkbook, and make a list of them."

I suggested that he have an investigator canvass the waterfront for witnesses right away.

"The Coast Guard told me inquiries were made, but no witnesses came forward," he responded.

"Lee, the Coast Guard's method of finding witnesses is to put the word out for anyone who knows something to contact them, which is not the same thing as a witness canvass. It doesn't seem possible that a thirty-four foot boat could go out fishing without somebody seeing it. I suggest you contact Muni Bait Shop in San Francisco."

Lee was not a fisherman, and asked me to explain.

"The Muni Bait Shop acts as the booking agent for the party boats berthed at Fisherman's Wharf. The party boats take sport fishermen out on salmon fishing trips as fare paying passengers."

He asked what the likelihood was that a lawsuit would be filed, bearing in mind the circumstances of no survivors, no witnesses, and the vessel disappearing.

"A lot will depend on what's in the Coast Guard report. If they determine the *Aloha* had not been properly maintained, or the legally required safety equipment was not onboard, those are obvious negligence issues. If Mr. Dowd did not have sufficient training to operate the boat, or was inexperienced in taking it out on the ocean, those would be negligence problems too."

I continued: "As soon as the trial is over I'll get back to you regarding potential liability issues, probably in a week or so."

When the trial ended, and I caught up with the pile of work accumulated on my desk, I turned my attention to the research work I'd promised Lee. The first case I looked at involved the *S.S. Marine Sulphur Queen*. The case had been extensively covered in the textbook for the course I had taken on admiralty law.

Reading the case brought back a memory of learning about sulfur tankers from a conversation that took place back in my days as a sailor. I had walked into the hiring hall in New Orleans, and a friend I'd sailed with before waved me over to join a domino game. Shipping was slow at the time. A discussion was going on about which ships were due to crew up, and the prospects of getting a berth on one of them. One of the players commented if we were in a hurry to get shipped out, he'd heard they were having trouble getting a crew on the *Louisiana Sulphur*. None of us had heard of the ship, and he gave a description of its usual run from loading ports in the Gulf up to the East Coast, carrying cargoes of molten sulfur. Tankers running coastwise clean their cargo tanks on the return voyage back to the Gulf. Tank cleaning is a lot of work, frequently involving twelve to fourteen hours a day until the vessel arrives back at the loading port in the Gulf. One of the other players cut in, saying the reason they have trouble getting crews on the sulfur ships was that they could explode. Everyone looked up from their dominoes, giving him full attention. He told us a ship called the *Marine Sulphur Queen* had sailed from a port in Texas for the East Coast, and nobody heard from the vessel again. It disappeared without a trace. Not a single soul onboard survived, and no bodies were ever found.

He looked at us, one at a time. "It's nice to make a lot of overtime, but it's nice to live too."

In the prolonged silence that followed, the domino game ground to a halt, everyone at the table deep in thought. Many of the men were old timers who survived many disasters at sea. What must have been running through their minds was the calamity sailors fear most, fires and explosions. Ashore, a fire can be fought for as long as it takes, and if the blaze gets ahead of the firefighters, they can back off. At sea, there's no escape.

After the game broke up my friend asked me to join him for a cup of coffee, and asked if I was considering getting a berth on one of the sulfur ships. I shook my head. If I'd said I was thinking about it, he would have done everything he could to dissuade me. I respected the dedication of men like him who willingly spent their lives at sea in a difficult and dangerous profession, not because of the wages, which were not a lot, but because they loved seafaring.

There is an undefinable attraction to the sea for some men. Mostly it's a lonely job, separating them from their families and friends for months at a time, entailing hard, dangerous work with long sea passages, sometimes as long as a month between ports. It's not for everyone, but for those who choose it as their profession, there is nothing else.

When I finished the research work, Lee and I met to discuss the results and review the information he had gathered. Referring to his notes, he said, "Here's what I've learned about the heirs of the guests onboard: Mr. Ang left a widow and five children. Dowd's brother in law, John Kennedy, was married, but they had no children. Werner Buntmann left two adult sons. His wife died before the incident."

Lee looked up from his notes. "Jay, you mentioned there might be some cases or statutes relevant to the liability issues. Tell me how they might apply to the *Aloha?*"

I gave myself a moment before responding, "One case in particular may be applicable: *In Re The S.S Marine Sulphur Queen.*" Lee had never heard of the case and asked me to outline its relevance. I told him the *Sulphur Queen* had sailed from a loading port in Texas bound for the East Coast. It disappeared without a trace, and there were no survivors and no witnesses to what happened to the vessel. Lawsuits had been filed by the heirs of the men onboard. During the trial, the judge established an important new legal precedent applicable to incidents where there are no survivors, no witnesses, and no vessel.

"The judge ruled that since some *prima facie* evidence had been introduced by the plaintiffs indicating the ship owner was negligent—"

Shaking his head, Lee cut in, "Jay, give it to me in English please."

I explained: "The legal term '*prima facie* evidence' means evidence that would establish a fact or a presumption concerning negligence on the part of the vessel owner, if such evidence was not countered."

Lee stared at me incredulously. "Let me see if I understand you correctly. Are you saying the usual rule of law that applies in automobile and other negligence cases, where the burden is on the plaintiff to prove that the defendant's negligence was the cause of an accident, will not apply to this incident involving Mr. Dowd's boat?"

I replied, "This rule of maritime law is what differentiates cases involving vessels from ordinary negligence lawsuits. If a *prima facie* showing of negligence is made by a plaintiff, a burden is then placed on the vessel owner to produce evidence that his actions were not the cause of the loss. In the *Sulphur Queen* case, the judge held that since there were no witnesses, no survivors, and no vessel, there was no way the *Queen's* owner could meet that burden and they lost the case."

The similarities between the loss of the *Sulphur Queen* and the disappearance of the *Aloha* were nearly identical. The portrait of disbelief on Lee's face made it amply plain he did not like the idea that the *Sulphur Queen* rule might apply if a lawsuit were to be filed regarding the *Aloha*.

# 4

A few months later, Lee sent a copy of his investigation file. A copy of the report prepared by the marine surveyor Francis Dowd hired to inspect the *Aloha* before he bought it was included. The few recommended repairs had been done prior to the purchase.

There was no notation in the file that the investigation work I suggested several times—to locate witnesses through the Muni Bait Shop—had been done.

The last item in the file was a copy of the autopsy report from the San Francisco County Coroner's Office on Francis Dowd. This came as a complete surprise. No one had mentioned anything to me about bodies being recovered. Mr. Dowd's body had been discovered in San Francisco Bay without a life jacket. The cause of death was listed as: "Unknown. Apparent drowning." Attached to the autopsy was the toxicology report. I read through it quickly. The last sentence leaped off the page: "Blood Ethyl Alcohol = 0.08%." Ethyl alcohol is the scientific term for the type of alcohol found in alcoholic beverages. A .08 finding would mean Dowd was legally drunk. I reread the "0.08%" notation several times to make certain the decimal point was in the right place. It was.

Lee had previously given me a copy of the memorandum he made of his meeting with Mrs. Dowd. I tore through my file, found the memo, and read it again. She had told Lee beer was occasionally brought onboard for his friends, but her husband did not drink beer, and according to her, no excessive drinking had ever taken place on the boat.

After reading the Coroner's report for the third time, I set it aside. When my blood pressure subsided enough to think clearly, I started reflecting on the realities of the situation. Why wouldn't Mrs. Dowd have said what she had to Carlson? Of course she'd told Lee her husband didn't drink on the boat. Three people she cared about deeply—her husband, her son and her brother-in-law—were dead, along with two other men, and she was now a widow. With all of this devastation on her shoulders, maybe she was entitled to rearrange some of her recollections. Mrs. Dowd would hardly be the first widow to engage in some form of protective self-denial about her late husband.

I told myself if a lawsuit were to be filed, there would be plenty of time to explain to her that the toxicology screening performed by the Coroner's office was an objective test to determine the amount of alcohol in a person's system, and she would not be helping herself by making statements that her husband never drank on the boat in face of objective evidence to the contrary. If she was as sensible as Lee said, I should be able to appeal to her sense of reason not to put her credibility in jeopardy by making statements that would be exposed as false by an objective lab test.

It was imperative to immediately engage the services of a toxicologist to go through the report to see if anything could be done. And not just any toxicologist, but someone thoroughly familiar with the testing protocols followed by the San Francisco Coroner's office, preferably someone who used to work there. If Dowd had two or three drinks in his system at the time of the incident, Houdini couldn't defend the case.

An attorney friend recommended Phillip Reynolds, the former chief medical examiner in the Coroner's office. I called Reynolds and engaged him as an expert consultant. He was noncommittal about what might be done until he had a chance to review the report. I told him it would be in his office that afternoon.

A few days later, Reynolds called back. "The proper protocols were followed, and the findings by the toxicology lab are correct."

I listened in stunned silence as his words dashed my hopes of finding some error in the testing.

"Turn to the page concerning the instructions given to the toxicology lab about what to use for the test sample." I found the section. It stated, "Red Purge Liquid."

He explained. "In lay terms, purge liquids means stomach contents, not blood. These fluids cannot be used to determine the presence of alcohol in your client's system at the time of death."

Hearing the tremor in my voice, I asked, "If the alcohol in this purge liquid wasn't from drinking, where did it come from?" and readied myself for an answer I didn't want to hear.

"Over a period of time, alcohol is produced in a deceased person's internal organs as a natural result of bodily decomposition. It will depend on how long the body was in the water."

"How much time are we talking about?" I asked, holding my breath.

He thought a moment. "Alcohol would be produced through decomposition within a matter of days, certainly after a week." He asked what the date of the incident was. I told him March 9th.

"Well," he responded, ". . . the body was found a month after that, so the chances are the alcohol in your man's body was the result of natural decomposition, not alcoholic beverage consumption."

"Could the Coroner take a different position if he were called as an expert witness by a plaintiffs' lawyer?" I asked.

Unaccountably, Reynolds began guffawing. I braced myself for some sort of macabre Coroner's Office humor I was not at all in the mood for. When he regained control of himself, he said, "He'd better not. In fact, I know he won't."

A moment of dread swept over me, envisioning Reynolds had called the Coroner and improperly interceded with him in some way. If that happened, it would be a disaster. He then finished his thought, "I know he won't because I trained him, and he isn't about to say anything that can't be supported medically."

This was a huge relief. If the .08% alcohol reading was attributable to drinking, it would have made the case indefensible.

After hanging up, I put a note in the file about our conversation. When I finished, I gave a silent apology to Mrs. Dowd for doubting what she had told Carlson about her husband.

# 5

One day before the statute of limitations would have barred the case, a lawsuit was filed on behalf of Jane Ang, Andy Ang's widow, and her five children.

The Complaint alleged Francis Dowd had negligently caused the death of Mr. Ang. It additionally alleged that the *Aloha* was unseaworthy. Under maritime law, the term 'unseaworthy' means that a vessel was in some manner improperly operated, equipped or maintained. The complaint also made reference to '. . . violation of Coast Guard regulations,' which meant the plaintiffs were alleging that the safety equipment required by law was not onboard the *Aloha*.

The lawsuit was filed by the Law Offices of David B. Baum, a prominent and very successful plaintiffs' firm in San Francisco. Martin Blake, a lawyer in the firm, would be handling the case. I had never tried a case against Blake, but had worked on several cases with him before and knew he would be a formidable opponent.

Blake was born and educated in England, including his legal education, and practiced there for a number of years before coming to the United States. He possessed a fine speaking voice which, in combination with his refined British accent and mannerisms, made a notable impression.

Lee informed me that since the matter was now in litigation, a claims specialist in the San Jose office, Marjorie Fraiser, had been assigned to the matter.

After filing the Answer to the Complaint, I turned to the urgent priority of trying to locate witnesses. At the top of the list was the Muni Bait Shop, the party boat booking agent, located at the foot of Russian Hill.

I had been there many times; it was always a special experience. Floor to ceiling shelving lined the walls. Even the ceiling had been pressed into use with fishing poles, dip nets, and rod cases hanging down. The well-worn display cases were the store's centerpiece, their glass tops scratched nearly opaque by hundreds of fishermen examining lures, hooks, and dozens of other items of fishing tackle on display. Muni Bait was not a place to go without a shopping list kept firmly in mind. I'd never visited the place and left empty handed.

Presiding over this realm of fishing fantasies were the Zydeck Brothers, John and Eddy, who customarily communicated with each other by bellowing from opposite ends of the store. I dropped by the shop one morning, occupying myself in selecting a few packages of hooks with pre-tied leaders I needed, and waited for Eddy to get off the phone.

He was arranging a fishing trip for someone. I watched as he made entries on a large printed form that I remembered from booking my own salmon fishing trips. When he finished writing, he read back the information he had just obtained from the caller ... the person's name and phone number, the name of the boat he had been booked on, and the date. He then hung up. The shop was now nearly empty, and I went up to the counter with the packet of hooks I needed and introduced myself. I came in only three or four times a year, and he didn't remember me.

To lead into my reason for being in the store, I began conversationally: "I've had good luck with the rod and reel outfit you sold me, and appreciate your advice to buy a Penn Reel for my new salmon rig. They really are the Cadillac of fishing reels; I've had no problems with it."

While he was ringing up my purchase, I continued: "I'm doing some investigation about the fishing boat with five men onboard that went down last March." He grunted a recollection of hearing about the incident, commenting it was the worst he could recall.

"You a lawyer?" he asked.

When I said "Yes," he continued: "What kind of investigation are you doing?"

The change in his demeanor after mention of the word lawyer told me I had about two minutes with him, and the conversation would be over.

"I'm trying to find someone who may have seen the boat that morning—"

He interrupted me. "Talk to the Coast Guard, they investigate those things."

"I have," I said, "but they didn't find any witnesses."

He grunted again, saying he was unaware of anyone who had knowledge about the incident, adding with a note of finality, "I don't see how I can help you."

Undeterred, I continued: "I've been booking my salmon trips with you for a number of years, and when I lived nearby I'd come into the shop to do it. I noticed when you booked me for a trip you'd take down my name and phone number for a particular boat. I'd like to look at your booking sheets for the party boats that were out on March 9th. Maybe someone onboard saw the boat that went down or knows something that would be helpful."

"There aren't any records," he said.

I repeated, "What I'd like to do is look at the sign-up sheets, the ones with the people's names and phone numbers."

"We don't have them," he replied firmly.

The conversation was going nowhere, and my time rapidly coming to an end. What was the matter with him! He had just made a booking not two minutes earlier. I was standing less than ten feet away, and he had to see me watching him write down the person's name and number. I didn't want to force the issue by pointing out the obviousness of this to him, but I had to get him off his position, and fast. A thought flashed about what the problem might be. I had defended enough small businessmen to know their record keeping was typically haphazard, frequently consisting of documents stuffed into shoe boxes and dumped in a dusty corner of a back room.

I spoke quickly, "I know you're busy, and I don't want to waste your time, but I'm defending this widow lady, and I have to do everything I can to find anyone who might know something. I'll be glad to pay for your time to look for the booking sheets. If you are too busy, just show me where you keep the records and I'll look for the day in question, right here in the store," quickly adding, ". . . under your complete supervision, of course."

Before I finished speaking, he was shaking his head. "Like I told you, we don't have records that far back, okay?" and handed me the bag with my hooks. The conversation was over.

I headed back to the office along the Embarcadero on the northern waterfront, angry and frustrated. It was a little before noon, and I decided to stop for something to eat at Red's.

Red's Java House is precariously perched on the edge of one of the piers. This tiny five table place makes a special grilled hot dog sandwich, actually two dogs served on a sour dough roll. I never ate inside at Red's, preferring to take my 'double doggie' and sit outdoors. The large open pier behind Red's provided a perfect place for lunch al fresco, and the quiet I needed to think. The salt air and watching the passing ships soon had the desired effect.

As I reviewed what happened, it dawned on me: if there were no records, there was probably a simple explanation why. This was partly a cash business for the party boat skippers, and the sign-up sheets would be kept only as long as it took to square up the accounts and then tossed.

Between the passengers onboard the party boats on March 9, plus the boat skippers and their crews, the sheets would have provided a hundred potential witnesses to contact. Surely someone would know something relevant to the incident, or at least seen the *Aloha*. It was too late now. I mentally crossed off this rich source of potential witnesses.

Next on my list was to contact the Coast Guard and arrange a meeting to go over their extensive investigation and report concerning the loss of the *Aloha*. The Coast Guard investigates most accidents involving injuries. The report involving the *Aloha* was particularly thorough because of the large loss of life involved. If the case went to trial, the report would be used by both sides. I noted the investigation report had been prepared by Chief Warrant Officer Dennis George, and signed off by Lieutenant Commander James McCartin. I called Officer George who readily agreed to meet with me in his office located at Coast Guard Headquarters on Alameda Island, on the other side of San Francisco Bay. When I arrived, the receptionist informed me Officer George was in a staff meeting.

In due course George emerged from his meeting. Extending his hand, he said, "I am sorry to keep you waiting. I have a conference room for us."

We walked down the corridor to a spartanly furnished meeting room. He had a file under his arm.

George had the kind of face that made guessing his age difficult, one of those perpetually youthful looking types that no one wants to stand next to when a class reunion photograph is taken. He could have been any age from twenty-five to his early forties. He opened the file which I interpreted as an invitation to get down to the purpose of my visit.

"I appreciate your meeting with me on such short notice. As I said on the phone, I am here concerning the loss of the fishing boat, the *Aloha*. I represent Mrs. Dowd who is the widow of the boat operator. A lawsuit has been filed claiming her husband was at fault, and I am defending her. The purpose of my visit is to go over a few things in the report."

He nodded and said he would be glad to answer my questions. I looked at the list I had prepared. "Were you the sole investigating officer?"

"Yes I was."

He had a copy of the report in front of him, and I directed his attention to a section at the bottom of the first page. "I see there is a notation

indicating that a certain Coast Guard form, identified as 'the long narrative form,' was not utilized."

He looked where I was pointing and nodded.

"What is that form, and why wasn't it used?" I asked.

He thought for a moment. "I felt since there were no survivors or witnesses, no real purpose would be served by utilizing the longer form."

I nodded and replied, "When I read the report initially, I thought perhaps you wanted to use the long narrative form and the idea had been
overruled."

I put this to him as an aside, but it was really a question. I didn't want
George to take offense, but if he had filled out the long form, even in rough
draft, I was very interested in seeing it. He shook his head.

As we conversed, I was trying to assess what impression he would
make if he were called as a witness. He was well spoken with no accent
indicating where he had been raised. I mentioned serving in the merchant
marine, and being on ships the Coast Guard had inspected, commenting,
"Sometimes it gets pretty hectic trying to get the ship's regular work done
at the same time the Coast Guard is onboard making an inspection."

He indicated the inspections I referred to were a large part of his duties, and he enjoyed visiting the big ships . . . "Although I don't always get
the level of cooperation I would like from the ship's officers."

When I responded, "So you get a little of that: 'Psssst . . . the inspector's here,'" he laughed heartily.

I returned to my list of questions. "Could you tell me what you did to
locate witnesses?"

"Inquiries were made, but no one came forward. If any witnesses had
been interviewed, I would have noted that in the report."

Trying to get him to elaborate, I asked, "Sometimes people claim to
know something, but when they are interviewed it turns out they just
heard something and not actually seen anything themselves, or merely
had an opinion. Did anyone like that come forward?"

"I don't recall that, but my practice is to keep notes on everything I do
during an investigation, including who I spoke with," and he began looking through the file.

After searching it thoroughly, he continued: "I did what I usually do,
which is to discard my field notes after the report is in final form."

His glance toward the wall clock indicated my time was about up. The
point had arrived anyway to put my main question to him. As casually as I
could, I commented on the tentative manner in which his conclusions had
been stated.

He showed no sign of being offended, and replied, "My conclusion was that the *Aloha* had been capsized."

I asked if he had any other thoughts about what might have happened, hoping he would speculate on other possible causes.

Keeping his face an unreadable blank, he said the loss could have been for any number of causes, but would not be drawn out on specifics.

Changing the subject, he asked, "Do you think this case will go to trial?"

I responded noncommittally that I had to treat every case as if it would, and be fully prepared.

He accompanied me to the end of the hallway. While we were walking out, he mentioned he had looked through the records kept at the Alameda base, and spoken with people at Coast Guard Headquarters in Washington; it appeared the *Aloha* incident was the worst sport fishing boat accident that ever happened in San Francisco.

As we shook hands, he seemed sincere when he said to call him anytime if he could be of further assistance.

Recounting our meeting on the drive back to the office, the thing that struck me most was his response when I inquired if he had considered any theories other than what was in his report and later rejected them, and he had not responded directly.

George had been helpful, not so much for the information he provided, but in eliminating the possibility that people not mentioned in his report had been contacted.

Having completed the investigation work that might have turned up witnesses through Muni Bait Shop and the Coast Guard, and come up empty, I turned my attention to preparing a strategy for the discovery phase of the case.

It would be at least a year, and more likely eighteen months, before the case inched its way up the list and received a trial date from the court. This was a wrongful death lawsuit involving a widow with five children, and there was going to be a massive amount of discovery work to do.

# 6

Engaging the right experts does not assure winning a case. Hiring the wrong ones almost guarantees losing it.

I would need experts to help me work up this case, and be available to testify in court if it went to trial. The need was in two areas: a meteorologist to provide expert opinions concerning the weather conditions and the size of the waves on the day of the incident, and another expert to testify about safe boat handling and navigation issues.

An expert must possess an unimpeachable reputation, and be thoroughly knowledgeable about their area of expertise. One other quality is a necessity, and hard to find. They must be able to speak in layman's English. Nothing is worse than an expert on the witness stand droning away, using scientific terminology unintelligible to the average lay person. A jury subjected to that initially becomes confused, then angry, and finally tunes out.

I immediately engaged the services of Captain David Seymour as an expert concerning safe boat handling. I'd worked with him on other maritime cases in the past. He had an excellent reputation, and was not only a licensed ship's captain, but also an engineer. One of Seymour's biggest assets was his ability to simplify complicated matters.

For an expert on wave formation and the weather, I contacted Rae Strange, an oceanographer and meteorologist from Santa Barbara. We had not previously worked together, but he came highly recommended. I called Strange and he agreed to be an expert. In our initial conversation I gave him the date of the incident, and explained that the *Aloha* had left San Francisco Bay heading for the Duxbury Reef area to fish. He said he would contact the National Weather Service and obtain the weather and wave data for the week of the incident. After reviewing the data, he would give me a preliminary opinion about the height of the waves that morning.

It had been a number of years since I had a case where the science of wave formation had been an important issue. As I listened to Strange outline the methodologies he would use to determine the wave heights, it quickly became apparent the little I remembered about how waves are formed had no relevance to this case. I would have to reacquaint myself with the physics of wave formation from the beginning.

I had been tempted to ask Strange to explain the basics to me, but rejected the idea. He had a busy practice, with neither the time nor the inclination to answer a lot of 'A B C' questions from me about wave formation. At the very least, he would expect me to know the fundamentals of the physics involved, and have a basic understanding of the relevant terminology as well.

In past cases when something of a technical nature came up that was unfamiliar to me, I found the most efficient way to learn the basics was to do a search for all the articles I could find pertinent to the subject. By the time I'd digested the material, I had sufficient knowledge to work with an expert.

After spending a few evenings immersed in my search, it became clear the *Aloha* case was going to be an exception to this method. The articles I was finding about wave formation were filled with scientific principles beyond my comprehension. The only option would be to fly down to Santa Barbara for a weekend, and have Strange tutor me in the basic science of wave formation from the beginning.

A few evenings later, I was walking past the local branch of the public library, and stopped to look at the display of newly arrived books in the window. Out of the corner of my eye, I noticed 'story time' taking place. A dozen children, age five or six, were in a semicircle around the reader. Rapt expressions wreathed their faces as the very animated reader enthralled them with the story. The scene brought back memories of story time when I was that age, and fond remembrances of the reader, Ms. Boye, a Norwegian lady with the gentlest voice imaginable. She also introduced us to the joys and uses of the library. "Boys and girls," she would say, ". . . all the world is in these books," dramatically sweeping her hand toward the shelves. "Think of it, everything you will ever want to know about any subject is right here in this room." She instilled my lifelong interest in reading.

In the midst of my reverie about Miss Boye, it suddenly came to me . . . I had been making a terrible mistake. When the technical articles proved to be unfathomable, what I should have been doing was looking in the children's *World Book*, or something like that. They would have articles about waves and weather patterns written in a plain and simple way. I rushed into the library.

It was an evening they closed early, and I had only twenty minutes to find what I wanted. Hurrying over to the children's section, I located the reference books, quickly found the World Book set, and pulled out the W volume. I flipped through the pages to the article on waves and began reading. The article was two or three pages, interspersed with lots of illustrations.

It took an effort to keep from bursting into laughter at the thought running through my head . . . 'This is the kind of reading even a man can understand . . . no big words, no undecipherable formulas, and no confusing diagrams.' All neatly and concisely laid out were the basics of wave formation. The principles I had spent hours trying to make sense of in the technical articles were now revealed in beautiful simplicity.

I checked the time, and began searching for an article about the weather. It was even more informative than the one on waves. As I began to absorb the basics, a feeling of exhilaration welled up inside me as a dawning sense of comprehension came about weather formation.

Suddenly, from behind me a purring sound intruded, breaking my concentration.

"May I help you?" a voice said.

Being only inches from my ear, I was so startled I nearly dropped the book.

It was a librarian. The way she said, "May I help you," sounded more like, "What are you doing here?"

First her tone, and then her increasingly suspicious look, made it clear that I was being assessed as if I were some sort of deviant loitering in the children's section. Doubting she would believe my explanation for being there, I stammered, "I . . . ahh . . . no, no thank you." I stood so quickly the book fell to the table as I bolted for the door, thoroughly embarrassed, and at the same time euphoric at my find.

On the weekend, I returned to the library. After first checking in with the children's librarian with an acceptable explanation for my presence, I spent half the day going through their large selection of children's reference works. They were just what I was looking for. If the case went to trial, I would be able to take the basics of the scientific principles I was reading, and present them in an understandable way to a jury who would have no background in the science of oceanography or wave mechanics.

Brimming with excitement, I made page after page of notes and spent the rest of the weekend absorbing the material I'd read. By Sunday evening, I had the basics of oceanography sufficiently in hand to communicate meaningfully with Rae Strange, and understand his theories.

The first thing Monday morning, I called Strange.

"Rae, I looked at the weather forecast for the 9th of March. The forecast predicted waves five to eight feet high, and wind speeds of ten to twenty knots. If the waves were only that high, they don't seem big enough to capsize the *Aloha*."

He thought for a moment before responding. "I've reviewed the data I obtained from the National Weather Service for the entire week, beginning with March 4th. What I think happened is this: a severe late winter storm that originated northeast of Hawaii a few days earlier, created waves that reached the California coast on March 9th. To find out for sure, I want to get the data from the wave recording buoys in the area."

I wasn't aware of any wave recording devices and asked him to explain.

"There are three specially equipped buoys anchored offshore that measure the height, speed, and length of the incoming waves. Each buoy has a radio transmitter that sends the measurements to shore stations where it's stored in computers. I want to get the data from all three. After reviewing it, I should be able to say whether the swells coming in that morning were big enough to have turned into breaking waves capable of capsizing the *Aloha*."

I asked what was involved in gathering the data and interpreting it.

"Each recording buoy is operated by a different governmental agency. Unfortunately, the data from these buoys is separately archived. One of the recording buoys is run by the U.S. Army Corps of Engineers who are responsible for keeping the Main Ship Channel dredged out for the large ships entering San Francisco. Another is operated by NOAA, the National Oceanographic and Atmospheric Administration. The data from the NOAA buoy is used by the National Weather Service which is a part of that agency. The third buoy is run by the Scripps Institution of Oceanography in La Jolla."

"How much time will it take to get the data?" I asked.

He exhaled in irritation. "I can't even begin to estimate how long it will take to get it from NOAA and the Corps of Engineers. But I have a friend at Scripps who can get their data to me in a few days. Once I have everything, it will take a week to analyze and send you a report."

I requested that he go ahead with his plan.

Next, I turned my attention to meeting Mrs. Dowd. Before doing so, I arranged to meet privately with David Ellison, the Dowds' family lawyer.

He was handling Francis Dowd's Estate, and had been a personal friend as well. If Ellison knew anything of a sensitive nature about Francis Dowd, it would be best if he told me about it without Mrs. Dowd present. As a lawyer, he would understand the necessity that I learn about any negative information, and also be aware that plaintiffs' attorney would have an investigator digging up anything of an adverse nature in Dowd's background.

I met Ellison at his office in Palo Alto, located in one of the new office parks that typify Silicon Valley. The building was a rambling one-story structure surrounded by stately Live Oaks. It would be a pleasant place to work every day. I had spoken with Ellison on the phone a few times, but this was our first meeting.

We settled into his spacious office, which had the comfortable feel of a living room. After a minimum of pleasantries, he asked about the status of the case. Then in a subtle manner, indicating he had put a good deal of thought into making sure he did not appear to be doing so, Ellison began diplomatically quizzing me about my knowledge of admiralty and maritime law, and my experience in handling boating cases. Fielding his questions had the same uneasiness of a job interview, but when he finally finished, Ellison seemed satisfied.

"Janet is going to need good representation; I'm glad you know this area of the law."

I asked Ellison to tell me what he knew about Andy Ang and why he was on the boat that day. He said Ang had a long standing business relationship with Raytheon. The purpose of his trip to the United States was to negotiate a new contract for the management services his company provided Raytheon regarding their manufacturing operations in the Philippines.

Ellison added that Dowd and Ang liked each other from their first meeting, and over time their status as business acquaintances grew into a personal friendship. He commented that Andy's son Dwight was educated in the United States as a physicist, and Dowd had been instrumental in getting him a job at Raytheon.

I asked how Mrs. Dowd was holding up.

"Under the circumstances, she is doing well, but I am worried about her. Three of her four remaining children live close by, and they are a great help to her."

He then informed me that claims totaling five million dollars had been made against the Estate concerning the disappearance of the *Aloha*, and Mrs. Dowd was understandably upset. Ellison wanted to know what the likelihood was that the case would settle.

In response, I said, "Like most personal injury cases, wrongful death actions usually settle, but only after months of discovery and investigation have taken place. Bearing in mind the complexity of the legal and factual issues, if this case settles it will probably be at the court ordered settlement conference, a few weeks before the date set for the trial to start."

I told him I needed to meet with Mrs. Dowd, and asked if I could meet her for the first time in his office. "She will probably feel more comfortable if you are present."

He readily agreed and said he would set it up for the following week.

In the hour it took to drive back to San Francisco from Ellison's office, I reflected on our meeting. I asked him directly if he knew of anything untoward concerning Francis Dowd, and he told me there was nothing he was aware of.

Ellison seemed sincere when he said he had confidence I would protect the interests of a family he was close to. When he said he did not want to involve himself in the defense of the matter, I was immensely relieved. Two lawyers trying a case is like having no lawyer.

There was another thing to think about concerning the upcoming meeting with Mrs. Dowd: a widow is like no other client. Every woman knows that the man who courts her will not be the same man she marries. But whether they are young or old, the recollections of widows about their deceased husbands are markedly different from the way they viewed the same man when he was alive. As a widow, Mrs. Dowd was going to have a heavy emotional investment in this case which could easily cloud her willingness, and maybe even her ability, to be candid about her late husband.

On the day of the meeting, Ellison met me in the reception area and walked me to his office. Mrs. Dowd was seated in one of the client chairs. She put aside a document she had been reading, and ignoring my "Please don't get up," pushed her chair back, and stood to take my hand. She looked younger than I expected, and attempted a smile as we exchanged greetings. If the circumstances were different, I sensed there would have been more warmth involved. As it was, my presence served as an unhappy reminder that she was a widow and a defendant in a lawsuit.

When we were seated, Ellison spoke first: "I have been explaining where the case stands at the moment. I've also outlined your background in maritime cases and your experience at sea, and how that will be of considerable help in understanding the practical aspects of boat handling and navigation." He then gestured for me to begin.

"Mrs. Dowd," I said, "I understand there is a list of everything taken in the burglary of the *Aloha*."

Ellison looked in his file, producing a list of the stolen items, and an inventory of the things that had been purchased to replace some of them: the radar set and antennae, the two-way radio, the flare gun and flares, the ship to shore telephone, and life jackets. When he finished reading the list, Mrs. Dowd entered the conversation for the first time.

"My husband and my son Gerald . . ." The mention of her son's name triggered her first overt emotional reaction. There was no reaching for a handkerchief or stammering; she simply stopped in mid-sentence, plumbing the depths of her emotions, the struggle for control racing over her face. Before Ellison or I could ask if she would like some water, she had herself back in check, continuing from the exact word where she had stopped speaking, ". . . drove up to the Sausalito marina several times just before the accident to work on the boat."

I quickly changed subjects. "Mrs. Dowd, could you give me an idea of how often the *Aloha* was taken out?"

"It was used for pleasure boating on the Bay with our friends and family, and the rest of the time by my husband for fishing. The fishing was for him; I did not care for it, and had only been out once."

I asked her to elaborate on anything she knew about the work that had been done to get the boat ready for the first fishing trip of the season.

She withdrew into silence for an extended period. I searched her blank face, unable to tell if she was having difficulty keeping her emotions in check, or searching her memory for the information I asked about before beginning to speak.

"My husband and son went up a few times to work on the boat. The only thing I recall is they were getting it ready for the start of the season. I'm sorry I can't be more helpful, but I had no interest in fishing, and nothing was discussed with me in detail about what they were doing."

Tentative as they always are, first impressions were starting to form about Mrs. Dowd. She struck me as an extremely well spoken, remarkably poised woman. A note in the file indicated Mrs. Dowd had been born and raised in Massachusetts, I guessed probably from an 'old money' New England family. A naturally private person not given to displaying her emotions, she was completely unpretentious as well, even down to her clothing choices. There was an almost Amish lack of adornment about her; no jewelry and a minimum of makeup, not even lipstick.

After discussing a few more details, it was time to bring the conference to an end. Turning to Mrs. Dowd, I said, "I feel privileged to represent you in this lawsuit. I'm sorry our meeting has to be under these unhappy circumstances."

As we said our goodbyes, I noticed she was struggling to control her emotions.

On the drive back to San Francisco I reflected on the meeting. Her look was one I'd seen before—the sad, mournful face of a widow who understood that every letter, every telephone call, and every meeting would be a reminder that the lawsuit kept her from completing the grieving process. Only time heals a broken heart. Losing a husband was burden enough, and I thought how deeply painful it must be for her to bear the loss of a son as well. Gerald was only nineteen; his life not yet begun.

# 7

The receipt of the first set of interrogatories from the Angs' attorney provided the impetus to have Mrs. Dowd meet with me in my office.

The interrogatories were not complicated; a phone call would have answered any questions she had concerning them. The real purpose of our first private meeting would be to get a sense as to what kind of witness she would make, and gauge what effect the litigation was having on her.

Most important of all, I wanted to learn whether Mrs. Dowd would work with me toward building the critical bond of trust that must come into being between lawyer and client in a lawsuit of this magnitude.

During my first meeting with her in Ellison's office, it was clear she knew little about boat handling or fishing. Although she might know nothing about fishing or boating, Mrs. Dowd would know her husband better than anyone else. No man married thirty years would have any important character traits kept secret from his wife. If there were any negative aspects of his personality that might have affected how he handled the boat, she would have known or at least had a suspicion about them. It would be instructive to see if she mentioned anything indicating he was a risk taker.

I would give Mrs. Dowd free rein to discuss everything of significance, and if it turned out by the end of our meeting that she failed to mention important details germane to the case, their omission would be a major red flag. Missing facts, for the most part, can be obtained from other sources. Missing candor is filled in by the other side at trial—with disastrous consequences.

On the day of her appointment, I paced back and forth in my office anxiously awaiting her arrival. A buzz interrupted my thoughts: Mrs.

Dowd had arrived. I met her in the reception area and we walked to my office. I pointed out several highlights of the downtown skyline and the harbor. The day was sunny, and San Francisco Bay a beautiful blue. When she finished admiring the view, I held out one of the leather client chairs in front of my desk.

Since her arrival, I had been trying to gauge her mood without success. She sat erect with an expectant look, waiting for me to begin.

"Mrs. Dowd. . . ."

She cut in. "Please, call me Janet."

"Thank you," I said, pleased with this gesture on her part, and began again.

"Your husband's Estate is the named defendant, but it is really he who is being sued. What he did, or did not do, is what this case is all about." She did not react. I launched into an overview of the various phases the lawsuit would go through.

"The discovery process will be very intense, taking at least a year, maybe more, to complete." I asked if she had been involved in a lawsuit before. She shook her head.

"Discovery has commenced in the customary way with a series of written questions, called interrogatories. They are sent by both sides seeking information, and requests for the production of documents. The last phase of discovery will be taking the depositions of each side's expert witnesses. After that a mandatory settlement conference will be scheduled by the court. A judge will preside over the settlement conference, and a serious attempt will be made to settle the case. If it does not settle, the case will go to court for trial in front of a jury." She had no questions.

"Janet, your husband is going to be on trial just as surely as if he were in the courtroom sitting next to me, and I will need to make him come alive to the jury. I'm hoping you will share with me insights into his personality so I can successfully defend him." She nodded.

"Please tell me about your husband's experience with boats, and give every detail you can recall. Why don't you begin with his earliest experiences, maybe even as a boy if his family had a boat?"

"Fran," as she called him, ". . . joined the Navy right out of high school. He was eighteen at the time. He served for four years, mostly at sea on submarines, as a sonar operator."

If his family had a boat, she knew nothing about it. "The first boat Fran owned was a ski boat used for family water skiing trips, and occasionally for fishing on nearby lakes. He enjoyed fishing, and always wanted a boat big enough to go out on the ocean for salmon. Eventually, he bought the *Aloha*."

"How frequently did he take the *Aloha* out on the ocean for fishing?" I asked.

"He went fifteen plus times a year with a number of friends who were his fishing regulars."

"Any problems with the boat that you were aware of?"

"None."

Next I asked what equipment had been replaced after the burglary.

She related that Fran bought replacement items which were temporarily stored in the 'boat corner' of the garage. Fran and Jerry had been up to the boat several times in the two week period before the incident, getting it ready for the first trip of the season. After the incident she noticed those items were gone, and assumed they had been installed on the *Aloha*.

"Please tell me what you know about your husband's relationship with Mr. Ang, and how it came about that he was on the boat that day?"

"Andy owned a company that managed the operations of Raytheon's assembly plant in Manila. Fran liked Andy, and over time they became personal friends. When Fran and I visited the Philippines, we were entertained by Andy and his wife, Jane. Before we made that trip, I learned Jane was a doctor and I was apprehensive about meeting her, but she was a cordial hostess." During the visit Janet learned they had the same number of children, two boys and three girls, all about the same age.

The Angs' home was in a very prestigious neighborhood in Manila, the equivalent of Pacific Heights in San Francisco. Several of the past presidents of the Philippines had homes in the area. Janet said the gardens of the Angs' house were quite extensive and meticulously kept, and the views overlooking the city and Manila Bay were spectacular. From her description, the Angs lived a life style only the extremely wealthy could afford in the United States. Jane Ang had a cook/housekeeper, and a gardener. Andy had a driver.

"Did you see Mr. Ang during his visit here?" I asked.

"Yes. Andy and Werner Buntmann joined Fran and me for dinner two days before the fishing trip. It was nice to see Andy again and hear about Jane and their children. . . ." Suddenly, in mid-sentence, she burst out, "Why won't Allstate just pay Jane Ang?" Her voice quivered.

Before I could respond, she added, "If Fran had been visiting in Manila and this happened to him, I would expect their insurance company to pay. That's what we have insurance for."

Her cheeks flushed crimson. From the look on her face it was evident she had been carrying this thought around for some time.

Trying not to exacerbate the charged atmosphere, I responded quietly, "Under the terms of the policy covering the *Aloha*, the company is not obligated to pay the Angs unless your husband was in some way negligent."

She stared at me in stony silence, with no indication she comprehended what I had said.

Using less legal phraseology, I tried again. "Only if your husband was careless, and caused the accident, will the company be obliged to pay."

In an instant her face transformed from fire to ice. A fog bank of uncomfortable silence enveloped the room. When she finally spoke, it was in a slow measured cadence.

"My husband was not a perfect man," she paused, her eyes flashing over my face, searching for comprehension before continuing, ". . . but he was never careless . . . and never negligent . . . ever."

She spoke in a tone etched in steely calmness making it abundantly clear that her words were to be taken as a statement of fact. I was completely taken aback. It was not anger that Janet was expressing, she was defending her husband's character. It seemed as if I had been meeting with two totally different women: one a staid lady from another era, and a completely different woman driven by 'she bear' protectiveness.

A few moments passed as I sat in stunned muteness, trying to make some sense of her words. After an uncomfortably long silence in which I failed to think of anything to say in response to her outpouring, I moved to another subject.

"How long had your husband been with Raytheon and what were his duties?"

Her expression immediately lightened.

"He joined Raytheon as a junior engineer right after graduation. A few years later, he was moved into the first of many management positions he held with the company, and eventually promoted to manager of their West Coast operations. He was a good leader and motivator, and felt he had not reached the epitome of his career."

I asked her to give me background information about Fran and herself.

"We both came from Springfield, Massachusetts. Fran came from a large family. His father came as a child from County Kerry, Ireland, and worked in a mill until he became disabled."

I envisioned Springfield as a small New England town of tall steepled churches and white picket fences, but she described an industrial town, more gritty than bucolic. The city had apparently reached its zenith around the turn of the century as a center of diverse manufacturing best known for the Springfield Armory which had produced military firearms since the Civil War era.

"My maiden name was Sullivan. My father, like Fran's, was also born in Ireland. He worked as a millwright. Mother was a homemaker."

This was a complete surprise. The impression I had from our meeting in Ellison's office was that she came from an old money New England family.

She continued: "I was an only child in an Irish neighborhood of large families. I hoped to go to the nearby parochial school, but mother and father thought I would get a better education in the local public high school, and that's where I went."

"Did the Dowds live close by?" I asked.

"Oh no . . . they lived over on Irish Hill."

Something in the way she spoke gave the impression her family lived in more affluent circumstances. She must have seen the reaction on my face and quickly added, "I didn't mean it that way . . ." and began fumbling for the right words.

The moment lengthened awkwardly. I volunteered, "So, the Sullivan's were a little more 'lace curtain,' is that it?"

She seemed puzzled. I mentioned being born in Chicago, and the more comfortable Irish families were referred to as 'lace curtain Irish.' The term was new to her and made her smile. "Now that I think about it, Mother did have some lace curtains."

"How did you and Fran meet?"

Her voice softened as she mentioned enjoying Irish step dancing, and through that interest met Fran. He was light hearted and fun loving, but about getting an education he was dead serious; more so than most of his contemporaries. Even at that young age he was determined to get somewhere in life, a trait she admired in him. He realized the only way he could go to college would be through the G.I. Bill, and immediately after graduating high school he joined the Navy. On completion of basic training, he was encouraged to take the special physical and mental examinations for submarine school and was accepted.

"I think he opted for the submarine corps partly for the adventure. I believe I told you he was eighteen at the time, and there was also the consideration of the extra pay for hazardous duty. He tested well in math, and after completing submarine school, the Navy sent him for further training to become a sonar operator. Fran liked the Navy. He was discharged four years later, at age twenty-two, as a Sonarman First Class."

Her face took on the soft glow of an altar candle as she continued. "We stayed close while Fran was in the service, and at some point I knew he was the one and we would be married," she added.

"In the meantime, I was in college studying for a teaching degree. We set a date, and right after he was discharged we were married. He was accepted at the University of Massachusetts in Amherst. He discovered a real flair for physics and made it his major." She stopped for a moment; the same look returned to her face she had used several times before: a combination of love and sharp introspection when speaking about him.

"Fran obtained good grades more by dogged determination than any innate brilliance, frequently studying for hours, well past midnight if necessary, until he mastered his course material."

Janet had obtained a teaching position in the local school system. Between her salary and his G.I. Bill benefits, they could afford to live in a nice place and enjoyed Amherst.

"Things were looking up for us. There was a good demand for physics graduates, and Fran interviewed with a number of companies. He learned the Raytheon Corporation, located in nearby Lexington, might be interested in someone with his background. He applied and was hired. Raytheon pioneered in the early development of radar and sonar, and his background as a Sonarman in the Navy was of interest."

She stopped again. A long moment of inner reflection passed. I finally had to ask her to go on. Practically stammering her words out, she continued, "In our last year at Amherst, I began having difficulties standing and walking, and sought help from a doctor. On one of the visits, he detected some odd symptomatology and ordered a battery of tests." They were shocked to learn she had come down with adult onset polio. The doctor was very concerned and referred her to specialists for further examination and testing. They were told she would have to be followed very carefully to make certain the disease did not progress to the point where there might be life-threatening consequences.

"Through it all Fran was my rock, and at the same time somehow managed to keep up with his course work and graduated with his class."

As she finished this extraordinary recitation, tears were one blink away from cascading down. She managed a small smile. "Of course it deepened our relationship far more than we ever expected."

Many of the details she divulged were extremely difficult to speak about, and none related directly to the case, but something critically important to the defense of the lawsuit had just occurred. Janet had taken the first step towards reposing her trust in me, that all important bond which has to exist between lawyer and client in an important case. Without this 'passing of the baton of trust,' the chance of success if the case went to trial would be virtually nonexistent. I was profoundly moved, and sensed Janet recognized we had reached a milestone as well.

After she left, I started to make notes of our meeting, but slowly put my pen aside, my mind overwhelmed by her extraordinarily candid words about her husband, and the impassioned manner in which she delivered them:

"My husband was not a perfect man, but he was never careless . . . and never negligent . . . ever."

I had no idea how prophetic those words would become.

# 8

The National Weather Service's marine forecasts, which the fishermen rely on, are broadcast on a special radio frequency that only carries the marine forecasts. The same weather report is repeated continuously until there is a material change in the weather. When a change occurs, a new forecast is taped, and is broadcast until the conditions once again change.

I called the National Weather Service and ordered a copy of the transcripts. When they came, I was stunned.

The forecast for Thursday, March 8, the day before the incident, mentioned overcast weather conditions and moderate swells. At midnight the forecast was modified slightly, calling for a continuation of the same general wind and wave conditions. It remained in effect until eight a.m. Friday, March 9. The forecast was then radically modified. Much higher waves were predicted, and a 'small craft warning' had been issued.

I grabbed the discovery file and searched for the response Janet had made to plaintiffs' interrogatories, hoping the answer that I knew would be there somehow would not be.

Finding the interrogatory I was looking for, I read it carefully. It asked: what time did Francis Dowd leave his house to drive up to the marina? In the rough draft answers Janet sent me, she had written down the men left the house at six-thirty, and I had put six-thirty in the final answers submitted to plaintiffs' attorney without independently checking its accuracy. What made it so galling was how easy it would have been on my part to ascertain that Janet had made a big mistake in her recollection about when the men left the house. The problem with her answer was the Coast Guard report indicated that on the night of the incident Janet told their dispatcher the *Aloha* sailed from the Sausalito marina at six-thirty. I should have noticed the discrepancy and clarified which statement was correct . . . did he leave the house at six-thirty, or leave the marina at six-thirty . . . before I sent out the answers to the interrogatories.

The small craft warning that was included in the N.W.S. eight o'clock broadcast created a real dilemma. If Dowd left his house in Los Altos at six-thirty, as I had put down, and it took close to an hour to drive to Sausalito, this meant he arrived at the marina at seven-thirty. It would have taken another ten minutes for the men to load their gear and warm up the engines, which would mean the *Aloha* did not leave the marina until 0740. I did a quick time and distance calculation and determined the *Aloha* would still have been within the protected waters of San Francisco Bay at the time the small craft warning was made at 0800, and he should have returned to the marina.

The issue of what time the men left the house was now critical.

I called Rae Strange immediately. It was essential to find out if there had been a significant increase in the height of the waves that morning. I could hear the urgency in my voice as I asked about the waves on March 9.

"I've received the data from the Scripps Institution buoy and reviewed it," he replied. "But I don't as yet have the data from the buoys operated by NOAA or the Army Corps of Engineers. It's very frustrating dealing with them. They have their own way of doing things, and quite frankly I don't know when I'll get their data."

I needed an answer now, not later, and pressed him. "Rae, can you at least give me a preliminary idea from your review of the Scripps data if the waves became appreciably larger on the morning of the 9th?"

A long pause ensued before he responded. "I think they increased in height," he paused again, and then in a firm tone added, ". . . but I don't want to speculate how quickly that happened. The answer will have to wait until I have the data from all the buoys."

Days later, Strange called back. "I've finally received the data from all three buoys, and analyzed it."

He then asked me to get the chart showing the entrance to San Francisco harbor, and a second chart that showed the offshore area.

I did as he asked, and switched on the speaker phone.

"O.K.," he said. "The swells that morning were coming in from due west. Look on the chart showing the San Francisco Bar. Do you see the area in blue around Four Fathom Bank and Potatopatch Shoal?"

"Yes," I said.

"This is my analysis. The swells coming in that morning were created by the storm I told you about, centered 1,500 miles northeast of Hawaii. The buoy data indicate the initial contingent of waves from that storm began arriving in the early morning hours of March 9th, around two a.m., and rapidly increased in height. Sometime between six and eight o'clock their height increased from four or five feet, to ten and fifteen feet. But they would have been rolling swells, not breaking waves."

We said our goodbyes, and I put the phone down, shocked with what I just heard.

What Strange said about big swells arriving that morning confirmed why the National Weather Service issued the small craft warning at 0800.

If it could be demonstrated that Francis Dowd left the safety of San Francisco Bay after the small craft warning had been broadcast, there would be no escaping that this was a clear act of negligence on his part.

# 9

I urgently needed to gain practical understanding of the technical information Captain Seymour and Rae Strange were inundating me with about the wave conditions existing on the morning the *Aloha* went down. To accomplish this, I booked a salmon fishing trip on one of the party boats to retrace the course Francis Dowd would have taken. I waited until the fishing report in the *Chronicle* indicated the salmon were schooling in the Duxbury area, and the tide would be flowing outward as it had been on March 9.

The boat left at six a.m. After assembling my rod and reel, I went out on deck. It was still dark out with a sharp wind blowing. The other fishermen remained in the cabin swapping fishing stories and having coffee. Alone out on deck, I began putting myself in Francis Dowd's mindset, trying to visualize what he would have seen and done that fateful morning. As we headed for the Golden Gate Bridge, I began looking for the navigation aids Dowd would have used.

The force of the outbound tidal currents, plus the darkness, would have made it prudent for Dowd, and the other boat skippers heading out on March 9, to keep a good distance from each other. I noticed the captain of the boat I was on did the same.

After passing under the Golden Gate Bridge, Fran's next navigational reference point would have been the lighthouse at Point Bonita, two and a half miles ahead. After passing the Point, the outgoing tide swirls in a counterclockwise manner. Dowd had been out a hundred times and would have known if he got too close while coming around Point Bonita, the current could suddenly cause the *Aloha*'s stern to swing around, heading her toward the rocks. He doubtlessly would have made a wide swing going around Point Bonita, giving his helm a good bit of left rudder to compensate against the push of the currents.

After rounding Point Bonita, small craft lose the protection provided by Golden Gate Channel and come into contact with the forces of the open ocean. Straight ahead is the Pacific Ocean. The next landfall is thousands of miles away in Asia. One last thing would have provided some protection to the *Aloha* from the full effect of the Pacific swells: the San Francisco Bar. This scimitar shaped sandbar lay less than a mile ahead. I could feel the boat rolling more heavily as we began rounding the Point, just as the *Aloha* would have.

After passing Point Bonita, I concentrated on the actions Fran would have taken. As he rounded the Point, the swells were spaced well apart allowing the *Aloha* to ride them with a nice easy gait, and setting his speed to take them comfortably. Upon entering Bonita Channel, he would have altered his course to a northerly compass bearing, keeping the *Aloha* well away from the Marin Headlands. It was still fully dark out. He would have looked for the next set of navigation markers he would use to go through Bonita Channel, which is two miles long and shaped like an hourglass.

At its mid-point, the Channel's width narrows to about nine hundred feet, marked by Buoy Four on the left to warn mariners away from the dangerously shallow waters of the Bar. The Channel's right side is marked by Buoy Three which cautions mariners to keep away from the sheer bluffs of the Marin Headlands. Number Three is also equipped with a flashing green light, making it much easier to see in the darkness. He would use that green light to navigate the Channel.

Careful navigation is required to avoid straying onto the Bar. If the swells are running high, the Bar's shallow depth can turn the smooth rolling swells into dangerous breaking waves. Over the years, the Bar has become the final resting place for dozens of ships and hundreds of men lost to these breakers.

The weather service records confirmed there was no fog on March 9, and the flashing green light on Buoy Three would have been clearly visible a little more than a mile ahead. The *Aloha* would arrive at Duxbury on time.

From what I had learned about the wave conditions on March 9, it seemed that as Fran progressed deeper into the Channel, the *Aloha* would have experienced a change in its movement through the water. What had been a rhythmic side to side roll would have had an increasing element of fore and aft pitching added to its motion as the boat progressed farther in. Fran would have eased the throttles back, slowing the boat's speed slightly to smooth out the ride for the four men in the main cabin getting the gear ready.

Standing on the foredeck, I could hear the murmur of voices and occasional bursts of laughter from the cabin, just as Fran would have heard in his position on the bridge, one deck above the *Aloha*'s main cabin. The fishing report in the paper had been favorable, and Fran shared everyone's optimism that they were going to get the season off to a good start. Bringing the ice chest back filled with fish would be a pleasure if they all caught their limits.

The *Aloha*'s galley table was pressed into service for making up the baits. The rolling motion caused the hooks to slide around on the table top, and everyone's hands were needed to keep things in place. The task of 'baiting up the hooks' requires a good deal of skill to do correctly. Salmon, even the hungriest, are very particular feeders. If the slightest scar mars a bait, the salmon will refuse it.

It was still dark outside, but the roll and pitch alerted Jerry, his Uncle John, Werner and Andy, that the *Aloha* had rounded Point Bonita. Duxbury was a half hour away. The excitement of the first trip of the season had all of them in animated conversation discussing fishing techniques, and the usual stories of past trips and 'the big ones that got away.'

As the *Aloha* pressed northwards into the Channel, it was still too dark to see the incoming swells clearly, but the *Aloha*'s side to side rolling motion would have told Fran the waves were coming mostly from the west. From the data Rae Strange gave me about the size of the waves that morning, I sensed Fran would be making steering changes with increasing frequency to keep the *Aloha* on course, and adjusting the throttle controls to maintain his speed. As the *Aloha* pushed deeper into the Channel, the regular rolling movement was becoming increasingly punctuated by an up and down pitching motion, requiring him to move his feet continuously to maintain a steady position at the steering console. The height and steepness of the waves seemed to be increasing as well, and for the first time Fran noticed a few breaking waves. Although their tops were not plunging over, they were too large to take head on. He counteracted their force by turning the helm slightly, taking the swells at an angle and adjusting his speed.

The gradual change in the sea state eventually had Fran steering with one hand on the helm while gripping the throttle controls with the other to maintain his position in mid Channel, well away from the Marin Headlands and the phalanx of rocks at the base of the cliffs.

I could not see the headlands clearly in the dark, but the rocks made their presence known by the constant roar of the waves breaking on them. Fran would have heard the sound too, and kept a respectful distance away. If there had been a sudden stoppage of the engines, or a rudder failure, the

*Aloha* would have drifted helplessly toward the bluffs. No one would have been able to respond to a radio call for help quickly enough to prevent her from being ground to pieces on the rocks.

As the distance to the midpoint of Bonita Channel closed, the *Aloha's* motion through the water undoubtedly changed. The westerly swells were rising in height and becoming more disordered. An increasing number of waves coming from the northwest and south were mixed in.

To maintain his course and speed, Fran had to be making constant helm changes. The wheel was responding sluggishly, requiring both hands to steady his course. He decreased his speed to smooth out the ride, but further reductions in the *Aloha's* engine speed were rapidly becoming a non-option. If he slowed down any further, some of the larger waves he was encountering might push the bow over too far, allowing the *Aloha* to slide sideways into the trough of a wave. If a big breaking wave came up while he was in that position, it could mean trouble. Making the constant speed and steering changes required precise timing which is hard to execute in the darkness. The swell's gray color made determining their size and characteristics impossible until Fran was practically upon them. There was no alternative but to pick his way carefully through the discordant wave conditions.

The boat I was on crested a big swell. I held onto the railing to steady myself as the captain immediately throttled the engine back. Fran would have done the same to prevent the *Aloha* from slaloming down the front of a wave too quickly. I envisioned Fran wedging himself into a firm position at the control console to avoid changing his footing every time a wave buffeted the vessel. Below, in the *Aloha's* main cabin, the increased rolling and pitching motion made baiting the hooks more difficult, and finally impossible. At the end, it had probably become a source of laughter as the men chased the hooks and baits sliding around the galley table.

As he drew nearer to the Channel's narrow midpoint, Fran and the flashing green light played tag with each other. He would be coming over the crest of a wave and Buoy Number Three would be down in a trough, invisible. A minute later both he and Number Three would be at the top of a wave and visually reconnect with each other for an instant. A moment later the *Aloha* would slide into a trough, once again losing sight of the green light.

The width of the Channel was steadily narrowing as the *Aloha* drew closer to the mid-point, and Fran would be growing concerned. The force of the waves was causing the bow to swing more ominously. Standing at the railing of the boat I was on, I thought about the weather data I'd reviewed for March 9. An increasing sense was coming to me that Fran had gone over a number of waves a little too fast, and instead of achieving a moment of equilibrium at its crest, the *Aloha* had gone over the top and slid down the face of the wave. And Fran needed those seconds at the top to scan the horizon for the flashing light to make sure he was in the Channel, and not drifting too close to the Bar. He waited for the next good size wave and slowed down at the crest, straining to see the buoy's light. He put aside worrying about adjusting the throttles, his eyes racing for some sign of the flashing green light. Where the light should have been, there was nothing but a shadow line of gray. He scanned again, this time widening the angle of his search . . . only gray. Darting his eyes back and forth, he widened the scope, anxiously searching for the green flash. The deck began slanting downward, telling him the *Aloha* was heading over the crest. He gave one more scan, this time sweeping the entire horizon from his port beam, to dead ahead, and then his starboard beam, the whole horizon . . . with no sign of the light.

As I stood on the rolling foredeck, the wind whipping spray from the bow in my face, I sensed what might have happened: after the third or fourth time not seeing the buoy, Fran Dowd was worried. He knew the light flashed every four seconds, and he had been at least that long on top of the wave and seen nothing. A quick look at the compass indicated he was maintaining the course he had set. This should have meant the *Aloha* was safely within the boundaries of the Channel. But where was that damned green light? The bow suddenly lurched downward. He instantly checked the helm to determine the direction of his rudders. They were where they should be, amidships. He then looked out the window straining to see forward. The off-balance position of his body told him the *Aloha* was racing out of control down the front of the wave he had just crested. Straining his eyes in the dimness, he could barely make out the steepening gray outline of the wave. At that moment he saw it: the nothingness.

Different from any experience he'd had on the *Aloha*, or in the Navy, Fran was staring in disbelief into what could only be described as a hole in the ocean. Instead of a trough at the bottom of the wave where it should have been, there was a gaping, bottomless maw. In the next few picture frames of time, measured in split seconds, the bottom of the hole abruptly became visible . . . with the *Aloha* hurtling into it in a nearly vertical free fall.

The bottom was rushing up like a punch being thrown in the ring . . . you see the blow coming, try moving to avoid being hit, but know it's going to land, and pray you don't get knocked out. There was not going to be enough time to avoid hitting the bottom in a staggering blow.

In reacting to imminent life threatening danger, the brain pushes all rational thought aside, replacing it with the most primal gut instinct . . . the will to survive.

In milliseconds, the shock of seeing the boat hurtling into the empty hole in the ocean would have triggered raw action in Fran. Spurred by pure reflex, he jammed the helm hard over to avoid hitting the bottom straight on. At the speed they were going, the bow would plunge in so deeply the *Aloha* might not be able to pull herself back up. With adrenaline fueled strength, Fran smashed the throttle levers forward, putting maximum power to both engines. They roared in response, giving full traction to the rudders in a desperate attempt to put the *Aloha*'s bow at an angle.

Inside the cabin, the lights flickered. Startled cries of 'hang on!' rang out as everything loose in the main cabin began crashing forward. The force was so great that the men's hands were ripped from whatever they had grasped, sending them cart-wheeling across the cabin until their spinning bodies slammed into something strong enough to arrest their movement.

A little less than a second was consumed in the actions Fran had taken. No one could have reacted faster. Many would have taken longer, and some, immobilized by fear, would have done nothing. There just weren't enough seconds.

The moment before the *Aloha* hit the bottom of the wave, something compelled Fran to look over his shoulder. At that moment, a nearly perpendicular wall of water above him was tipping forward just as the bow plowed into the trough, piercing the water like a surgeon's scalpel, plunging half her length into the wave's trough. An instant later, the wave's crest collapsed, hurling tons of green water downwards, smashing the door to the main cabin as if it were made of paper. In seconds, hundreds of cubic feet of water burst inside; an instant later flooding the engine spaces. The engines stopped, immersing the cabin into darkness. The raging water surged into the fore cabin where the sleeping quarters were located. Dead in the water and nearly perpendicular, the *Aloha*'s exposed stern caught the remainder of the wave, throwing her end over end in a pitch-pole motion. Filled with water, the boat lost her buoyancy and began reeling downwards.

The brute power of the wave pried Fran's hands from the wheel, flailing him about in the flying bridge before flinging him out to drift to the surface.

The instant the main cabin door burst open, the four men inside knew the peril they were in. Their collective reaction was instinctive and instantaneous ... get to the surface. The only way out was through the cabin doorway, and then kick their way to the top. Other than a few pockets of trapped air, the cabin was filled with water. The fifty-five degree temperature shocked their systems, numbing their muscles. There had been barely enough time for a few shouts before the flooding, and then darkness. Not darkness in the ordinary sense, but the seldom experienced sensation of a complete and total absence of light. The four men were spatially disoriented as well. They knew their positions when the water rushed in, and the location of the cabin door, but in the tumult of the boat pitch-polling end over end, where were they now? In the few seconds it took to flood the cabin, there was barely time to suck in a few precious gasps of air and make a desperate attempt to get to the surface.

Darwin suggests that man evolved from creatures that once inhabited the sea. In apparent corroboration of his theory is the fact that man has no greater fear than drowning. It is neither slow nor painless, but quick and frightening, one step from being terrorized. Someone gripped with terror becomes immobilized, unable to act. But that same person, facing a situation where there is a chance of survival, reacts quite differently. Instinct takes over, pushing fear into a state of suspended animation. In these circumstances, people become like the mother who lifts the back end of a car pinning her baby, or the acts of incredible heroism performed by soldiers in combat that no one, including themselves, thought they were capable of doing.

The downward gyration of the *Aloha* expelled the few remaining pockets of air, and the men began breathing in seawater. As their struggling gradually ceased, they entered a final dream-like state, grabbing onto anything they could find; a sailor's last bond with his vessel.

Striking the bottom in a reverberating shudder, the boat gently rocked on the sea-bed, preparing a final resting place for herself. The men entombed inside were now in death's repose, their valiant struggle to live concluded. They appeared asleep, resting in silence. In a short time, the sea overhead would revert to gentler swells, leaving no trace of the men or the boat that had intruded into its realm.

As it is with all living things, there comes a time for a vessel to die. At the moment the first hint of sunlight became visible over the Marin hills, erasing the last trace of the stars from the fading night sky, the *Aloha* died.

It would have been 6:35 a.m.

# 10

A few weeks later we had a setback. Janet called informing me that the radar set, which Fran purchased to replace the stolen one, had been found in another storage area of the garage. From several conversations with her about the subject, I'd been under the impression all of the stolen safety gear had been replaced. For whatever reason, Fran had not installed it on the *Aloha*. During the call, Janet questioned me at length about the significance of the radar set not being onboard. She was upset, and I tried to ease the anxiety resonating in her voice. I told her that radar has its uses, principally in conditions of heavy fog, but I had confirmed no fog was present that morning. I also let her know that radar was not a mandatory piece of safety equipment like life jackets, fire extinguishers and signaling devices, and many boats the size of the *Aloha* did not carry radar. Her "I see" response didn't sound like she was at all convinced by my explanations.

A week later Janet called again, her voice sounding more relieved than excited as she told me, "I've been looking through some old paperwork about the boat, and found documents showing that Fran ordered two radar sets, not one."

The inference was obvious: two radar sets had been ordered, and since only one was in the garage after the incident, the other must have been installed on the *Aloha*.

I had to be down in San Jose the next day and said if she would be home, I would come by and pick up the documents. She agreed, giving me directions to her house.

Her home was a modern, one-story ranch house at the end of a cul-de-sac. The trees and gardens in the entire block gave the appearance there

45

was a friendly neighborhood rivalry for best landscaped home.

Janet met me at the door before I could ring the bell. She was casually dressed, mentioning she had been doing housework. I had not thought of her in terms of around the house chores, but part of Janet's appeal was her lack of pretension. We sat at the kitchen table where the documents were spread out. She offered coffee. Sensing she was anxious to begin, I declined.

She handed me a letter from Raytheon's Marine Sales Division containing a series of product code numbers. Attached was a memo with two invoices. The first invoice was for the radar set found in the garage after the incident. The second was for a different model.

Pointing to the second invoice, she said, "Since this radar set was not in the garage, Fran and Jerry must have installed it on the *Aloha* on one of the trips they made up to the marina getting the boat ready for the fishing season."

Janet was plainly relieved at this vindication of her husband. I told her this was welcome news, and thanked her for her diligence.

We were almost finished when the door opened unexpectedly. A young woman about 20 entered whom Janet introduced as her youngest daughter, Tracy. Janet was obviously surprised, remarking she had not expected her. During the introductions, I had the impression Tracy knew I would be there, and her arrival was not accidental.

Brushing aside the pleasantries, Tracy wanted to know what was going on in the case. I responded, "Everything is coming along fine." This generalization did not suit Tracy who began pressing for details.

Sensing her daughter was sailing into unacceptable waters, Janet intervened.

"We have a few more matters to discuss. I'll be free in a few minutes." Janet's face plainly portrayed 'you may leave the room now.'

Her daughter was not easily deterred, and she asked more pointed questions. Another stern look from her mother had the desired effect. But before leaving, she gave me a final look of perusal . . . as if I were someone with a pencil line mustache trying to sell her mother aluminum siding.

After she left the room, I gathered up the papers in awkward silence. When I finished, I said, "Well, I hope I passed inspection."

It took Janet only a moment to digest my remark, and become amused. An instant later her expression turned contemplative.

"Tracy has been so good, and so dear to me. I don't need this, this. . . ." She paused, searching for the right word. I gestured toward myself to interject. When Janet nodded, I supplied, "Babysitting?" Janet bobbed her head, smiling, and walked me out.

At my car, her mood changed once again. "I don't want Tracy to do this. . . . But it is so very, very sweet of her. She has been wonderful to me." Janet smiled in a way I had not seen from her before, the smile of a mother especially pleased with something a child has done. Her children were Janet's bridge to happier times in the past.

As we were about to say our goodbyes, her face turned pensive. "Jay, thank you for all your help; I appreciate everything you're doing."

Over her shoulder, I noticed Tracy standing in the open doorway, hands on her hips, watching attentively.

The radar sets were expensive, and why Fran would have ordered two was a question I kept asking myself, and been unable to answer. If the purchase of two sets seemed odd to me, it would be to Blake as well. I called John Geaghan, Raytheon's liaison counsel at home office, and said I needed to contact the person Dowd had spoken with to find out why two radar sets had been ordered.

As we ended our call, Geaghan mentioned that Raytheon had established a scholarship in Fran's memory for students majoring in physics to attend his alma mater, the University of Massachusetts. Janet had flown back for the inaugural ceremony, and a special reception was held afterwards honoring her and the memory of Fran.

A few days later Geaghan called back referring me to Bob Miller, Raytheon's West Coast Marine sales manager in Tacoma, Washington. I called Miller. "I remember Mr. Dowd calling me. He said his radar set had been stolen, wanted to replace it, and gave me the model number. I told him that particular model had been superseded and recommended he buy the updated model, which he did."

Cutting him off, I said, "But I have two invoices in front of me, for two different model radars."

"Mr. Dowd told me the adjuster handling the burglary claim required documentation showing the cost of the old set. The invoice you're looking at is for the old model, the one that was stolen. It's not an actual order."

Plaintiffs' attorney had sent discovery requests concerning the safety equipment onboard, and I responded that the stolen set had been replaced. I called Blake to tell him the information I sent was incorrect, and that the *Aloha* had sailed without radar onboard.

Sometime later, a copy of Francis Dowd's medical records arrived. I read through them carefully. He had undergone annual checkups and was in good health. There was no indication that he had suffered from blackouts, seizures, or been treated for any psychological problems. Any of them might have created an issue. There was even a note that he had been a boxer in the Navy. I thought to myself that he was likely good at it too. Any boy growing up in a neighborhood called 'Irish Hill' with a name like Francis probably had all the fights he wanted as a kid. . . . I wondered what his mother had been thinking.

# 11

In the ensuing months, conflicted as I was about the wisdom of my decision, an awareness gradually came over me of wanting to try this case. The exact time of this decision was uncertain, but the reason for it was clear: the fervent avowal Janet had made about her husband.

For Janet the issues were straightforward and uncomplicated. The lawsuit Jane Ang filed called into question the way Fran led his life, and there were two possible resolutions to the cloud that had been put over his name: settlement or trial. I explained that under the terms of the policy, it was in the sole discretion of the company whether or not to settle the case, and for how much, telling her insurers frequently settle cases to avoid the risk of getting hit with a run-away verdict if a case went to trial. I also pointed out that settling the case was not an admission of liability, and the settlement documents would say so.

Every time I broached the subject of settlement, she stared with the same fiercely protective 'she bear' look she used in our first meeting. Her face unmistakably communicated to me: the company wouldn't pay unless they thought Fran was at fault, and if the price of settlement was tantamount to an admission that he was negligent, then the case should go to trial. Anything else would be an unthinkable dance with the devil.

If what Janet said in our first private meeting, "My husband was not a perfect man, but he was never careless . . . and never negligent . . . ever," had not been so categorically emphatic, I would have regarded her words as the emotional reaction of an overwrought widow and forgotten them, but what she said had not receded from my thoughts. Every time I picked up the file, her words echoed in my mind.

As the trial date drew near, the thought that had been plaguing me for months intensified. Had I, as Janet's lawyer, properly discharged my pro-

49

fessional responsibilities to her? My duty was to think objectively, particularly in situations like this where clients can become so swept up in the litigation process that they are not thinking clearly for themselves. Her husband, her son, and her brother-in-law were all dead, and a trial was not going to bring them back. The only thing a trial would resolve was whether her husband was responsible for this tragedy.

If it had been only Fran who died, in time Janet would come to terms with that. He had lived a full life, and fishing was something he loved. But if a jury attributed the death of her son to her husband, it would be a death knell to her soul.

For Janet, the case seemed to have descended into a life and death struggle for survival, and in circumstances like these, clients can drift into a self-protective state of delusion.

Like a wound that wouldn't heal, I kept asking myself if Janet's best interests would be served by going to trial, with the crushing emotional price she would pay if the jury found her husband negligent.

I had explained that $1,100,000 of coverage was not a lot in a wrongful death case, and if there was an excess verdict, the possibility existed it would have to be paid out of the Estate. Even after I explained this potential financial disaster, she remained resolute. To Janet, honor was more important than money. It did not seem to be only his honor that was at stake, but hers as well.

In the end, despite my misgivings about not pursuing settlement, I decided if Janet was willing to assume the financial jeopardy imposed by the five million dollars in claims made against the Estate, and the immeasurably greater emotional risks she would bring upon herself by going to trial, I could do no less.

Perhaps the only bulwark Janet had against emotional devastation was her unwavering belief in her husband's character, and she would trade neither her self-respect, nor her convictions, for the false comfort of a compromising settlement.

A gauntlet had been thrown down challenging his honor, and nothing was more sacred to her.

Hell did hath another fury.

# 12

Under the rules of court, discovery closes thirty days before the date set for the trial to start.

A few weeks before the closing date, I learned from the plaintiffs' answers to our last set of interrogatories that they had found a witness named Taylor McGee.

McGee was identified as the owner of a party boat berthed at the commercial wharf in Sausalito. I called McGee several times. He was never in. I left my name and number on his answering machine without a call back. With time running short, I took Marsha with me and drove to Sausalito on a day I knew he would be out fishing, and waited until he returned from his trip. When all his passengers disembarked, we walked down the dock and asked to come aboard. He agreed, and helped Marsha over the railing. I explained who I was, saying his name had been disclosed as a witness, and I wanted to speak with him concerning what he knew about March 9. His attitude changed instantly. He said he was busy, and didn't want to talk to me anyway. Turning his back, he resumed hosing down the deck of his boat. I stepped forward into the path of his work, the water splashing my shoes.

"Captain, I can see you're busy, but we have to talk. I can either take a statement from you now, which will take fifteen minutes, or subpoena you for a deposition in my office in San Francisco, which will take all day." His eyes blazed with the intensity of fanned charcoal, but faced with this alternative, he grunted an assent.

I told him Marsha was a licensed investigator, and would write down his information. He would have the opportunity to read the statement and make any corrections before signing it.

McGee confirmed being out on March 9, and fishing in the Duxbury area. I listened in stunned silence as he stated that his intention was to go through Bonita Channel to get to Duxbury, but the wave conditions in Bonita Channel were too rough, and he had instead gone out via the Main Channel.

His statement was not as comprehensive as I wanted, but I'd said fifteen minutes, and he kept looking at the time. When we finished, he read the statement quickly before signing. He immediately stood, turned his back to us, and resumed his work. We left the boat without exchanging goodbyes.

On the drive back to the office I asked Marsha to read his statement to me again, and was stupefied by what he'd said.

This last minute discovery of Captain McGee motivated me to make another attempt to locate witnesses at Fisherman's Wharf in San Francisco.

Second only to Disneyland, Fisherman's Wharf is the most heavily foot-trafficked tourist destination in California. The seafood restaurants, built over the old piers, are one of the Wharf's mainstays. The working pier closest to the pedestrian promenade is used by the party boats that cater to sport fishermen. Beyond the party boats is the pier reserved for the commercial fishing fleet. The majority of the commercial boats are owned by fishermen of Sicilian descent. Their brightly painted and immaculately kept boats are themselves a tourist attraction. For the most part, the boats are named for the owner's wife or a patron Saint.

Years earlier, I had done a case for Ronald Pezzolo, the buyer for Alioto's No. 8, the best known restaurant on Fisherman's Wharf. The dining tables of this venerable San Francisco landmark overlook the fishing boats tied up at the Wharf. Ron's office was located on the long pier used by the commercial fishing fleet. His office looked out over the piers, and at a glance he could tell which boats were in and whether the owner was onboard. As Alioto's buyer, he dealt with the fishermen every day.

In the mid-period of the discovery phase, I had called Ron giving him the details of the case, and asked him to let me know if he learned about anyone with knowledge regarding the *Aloha*. Sometime later he called, letting me know someone had been around questioning the fishing boat captains about the incident. From the description he gave, it was Hal Lipset, plaintiffs' investigator.

I wanted to learn what Lipset had been asking the fishermen about. Due to the amount of time it would have taken Ron to talk with the dozens of commercial fishing boat captains, I decided not to bother him and make the inquiries myself. Some of the happiest days of my life had been at sea, and I welcomed the chance to visit the waterfront. I enjoyed the look and sounds of the docks, the salt air, and mostly the people who earned their livelihoods in and around it.

It didn't take long to discover that the captains were a very uncommunicative group. I would receive a polite hearing for a few minutes, but no information. As soon as the words 'lawsuit' and 'lawyer' were mentioned, the façade of interest continued, but their faces told a different story. After getting nowhere with them, I called Ron and arranged to meet him at his office.

While I was relating my attempts to get information from the captains and coming up with nothing, Ron said, "You should have come to me in the first place," waving away my explanation of not wanting to take up too much of his time. I recounted that most of the fishermen were polite, but very closed mouthed.

"These Sicilians," he said, gesturing toward the boats bobbing up and down outside his window, ". . . they only trust each other," and began laughing.

I chipped in, "So you only trust yourselves, is that it?"

His smile vanished. "Me," he said, suddenly in earnest, ". . . Sicilian?"

Thumping his chest, he said, "My family, we're Genovese, from Genoa . . . and we don't trust nobody."

I couldn't resist saying, "Not even each other?"

"*Especially* each other," he retorted, and started howling.

When he calmed down, he said in a serious vein, "So how can I help?"

"Ron, could you find out what plaintiffs' investigator was asking about, and what, if anything, the captains said to him?"

"I'll be glad to do it," and lapsed into silence before continuing. "If that investigator comes nosing around again, you don't want them to talk to him, is that it?"

I thought for a moment before replying. "Ron, the captains have the right to talk to anyone about the case, if they want to. But they also have the right not to talk as well. It's their choice."

He nodded, understanding. "I see most of them every day, and will let you know right away what I find out."

I thanked him again for his help as we said our goodbyes.

Mrs. Ang had flown in from the Philippines, and I took her deposition in Blake's office. When I arrived, Blake told me David Baum would be sitting in during the deposition. I assumed this was to give assurances to Mrs. Ang that Baum, as the principal of the firm, was involved in her case.

After a few minutes, Blake showed me into the deposition room and introduced Mrs. Ang. She remained seated, looking at me appraisingly.

What immediately struck me was her perfect porcelain skin tone. She was dressed flawlessly in a classic designer suit, and her hair salon styled.

I had been told there would be no need to arrange for an interpreter, and it quickly became apparent she was fully fluent in English. Mrs. Ang confirmed what Janet had told me about being educated as a medical doctor, but never practiced.

She testified at length about her husband's humble beginnings in China, and eventual arrival in Manila. By hard work, Andy obtained an education and became successful in business. Prior to her husband's death, she had not participated in his business affairs. Since then, she had assumed the presidency of the company. Mrs. Ang had a general understanding of the company's activities, but despite persistent questioning, she provided nothing substantive about its operations and profitability.

After concluding my examination, my thoughts were that she had undergone hours of preparation, and been carefully instructed not to give expansive answers concerning Andy's business affairs. She maintained her composure throughout the deposition, coming across as a sophisticated and determined woman, accustomed to being given a great deal of deference.

The trial date was rapidly approaching, and I asked Marsha to make one more attempt to find witnesses at the Sausalito marina. She contacted the marina manager and received permission to enter the section where the *Aloha* had been berthed.

I was out of town for a few days, and during one of my calls home Marsha excitedly told me she had finally found a couple who lived on their sailboat in the same section of the marina where Mr. Dowd's boat had been berthed. Marsha met with them, and they had information that seemed helpful. Knowing I would want to talk with them, Marsha arranged a meeting for that weekend on their boat when they would be available.

On Saturday we drove to the marina, and walked down the floating dock toward their berth. As it was a sunny afternoon with a brisk breeze blowing, it crossed my mind they would have preferred to be out sailing rather than meeting with me, and I readied a thank you. Marsha pointed out their boat up ahead. More than two people were sitting in the open cockpit of the sailboat she indicated.

A few steps further along, periodic bursts of laughter could be heard. As we approached their berth, Marsha whispered that the man who had just stood was Rod Thiessen. Seated next to him was Karen Burns who also lived on the boat. Ceremoniously welcoming us aboard, Thiessen commenced regaling their two guests about 'the lawyer and the investigator.' I noticed an empty wine bottle.

It quickly became evident they were in no condition to give a statement. Keeping my irritation in check, I said we would come back another time when they were less busy. I excused myself and helped Marsha off the boat to a chorus of entreaties that we stay and have a glass of wine with them. As we retraced our steps down the dock, considerable laughter erupted from the boat.

By the time we reached the Golden Gate Bridge, I'd cooled off enough to start thinking clearly. I asked Marsha, "When you interviewed them, did they observe you writing down what they were telling you?"

"We were seated close together, and they could not have missed observing me making notes of what they said."

I told Marsha I wanted them subpoenaed, and if their testimony at trial differed from what they had told her, I would call her to impeach them. My anger was welling up again, thinking about how they had wasted my time.

As gently as she could, Marsha said, "Honey, a lawyer calling his own investigator to impeach witnesses that he put on the stand is not likely to be a successful strategy at trial."

When I finally stopped swearing, I gave a resigned sigh and said I would think about it, but I knew she was right.

After additional attempts to meet with them were unsuccessful, I had no choice but to have them subpoenaed. We were running out of time, and I decided to have Marsha go to the marina, wait until she found them onboard, and serve them. The plan had one advantage: their boat was at the end of a long floating dock, and even if they saw Marsha coming, there was nothing they could do to dodge her other than diving over the side and swimming away.

On a weekday morning before daybreak, Marsha drove to the marina, found a place in the shadows, and waited. In the overhead lighting, she saw someone coming from their sailboat wearing a bathrobe; it was Thiessen heading for the shower and changing room located at the head of the dock. When he came through the gate, Marsha stepped forward and handed him the subpoena. Thiessen protested that he did not have access to a car and had no way to get to the courthouse. Marsha said to contact the office and arrangements would be made for his transportation.

A short time later, Karen Burns came down the dock. As Marsha stepped forward, Burns recognized her and ran for the women's shower room. Marsha followed her in and an angry scene erupted. I envisioned a hair pulling cat fight, but Marsha said it had not come to that. Ms. Burns was furious, saying she was refusing to accept the subpoena and would not come to court. "How dare you invade my privacy like this," she added.

Marsha persevered with serving the subpoena, explaining calmly to Burns that she was under a court order to appear, and then she left before the situation deteriorated further.

There was another important trial preparation matter to do. I had been through Bonita Channel a number of times on party boats, but I wanted Captain Seymour to show me firsthand what effect the tide and currents would have had on the *Aloha* as it went through Bonita Channel. Seymour chartered a party boat similar in size and speed as the *Aloha* to take us out to Duxbury and back.

The trip was scheduled for early November on a Sunday. We followed the course Francis Dowd would have taken: going under the Golden Gate Bridge toward Point Bonita, rounding the Point, and then through Bonita Channel to Duxbury.

On the way back in, Captain Seymour shuttled back and forth from the open stern deck to the main cabin where his charts were spread out, familiarizing himself with the various landmarks and navigation buoys in the Channel. He didn't need my help, and I went up to the flying bridge to speak with the boat's captain. When I mentioned I had been in the merchant marine, he warmed up considerably and asked if I would like a turn at the wheel. While we were talking, I noticed a small book from the Department of Fish & Game. It didn't look like fishing regulations. When I inquired, he said, "Fish & Game requires all of us party boat captains to keep track every time we go out fishing, and send them a report once a month."

My antenna went straight up. I asked, "What do you have to do?"

He picked up the book and turned to the report form. There were blank spaces to fill in for each day they went out, how many passengers were onboard, the number of fish caught, and where they had been fishing.

"How specific do you have to be about where you went fishing?" I asked.

"That's the easy part," he said, flipping to the back of the book, "you just use these grids," pointing to a map of the entire California coast that had been sectioned into separately numbered grid boxes. "See here, that's Duxbury Reef, and its grid number. So if you fished there on a particular day, you enter that number on the form you send to Fish & Game." I asked if he had an extra copy of the book. He did not, but when we got back to the dock, he went to the marine supply store and made a copy of the report form and the page with the grid map for me.

On Monday morning, I called Fish & Game. For two frustrating days, I dealt with bureaucrats passing me from one department to another before I finally located the custodian of records down in Long Beach. I gave him the date I wanted, and the five grid boxes for the Bay Area. He began a long complaining monologue that the storage area where the records were kept was a mess, and he only had time to search the records for two of the grid areas. I narrowed my request to Duxbury and Point Reyes. He said it would take a few days, and abruptly ended the call.

At the end of the week he called, reporting that five party boats had been out on March 9, but when I asked for the captain's names he refused, citing privacy act considerations. He'd said nothing about this in our prior conversation. Despite my pleas, he would not change his position. Finally, he agreed 'to think about' notifying the boat captains, telling them I wanted to talk with them. From the tone of his voice, it sounded more like a 'brush off' than something he would actually do. When I put the phone down, I didn't think it was going to happen.

# 13

In the week before the trial was set to start, I was on the phone when my secretary rushed in pantomiming that an important phone call was on hold. I was about to ask her to take a message when she mouthed that one of the fishermen I was looking for was on the line, and he wasn't going to wait very long. Putting the person I was speaking with on hold, I gave her my full attention. She hurriedly outlined that the man on the line was responding to a letter the Department of Fish & Game sent him about being out fishing on March 9. I didn't need to hear any more. I immediately reached for my yellow pad, and punched in the right line.

"Thank you for your call. You must have received a letter from the Department of Fish & Game."

The reply was a cryptic "Yes," followed by silence.

I introduced myself and said I wanted to speak with him about the weather conditions on the date mentioned in the letter.

The caller interrupted, "Your switchboard said 'law offices.' Are you a lawyer?"

"Yes," I said.

Anticipating his next question would be, 'what's this all about,' I continued: "Captain, the report form you sent Fish & Game indicates you went fishing in the Duxbury area that morning."

He confirmed being out that day.

"I'd like to know a little bit about the weather conditions that morning, and if you saw any other boats?"

There was an extended pause. In the silence, I heard the raucous cries of seagulls in the background. He was calling from someplace on the waterfront.

"Is this about a lawsuit?"

I acknowledged it was, and said, "If you would let me have just a few minutes of your time, I can explain what this is all about." No response.

It dawned on me I did not know his name.

"By the way, Captain, I didn't catch your name."

Ignoring this gambit, he said, "Are you suing somebody?"

My time was running out with this man. I sensed he was about to hang up.

"Captain, I represent a woman who is being sued. Her husband and some other men were out fishing and his boat sank. Everyone onboard drowned. Some of the heirs have sued, claiming her husband was responsible. I would really appreciate just ten minutes of your time. Anything you might know could be helpful. I can come to you right now; my widowed client would really appreciate it."

I had been speaking so quickly, I was out of breath.

More silence followed. He began sighing into the phone.

"I'm kind of busy right now," he temporized.

Trying to keep calm, I repeated, "Captain, I can come to you. I promise it won't take more than a few minutes of your time, if you will just tell me where to meet you."

There was a long pause. The sound of his steady sighing was blocking out the noise of the seagulls. "All right, if it will be short. Like I say, I'm kind of busy."

Before he continued, there was another spate of breathing into the phone. "Can you meet me in an hour?"

"Yes," I said.

"Then come to my house," and he gave me an address in the Inner Sunset district. While I was thinking of a new approach to learn his name, he hung up.

I stared at the phone, envisioning that I was going to have a nice drive out to a vacant lot.

After finishing a few matters, I gathered up a chart and tide table, along with a blank subpoena, and headed for the Inner Sunset address given to me by the reluctant and still nameless captain.

When I turned onto his street, I noticed most of the houses had small, meticulously kept front gardens. The entire neighborhood looked as if it had just gone through the wash.

The house I wanted had a garden decorated with what appeared to be religious statuettes tucked in among the flowers. The roller blinds in all the front windows were pulled down to be precisely level with each other. Lace curtains adorned the bay window. I found a parking space down the street and walked back to the house, not noticing anyone peering out of the windows. Straightening my tie, I went up the steps.

The doorbell seemed loud as I pressed it and waited. I was about to push it again when the door opened. Standing in the doorway was a man who appeared to be in his mid-sixties, with a full head of silvery hair. His face coloration was the same as his quarry, the unique pink-red of salmon. He was medium height and barrel chested.

"Good afternoon, Captain. I'm Jay Jacobs. Thank you for calling the office, and agreeing to see me on such short notice."

As I was speaking he looked me over, taking my measure. I paused to let him introduce himself. When he did not, I continued: "The boat involved in the incident was going to Duxbury." I paused again to give him a chance to speak. Still nothing.

"Tom Stienstra's column in the newspaper indicated the salmon were biting, and the Duxbury area was the hot spot. It was my client's custom to rely on Stienstra's column in the paper for ideas about where to go." I added, "After leaving the marina, he would also monitor the chatter of the other boats on the two-way radio for further information."

He nodded his head to those things routinely done by all fishermen.

I went on, "Since you were out that day too, I thought you might have seen something."

This one-sided conversation was taking place at his doorway. He had opened the door no wider than necessary to accommodate his stance.

"Captain, would you mind showing me the usual course you take to get out to Duxbury?"

When he nodded, I took the chart from under my arm and asked as casually as I could, "Do you have a table I can put this on?"

From the way he was acting, it would not have been a surprise if he said, 'Just a minute,' closed the door, and returned with a card table.

"Oh sure," he said, quickly followed by the hoped for words, ". . . come in."

The interior of the house was even more immaculately kept than the outside: whoever the still anonymous captain might be, he was obviously not a bachelor. A few steps past the foyer was the formal dining room with a table large enough to comfortably seat eight or ten. He gestured toward it. I unrolled the chart and he found some glass objects to hold the edges down flat.

"Would you show me what course you usually take to Duxbury?"

He gave no indication of wanting to sit down and we stood leaning over the chart. He began at Fisherman's Wharf tracing his course on the chart, narrating as his finger moved past various well known landmarks.

Before he got to the Golden Gate Bridge, I asked, "Do you normally dock at Fisherman's Wharf?" He nodded and continued, taking himself under the Bridge, moving his finger along the north side of Golden Gate Channel toward Point Bonita. When he got to Point Bonita, he stopped his narration, abruptly stepping back from the table.

"I want to know what this is all about. Why are you asking all these questions?"

"This is the situation, Captain. On March 9th, two years ago, a boat with five men went out fishing. There were no survivors—"

He interrupted. "Who is suing, and what are they suing for?"

"Some of the heirs are suing Mrs. Dowd, the widow of the boat owner, claiming that her husband sailed his boat into big waves and it sank, either on the Bar or in Bonita Channel. I am defending her."

He thought for a moment, scratching the day old stubble on his cheek,

"Well, there can be big waves out there; big enough to sink a fishing boat." He paused, looking at me intently.

"What is it you want from me?" Jabbing his finger in my direction, he added, "I'll tell you right now, I'm not coming to court," and tightly folded his arms across his chest.

There was something important I needed to know.

"I'm sorry, but I don't know your name."

Now it was my turn to wait for him to speak. As the seconds ticked by, he actually seemed to be debating with himself whether he was going to tell me.

"Phelan," he finally said with an aggravated sigh, ". . . Jim Phelan." Once again stating, "And I'm not coming to court," his voice several decibels louder than before.

I was confused. He seemed willing to be of some help, but that willingness apparently stopped short of being pulled into court as a witness.

"Captain, my purpose in meeting with you is to learn what information you may have that might be helpful in defending Mrs. Dowd." His expression didn't change, but he offered no further objections, and I continued, "By any chance did you see this boat, the *Aloha*, that morning?"

I handed him a photograph which he studied closely.

"No, she doesn't look familiar." He paused for a moment.

"Tell me again why your client is being sued."

"The claim is that her husband was negligent."

My response was deliberately vague, hoping he would ask for details so we could have a real dialogue. His face remained blank, and he said nothing.

I resumed my questions about the morning of March 9. I didn't get very far before he once again interrupted. "What is it that you want from me?"

It suddenly came to me what the underlying problem was. He was a captain, with the same self-assurance he would have as if he were in the wheelhouse of his fishing boat, maneuvering in tight waters. He wanted answers about any uncertainties he had, and now.

Maintaining steady eye contact, I asked, "Captain Phelan, did you take the Main Channel or Bonita Channel to get out to Duxbury that morning?"

"I took Bonita Channel," he answered without hesitation. Bending down to the chart, he continued tracing his course. I watched his finger move around Point Bonita, into the Channel, past the mid-point between Buoy Three and Buoy Four, coming out at the north end of the Channel by Buoy Two.

We were now at the cusp, and I had the critical question ready.

"On your way out to Duxbury, were there any unusual sea conditions you had to deal with? Big waves, anything like that?"

He looked at me in extended silence, searching my face, his lips moving in a faintly pursing manner before finally speaking.

"There were breakers on the Bar, but the Channel was clear."

I asked, "Are you talking about the north part of the Bar, around Four Fathom Bank?"

He nodded. "That's right. There were breakers on Four Fathom Bank and the Potatopatch, but the Channel itself was clear and I went through."

It was beyond remarkable he could remember what course he had taken two and a half years earlier. He would have taken his boat out several hundred times since then. There was no reason for the details of the trip on March 9 to remain in his memory, but somehow there was a ring of truth to what he said.

"Captain, I'm surprised you can remember that kind of detail from two and a half years ago."

Setting his jaw firmly, he gave me the same assessing look captains give crewmen signing on a vessel. This ritual had taken place every time I reported to the bridge of a new ship with my shipping papers.

His eyes darted around my face before he began to speak. "I didn't remember going through the Channel. I looked it up in my log book."

Log book! Trying to suppress my excitement, I asked quietly, "Captain, may I look at your log book?"

His response was silence. The same assessing look came over his face again, but not for long.

"Look," he said brusquely, "you said something about a trial, what's that all about?" Before I could reply, he shot in again, "And I'll tell you right now, I'm not coming to court."

I abandoned any further thoughts of trying to win him over with incremental small talk. His bluntness made it impossible to put off stating what role I had in mind for him.

I nodded my head slowly.

"All right Captain, I'll lay it out for you." I looked toward the dining room table.

"Telling you the whole story is going to take a few minutes. May we sit down?"

"Oh, sure," he said almost apologetically. It was the first time since opening the front door he had acted remotely like a host.

I provided the basic facts, beginning with the time the *Aloha* left the dock in Sausalito, who was onboard, Dowd's experience with boats, and summarized the Coast Guard report. I finished with a summary of the plaintiffs' negligence contentions, and told him the trial was coming up next week.

He stared at me, digesting my words, deep in thought. When he finally spoke it was in a completely different tone from what he'd used before. "I don't want to come to court."

I could practically hear the Hallelujah Chorus booming in my head. 'I'm not coming to court' had changed to 'I don't want to come.'

It was the turn I had about convinced myself he wasn't going to make. There was a test question that would determine whether he really had.

Speaking in a low voice, I repeated the question I'd asked earlier that he had ignored. "Captain, would you show me your log book?"

For a moment he remained motionless, lost in thought, and then abruptly strode to the credenza where the Sunday china was kept, retrieving his log book. He turned to the month of March and handed it to me.

I was taken completely aback. His 'log book' turned out to be nothing more than some sort of advertising calendar. At the top was a picture of dogs playing cards. Below the picture was the name of a neighborhood merchant. Attached underneath was the calendar. Each day of the month had an inch and a half box for notes. For March 9, there were two cryptic notations: "5/9," and "Breakers on the Bar—Duxbury," all in stubby block lettering.

It took every bit of concentration I could muster to ask, "What does the "5/9" entry mean?"

"I had five passengers and we caught nine fish."

I then inquired about "Breakers on the Bar."

"It means there were waves breaking on the Bar, but the Channel was O.K., and I took it out to Duxbury."

It took a determined effort to avoid conveying the importance of what he had just said. Keeping my voice steady, I asked, "Captain Phelan, I see where it says 'Breakers on the Bar,' but how do you know you went through Bonita Channel since it doesn't say that?"

He replied without hesitation: "Because if I'd gone out Main Channel, I would have put that down."

He was saying just the opposite of what Captain McGee had said about Bonita Channel being full of big waves, causing him to take the Main Channel out to Duxbury. I wanted to tell him the importance of this information, and how helpful it would be to have him testify, but hesitated. I had not yet asked if he had been contacted by plaintiffs' investigator, and wasn't at all sure about how much I could tell him.

I was still grappling with what to say when he burst out, "A man comes to court, and you damn lawyers make a fool out of him . . . make you look like a liar!"

His face flushed to a deep crimson, angrier now than any time since I'd been in his home. In his state of mind, one false move on my part and he would order me out of the house. I had to say something, and fast. But what!

I didn't blame him for his feelings. A person called to give testimony in court expects to perform their civic duty and answer questions about what they know. For their trouble they are subjected to prying personal questions, their character is impugned, aspersions are made about their impartiality, and if their education is limited, insinuations are made that they are unintelligent. Cross-examination is intentionally done in a manner to cast doubt about their veracity, frequently in a ridiculing manner.

"Captain Phelan, nobody's going to make a fool out of you, and here's why. You're a neutral witness, you're not taking sides, you don't know any of the parties, and you have no interest in the outcome of the case. If you stick to what you know, you will more than hold your own. Nobody is going to push you around in court."

He wasn't mollified. "What about the other lawyer? He's going to be asking questions too!"

I shook my head. "If you stick to what you know, what you saw, and what you did, there is nothing to get tripped up on."

He put his hands on his hips. In a tone equally bellicose and accusatory, he said, "And if I don't agree to come, you're going to give me a subpoena anyway . . . isn't . . . that . . . so?"

It was a statement, an accusation, and a question, that he wanted answered right then.

"Captain, I have a subpoena right here in my pocket," patting my suit coat, ". . . and to be perfectly frank it was my intention to serve you with it if you had any information that would help me defend Mrs. Dowd."

We were looking at each other squarely in the eye.

"I'm not going to kid you about this. You have information I need."

He seemed to be taking this quite calmly. From the sound of my voice, I was the one becoming agitated. I continued: "But I'm not going to force you to come to court. You have to be willing to come."

"And what if I say No," he declared truculently, jutting his chin out.

I shook my head. "The reason I'm not going to force you to come is this. If I make you come against your will, you could hurt Mrs. Dowd if you wanted to."

I had more to say, but it would have been mostly repetition, and I stopped.

In a low voice, I said, "It's your decision, Captain."

It was time for silence. His eyes burned holes in me, staring intently. As uncomfortable as it was, I had to look back in the same manner. If I broke eye contact with him, even for a second, I would be finished.

An interminable pause ensued before he finally spoke.

"All right, I'll come."

A long moment passed, his eyes fixed on me, unblinking, before he spoke again. Pacing his words in a slow, steely manner, "But, don't you make a fool out of me."

I felt a verbal noose slipping around my neck.

"Yes, Sir," I responded, in an equally firm tone.

For the first time we shook hands; the sandpaper grasp of a fisherman's hand, rubbed raw from years of exposure to the elements.

I filled out the subpoena and handed him a check for his witness fee and expenses. He stared at the subpoena in silence. He had made his decision, but from the expression racing over his face, he must have been wondering why he had called me in the first place when he didn't have to.

His mind seemed elsewhere, half listening, as I went through the areas I would question him about. When I asked if he had any questions, he shook his head and walked me to the door in silence. We said brief good-byes, and I descended the steps. At the bottom I turned to wave at him. The door was already closed.

I was halfway back to the office before it came to me that when the captain said he would come, and we shook hands on it, he was the one who extended his hand first.

# 14

Five days before the trial date, the mandatory settlement conference took place. On the drive to the courthouse, I went through the innumerable conversations I'd had with Janet regarding settlement. The two factors that motivate most clients to want a case settled, the innate fear of going to court and the risk of monetary loss, seemed to have no influence on her thinking. She showed no signs of wavering in her determination to go to trial.

I arranged to have Marjorie Frasier meet me at the courthouse. While waiting for her, I reviewed the approach I would take with the settlement conference judge. She arrived, and after exchanging greetings she asked if I had any last minute thoughts about the case. I shook my head. Marjorie commented that this was going to be an 'all in' or 'all out' case, meaning either a defense verdict or a very large verdict for the plaintiffs, and looked at me in extended silence, making no attempt to hide she was studying my face for a reaction. I walked to the bulletin board and found our case on the settlement conference list. The judge was listed as Phillip Young, a new name to me. We walked to the assigned room; the door open. The judge motioned us in. Blake was already there.

We were hardly seated before the judge began to speak. "I've reviewed the entire court file," and recited the things he'd read and considered. His grasp of the details indicated he had spent considerable time familiarizing himself with the facts.

The judge then told us he would begin by meeting with us separately, and Blake would go first. Marjorie and I stepped outside.

In fifteen minutes Blake emerged. As we walked in the judge, who was pacing back and forth, gestured for us to be seated.

"The wave is the big issue, isn't it?" he said, continuing to pace.

"I agree, Your Honor, but the—"

With a flick of his hand he cut me off. "Boats don't disappear for no reason. The jury will know something happened, and if they decide Dowd was negligent, you're going to get hit with a big verdict. $1,100,000 isn't a lot of coverage in a wrongful death case, particularly with Mrs. Ang being a widow with five children.

"Your basic problem is this: something happened, and plaintiffs have solid evidence from those data buoys that big waves were breaking on the Bar that morning." He let his words sink in for a few moments before continuing. "Plaintiffs' attorney tells me he wants the policy limits of $1,100,000 to settle this case." Before I could say anything, he went on quickly, "I don't think he's in cement on that figure, but he's not going to bid against himself either."

Changing to a persuasive tone, "Just give me an opening offer; something to get negotiations started."

"Based on the information I have at this point," I said, "I don't plan on making an offer."

Irritation immediately began to show around the edges of his face. In a strained effort to speak evenly he continued: "Since there are no survivors, and no witnesses, this case is going to turn on the testimony of both sides' expert witnesses. Right?"

I nodded.

Having gained my acquiescence to that plainly correct observation, he went on: "If it turns out that the opinions of the expert witnesses are a close call in the minds of the jury concerning whether or not Mr. Dowd was negligent, do you think they're going to turn a widow with five children out with nothing?"

The answer to that statement was so obvious he didn't even wait for a response. It was food for thought. He ushered us out, beckoning to Blake.

In a few minutes, we were summoned back in. The judge got right to the point.

"If Blake has a smoking gun, he wouldn't reveal it to me." Pursing his lips, he added, "I don't think he has one, and quite frankly, I don't think he needs one either," and wasted no time telling me why.

"This case has liability exposure, and the damages are easy to calculate. Many verdicts have come in with a lot less direct evidence than this case."

The settlement negotiations were not proceeding in the usual manner of plaintiffs making a large settlement demand, and the defense responding with a low offer. At that point, negotiations begin in earnest. By making no offer at all, I was not following the script and the judge's mercury was rising.

Dropping his voice, he spoke imperatively: "You have to make an offer."

"Unless plaintiffs' attorney discloses something I am unaware of, I'm not prepared to make an offer," I repeated.

The judge's displeasure was immediately evident. Standing abruptly, he ordered me to send in plaintiffs' counsel.

"I think Blake must have told the judge something in confidence," I said to Marjorie as we sat in the hallway . . . "and he's trying to get Blake's permission to let him use it on me."

In a few minutes we were summoned back in while Blake waited outside.

"There are no new facts, and there are no new witnesses. I asked Blake directly about both, and the answer was 'No.'" The judge was speaking in the short agitated bursts of a man whose patience was at an end. The icy look on Young's face made it very plain that there were going to be no more 'candlelight and black nighty' attempts at persuasion from him.

"This is not a case of no liability. You face exposure here. There are big damages and appealing plaintiffs."

The judge, who had been pacing back and forth since we came back in, abruptly sat down, staring intently for an unnervingly long time before slowly and deliberately speaking: "Blake isn't going to try this case." He paused, moving his eyes back and forth between Marjorie and me. "Baum will be trying this case for the plaintiffs."

If he had said there was a death in the family, I would not have been more shocked.

The judge continued in a lowered voice: "I see Baum's name regularly in *Jury Verdicts Weekly*, always getting million dollar verdicts." He said nothing further. He didn't have to. The expression on his face stated just as plainly as if he had spoken aloud: 'I've never heard of you before, or read about any big cases you've tried.'

Without further comment he went to the door and called Blake. When Blake entered, Young tersely announced the settlement conference was over, ordering us to report to Department One on Monday morning, ready for trial.

Marjorie and I walked out together in silence. I was practically in a daze. She finally spoke, "Is there anything you learned today that changes your thoughts about the case?"

I took note of the open-ended nature of the phrases 'anything you learned today' and 'changes your thoughts.' It was not clear if she was inquiring about Baum trying the case in her question. I shook my head.

After discussing a few other matters, Marjorie said she had to get back to the office. As we were saying goodbye, I forced myself to say, "I'll be ready."

On the freeway, I kept turning over in my mind what Young said. As insulting as the judge's words had been regarding Baum trying many million dollar cases, and never even hearing about me, I knew what he said was true . . . Baum was going to try this case.

The realities about what had just happened started falling into place. It is common knowledge that most of the cases handled by the tiny percentage of trial lawyers in the top echelon of the plaintiffs' bar, like Baum, are 'referrals,' sent to them by the large pool of lawyers who lack the skills to handle million dollar cases. Getting big verdicts makes good reading in *Jury Verdicts Weekly*. To keep their names in the forefront of the minds of that pool of less experienced attorneys with cases to refer, the plaintiffs' lawyers in the top tier carefully select two or three cases to take to trial each year. A lawyer of Baum's stature would never take a case to trial if there was any chance of losing it. Publicity is a two-edged sword, and the negative publicity of losing cases would soon dry up his primary source of income . . . referrals.

I noted Blake had not looked upset when the case didn't settle. The notion began to dawn on me that Baum had been planning on taking this case to trial all along, and I had been set up as this year's sacrificial lamb.

What galled me most was that Judge Young figured out in fifteen minutes that Baum would try the case. I had been working on it for over a year and in all that time, the idea of Baum's involvement had never even entered my mind.

Back in the office, I called Janet. I told her the case had not settled, and listened carefully for any change in her determination. She took the news calmly without uttering a single anxious word about going to court.

From the time I arrived in the office, I avoided doing something I knew would be counterproductive, but could not put out of my mind. Chiding myself for succumbing, I finally went to the office library, pulled out the Martindale lawyer's directory and looked up Baum. He was a graduate of Northwestern University law school, and had been in practice twenty-nine years. This was in stark contrast to my ten years of experience.

The list of his professional accomplishments was a long one. He had written numerous articles for academic and legal journals, and authored a well-known book on trial preparation. He had also served on the boards of various national, state, and local trial lawyers' associations, including president of the California Trial Lawyers' Association, the largest organization of its kind in the country.

I then looked in *Jury Verdicts Weekly* and read the write-ups of Baum's trials going back a few years. He'd tried around two cases a year. They shared a common theme: the jury rendered a verdict for his clients usually two or three times larger than the amount the defendants had offered at the settlement conference. There was a simple message for defense lawyers to draw: not accepting Baum's settlement demand was a decision they would soon regret.

On Monday morning I was going to be a participant in my own funeral, and Janet's life would be ruined in the process. I felt like I had just read the epitaph to my career.

# 15

In the hour it took to drive to San Jose on Monday morning, thoughts about everything that might happen churned through my mind.

I'd tried about forty cases. I had my share of losses in the beginning as I honed my skills, testing myself in the only arena that counts, the courtroom. What my father said many times resounded inside me now, "You are on trial as much as your client. You have to trust yourself; there's nobody else."

Department One was crowded with lawyers wanting, with one exception, to be assigned a courtroom for trial. I found a vacant seat near the back, clinging to the hope that Blake would be there by himself, and waited for the judge to appear. After a short delay the clerk rose. In a voice louder than her diminutive size suggested, she called the noisy courtroom to order.

"All rise. Department One of the Superior Court of California, in and for the County of Santa Clara, is now in session."

The bailiff opened the door to chambers and the judge strode toward the bench. The clerk waited until he was seated before completing her cry. "Please be seated and come to order. Court is in session."

The judge cheerfully addressed the courtroom: "Good morning everyone. I'm sorry to have kept you waiting." He then directed the clerk to call the trial docket.

She nodded, and turned to face the courtroom. "When I call your case, state your appearance, and give your estimate of the length of the trial."

Halfway down the docket, the clerk called, "Ang vs. Dowd." When I rose to state my appearance, my worst fear was confirmed. I saw Baum, and Blake was with him. Baum spoke.

71

"David Baum and Martin Blake for plaintiffs. Two weeks, Your Honor."

It was my turn.

"Jay Jacobs for defendant Janet Dowd, Your Honor; ten to twelve days."

In the next half hour, the lawyers for the cases ahead of us were called into chambers so the judge could prod them into making one last attempt to settle.

When the clerk called out, "Ang vs. Dowd," I gathered up my briefcase and headed for chambers.

"I see this is a wrongful death case," the judge said as he picked up the docket sheet, ". . . a two to three week trial. Is that right?"

We nodded.

He then examined our settlement conference statements at length.

"It doesn't appear you got very far at the settlement conference."

Looking at us pointedly, he asked, "Do you think another settlement conference might help?"

He barely finished before Baum began speaking in a terse tone of finality: "No, Your Honor, the time for settlement discussions is over. Plaintiffs are here, ready for trial."

"All right," the judge said, resignedly, ". . . I'm sending you to Department Six for trial." Without further comment, he signed the docket sheet. He had washed his hands of us; we were no longer his concern.

I retrieved my luggage cart with my court bags, and headed for the elevators.

As I got off, I looked at the directory on the wall. The occupant of Department Six was a new name, Judge David W. Leahy.

Pushing my cart through the door, I paused to look the courtroom over.

The walls were paneled in dark wood giving the courtroom an almost cave like appearance. Immediately in front of me were four or five rows of seats for spectators. Past the spectator area, separated by a wooden railing, was the 'well' of the courtroom with the clerk's desk, and a smaller desk where the court reporter would sit, making a transcript of the proceedings. Above the well was the elevated bench the judge would preside from. To the right was the jury box with its twelve swiveling chairs. Adjacent to the judge's bench was the witness box. It too was elevated, but not quite as high as the judge's bench. On the wall behind the bench was a six foot high replica of the Great Seal of California. Immediately past the barrier separating the spectator area were two well-worn tables for the attorneys.

Baum and Blake were already seated at the counsel table closest to the jury box. I took my cart to the table for defendants and removed the files I would need. Walking to the clerk's desk, I introduced myself to her and the court reporter, telling them I would be representing Mrs. Dowd. The clerk said the judge was reviewing the file and would see all counsel in chambers in a few minutes. While we were speaking, the bailiff entered.

The courtroom bailiffs are a part of the county sheriff's department. They are usually older men who suffer from bad backs after years of riding around in patrol cars, and assigned courtroom duty to see them through to retirement. In marked contrast, our bailiff was an attractive woman about thirty.

In fifteen minutes, the judge called us into chambers. Dominating the room was his oversized desk, clear of everything except the file open in front of him. After introducing ourselves and identifying who we represented, the judge gestured us to the chairs in front of his desk.

"Is it correct that this is a two to three week trial?" he asked in a well-modulated voice.

We confirmed it was.

"We will not be in session this Thursday and Friday for the Thanksgiving holiday. We will also be out of session Monday, Tuesday, and Wednesday of next week. I have long standing appointments which I must keep."

The judge pulled a calendar from his desk, and opened it to December.

"I think we should tell the jury panel this trial could go to Friday, December 12th, and to be safe I'm going to tell them it might extend a few days beyond that, in case your estimates are off."

He looked at us carefully. "Do you see this case taking more than three weeks to try?"

We shook our heads.

"I hope being out of session those three days next week will not create problems for your witnesses."

We thanked him for his consideration and indicated there should be no difficulties.

While the judge had been speaking, I looked at him carefully. He appeared to be in his mid- to late-fifties, and while not a strikingly handsome man, there was a distinguished look about him. He spoke deliberately, giving himself time to think before speaking.

So far the judge was making a good impression, but I quickly reminded myself these were all first impressions. Trial court judges have more power than the officials of any other branch of government. If they choose to abuse their considerable discretionary powers, little can be done about it. In a very real sense, he was going to rule our lives for the next three weeks.

He asked if there was anything about the facts or the parties that might result in a lot of people being excused from the jury panel for cause.

This was a good question. Some cases receive so much pretrial publicity that seating a jury is difficult. As had been done in San Francisco, the loss of the *Aloha* was a front page story in the newspapers, and on the evening televised news in San Jose.

Baum began to speak, and I moved my chair slightly to see him clearly.

"Your Honor, at this time the plaintiffs withdraw their jury trial demand, and wish to try the case before you without a jury."

The judge seemed surprised and asked, "Was it your jury demand?"

Blake answered, "Yes," handing him a copy of the trial setting order.

Judge Leahy leaned back, studying it carefully. When he finished, he looked at me for comment.

"We will pick up the jury demand, Your Honor," I said promptly.

Blake pointed to the document. "The demand for a jury trial was not a joint demand," he said. "The defendant did not request a jury; only we did. Since the defense did not request a jury at the trial setting conference, it is too late for them to request one now."

Baum's announcement, withdrawing their jury demand, was a surprise. Blake's statement that I had not made a backup request for a trial by jury came as a complete shock. There had to be some mistake. I had never tried any case without a jury, even when I was trying simple intersection accident cases. Most definitely I would not have waived the right to a jury trial in a case of this magnitude. I asked if I might look at the order. The judge examined the court file and found the original order. After studying it, he handed it to me.

"Mr. Jacobs, it would appear you did not make a jury demand . . . ," he paused, "and both sides signed the order. Do you have anything different from what appears in the original order?"

"Let me get my copy," I said, and went back into the courtroom to look through my files. My stomach told me my copy was going to be no different from the original the judge just showed me.

I found my copy. As I expected, the box for a jury trial had been checked 'yes' by plaintiffs, but 'no' by me, and my signature was on the form. Staring at my copy, I tried to recollect what possibly could have happened at the trial setting conference. Maybe the clerk had checked the wrong boxes on the form, and I signed without reading it carefully. I quickly rejected that possibility. The clerks are too busy for that; the form is filled out by the attorneys themselves.

I walked back into chambers with no explanation to offer. Baum's face had the same expressionless, measuring look of appraisal he used in his office during Mrs. Ang's deposition. The judge waited for me to speak, but nothing was coming. I sat numbly, the three of them staring at me as I struggled to think of something to say. Silently, I repeated to myself: Dammit! Dammit! Dammit! I was in an untenable position. To gain time, I asked to look at the original order again, trying to come up with a way to extricate myself.

"Your Honor, I always ask for a jury, and my client wants a trial by jury in this matter." My voice was dropping. The judge leaned forward to hear me as I continued. ". . . I have never tried a case without a jury."

Something finally came to mind. "Would it be possible to have the court reporter who was assigned to the trial setting department that day look at her notes? I may have asked for a jury on the record."

The judge shrugged with one shoulder, and spoke to the clerk through the open door.

"Call the court administrator's office. Find out which reporter covered the trial setting conference calendar for this date. Tell them I need to know right away, and find out how long it will take."

We sat in silence. I could hear the clerk on the phone. She came to the door and said it would take about ten minutes. Luckily, the notes had not been sent to storage.

The reporter arrived shortly with her notes. She found the record of our case and started reading. We had stated our appearances, and given our estimates of the number of days necessary to try the case. The conference judge asked if we had agreed on a trial date, and set the date we requested. The last item was the assignment of the settlement conference date. No request had been made by me on the record for a jury trial.

The judge tilted his chair back, silently scrolling through the issues he would have to decide. The facts were straight forward: plaintiffs' counsel had asked for a jury, I had not, and plaintiffs had just now withdrawn their jury demand. The question Judge Leahy would have to decide was: by failing to request a jury at the setting conference, had I waived my right to ask for a jury trial now? He turned to Baum and Blake, and asked if they were willing to stipulate that I could request a jury at this time? They shook their heads simultaneously, "No."

The judge removed his glasses, and began slowly rubbing his forehead. "I think this should be on the record."

We went back into the courtroom sitting at our respective counsel tables. While we were waiting for the court reporter to set up, I glanced at the unoccupied chairs in the jury box. I couldn't imagine trying this case with those twelve seats empty.

When the court reporter was ready, the judge came out of chambers wearing his black robe. We stood as he took the bench. In a voice markedly different from the conversational tone he used in chambers, he said somberly, "Clerk, call the case."

Even though we were the only ones in the courtroom, she stood to recite the full name of the case with the same formality as if the parties were present, a jury was in the box, and the spectator section filled with onlookers.

After asking us to state our appearances for the record, the judge said, "Mr. Jacobs, do you wish to be heard on the matter of a demand for a trial by jury in this matter?"

I stood to address the judge.

"Your Honor, this turn of events has come as a complete surprise. I don't know what could have gone awry. I have tried around forty cases, and not one has been without a jury."

Slowing my pace, I continued. "This case is of considerable importance to my client, and she wants a trial by jury. I know you are concerned that the case proceed in a timely way, but I request that you allow us time to research the legal issues and prepare briefs on this important matter. We can submit our briefs to you in the morning, after which you can hear argument, and make your ruling on my request that the case be tried by a jury."

The judge turned to Baum and Blake.

"Gentlemen?"

They conferred in whispers. When they finished, Blake spoke. "As the court pleases, Your Honor."

The judge tilted his chair back, staring at the ceiling in deep concentration for an unnervingly long period.

Shifting his look toward me, he said, "By the look of surprise on your face, Mr. Jacobs, there is no doubt in my mind that you were expecting this case to be a jury trial." He paused. "I will let you brief this matter."

He ordered us to submit our briefs to the clerk no later than nine o'clock; he would read them, and then hear argument. He left the bench.

I felt a wave of temporary reprieve pour over me. I had no idea whether Blake's statement that my failure to ask for a jury at the trial setting conference was a permanent waiver, barring me from requesting one now.

I began putting the files away, my mind racing about the events which just transpired. Thoughts began emerging of the potential consequences I faced with an escalating sense of foreboding about what might happen in the morning.

The reason I always asked for a jury was simple: I did not want one person, even a well-intentioned judge who is trained to disregard appeals to his or her emotions, to decide a case. A jury deliberates as a group, each person acting as a damper on the excesses of their fellows. I trusted twelve people, with their different perspectives on the evidence and different perceptions of the witnesses, much more than one person acting alone, trained judge or not.

I called Janet to let her know we had a courtroom, and would be back in session in the morning to argue motions. I told her it would not be necessary for her to appear at nine o'clock if she could be in court on an hour's notice. She agreed.

"Good luck," she said as we finished our conversation. By then I was thinking more in the terms of a miracle.

The first thing I did back in the office was phone a colleague in San Jose to ask about Judge Leahy. He told me before going on the bench that the judge had been a labor lawyer representing unions. Leahy had been appointed to the bench by Governor Jerry Brown, and also been the county chairman of Brown's gubernatorial election campaign. My friend had tried a few cases in front of Leahy and said, "With his background I thought he would be pro-plaintiff, but I got a fair shake in front of him."

He paused for a moment, his voice taking on a distinctly cautioning tone as he continued. "There is one thing to watch out for with Leahy. I think the judge has some sort of back problem. When he starts shifting around in his chair, he's probably in a lot of pain ... when you see that happening, make certain you're not the lawyer he's getting ready to unload on."

Most of my afternoon was spent in the library researching the jury demand issue. At five o'clock I forced myself to quit. Ordinarily, I would have continued my research work, but it was going to take several more hours to get the brief in final form. It was time to stop reading and start writing.

By seven-thirty I had it ready. Sitting at the computer, I typed it out. Bearing in mind the limited time I had to get the brief written, it was good, but far from perfect. Its principal fault was not an insignificant one ... it was way too long. It only takes a few hours to draft a ten page brief, but twice as long to pare it down to two or three pages. Whatever was going to happen the next day was going to happen with the brief as it was now. I took everything home.

Marsha had her dinner earlier, but sat with me as I ate the meal she kept warm. After dessert, we cleared the table and I began preparing for the next day, not going to bed until midnight. My last conscious thoughts were about Janet.

It was still dark when I went out for my morning run at six o'clock, and I had the park to myself. Marsha had breakfast with me and helped me pack everything.

"Good luck with the motion," she said, leaning in to kiss me as I backed the car out of the garage. I spent the one hour drive to the courthouse going over the arguments I would make to Judge Leahy.

Arriving in San Jose, I parked the car in a lot, and walked the few blocks to the courthouse. A breeze stirred the Gingko trees, freeing a few of their remaining leaves to float down around me. The movement of the shimmering golden colors lifted my spirits.

Baum and Blake arrived shortly before nine, and we exchanged copies of our briefs. When the judge finished reading them in chambers, he came on the bench. The clerk called the empty courtroom to order.

Greeting us with a cordial "Good morning," the judge stated for the record that he had read and considered our briefs.

"Mr. Jacobs, do you wish to be heard?"

I stood. "Your Honor, I have nothing to add that is not included in my brief, but I would like to make one comment, if I may." He nodded.

"I have searched my mind for some explanation why I did not check the box requesting a jury. Failing to do so was an inadvertent error on my part, and I want to apologize to the court and counsel for any inconvenience this may have caused. I have always thought this case would be tried before a jury, which is Mrs. Dowd's wish."

There was no reaction from the judge. He nodded in their direction. Blake rose and began ticking off his arguments. "Counsel signed the trial setting conference order, and checked the 'No' box waiving the jury he now claims to want. It is unknown whether this last minute request is merely a change of mind on his part. There is ample authority to deny defense counsel's request, and we ask the court to exercise its discretion and deny this last minute application. If this was an inadvertent mistake, he has had months to notice it, notify the court, and have it rectified."

The judge looked to me for a response. I had to steer the argument away from why the 'Yes' box had not been checked, and get Judge Leahy focused on the issues in my brief.

"Your Honor, I cannot explain why the 'Yes' box requesting a jury was not checked by me. Yesterday's withdrawal of the jury demand by plaintiffs came as a complete shock. But why that box was not checked is not the issue for you to determine. The issue to be decided is this: does the court have the discretion to deny Mrs. Dowd's demand for a jury?"

I was speaking too quickly and slowed my pace. "I would like to call your attention to the *Bishop* case which I appended to my brief. The appellate court in that case held it was reversible error for the trial court judge to deny Bishop's request to have his case tried by a jury, even though the request was made on the eve of trial."

The displeased expression on Judge Leahy's face reflected the dilemma the *Bishop* case put him in. The statute states that a trial court judge has discretion to either grant or deny a last minute request for a jury trial, but the holding in the *Bishop* case stated it would be a reversible error if Judge Leahy did not grant my request.

The judge tilted his big leather chair back, rocking it gently, deeply engrossed in thought. We stood silently. It was clear he wanted no more argument, and his ruling would be forthcoming soon. He picked up one of our briefs, flicking through several pages. Setting it aside, he resumed staring fixedly at the ceiling. The only noise in the tomblike silence enveloping the courtroom was the gentle squeaking sound emanating from his big chair.

Lowering his head slowly, he said, "Is the matter submitted, gentlemen?"

"Yes," we muttered.

This is the high anxiety moment of any motion, particularly when the stakes are so high. Once a lawyer states 'submitted,' the judge will permit no more argument and make his ruling.

The judge shifted in his chair several times before speaking.

"I'm going to grant defendant's request for a jury trial." A rush of air flooded into my lungs. I leaned against the table to steady my legs which didn't seem to be cooperating.

Turning to Baum and Blake, he spoke in a changed, almost querulous, tone.

"The *Bishop* case was tried right here in Santa Clara County in front of Judge Kennedy, just down the hall. I remember him discussing the appellate court's ruling with me."

Keeping his focus on them, the judge continued in the same purposeful tone.

"I'm surprised you didn't find that case."

There seemed to be a distinct note of reproof in what he'd just said. If the judge was making the point I thought he was, this was no trifling matter. The cases mentioned in their brief were much older than the cases

I cited. Citing cases to the court which are no longer a correct statement of the law, because they have been overturned or modified, is misconduct.

The look on Judge Leahy's face, when he stated he was "surprised" they had not found the *Bishop* case, I interpreted to be a subtle warning: 'don't try this with me again.' I made a mental note that any brief we submitted to Judge Leahy was going to be read carefully, and he would research any legal citations we made before making his rulings.

The judge turned to the clerk, and said, "Call the jury commissioner's office. Have them send a panel up at one-thirty."

With a last meaningful look at Baum and Blake, he left the bench.

# 16

During an earlier break, I called Janet asking her to be in court at eleven o'clock. Just as we finished arguing the motion, I noticed her sitting in the spectator area. After the judge left the bench, I stepped past the railing to greet her.

Janet stood as I approached, and I noticed what she was wearing . . . a stylish pant suit. The top had tiny glittering sequins woven into the fabric, set off by a silver necklace. Her outfit was fine for a social occasion, but not for court.

On every prior occasion, Janet had worn simple, low key dresses, even when we met at her home. She had to be feeling anxious, and I did not want to increase her angst, but her outfit was not going to be well received by the panel. This was my fault for not advising her. If it had been close, I would have kept my silence, but it was not.

I cleared my throat nervously. "Janet, the majority of the jury panel will be working people. You will be sitting next to me at the counsel table throughout the jury selection process. They will be looking at you carefully, making first impressions." She stared expressionless, waiting for me to get to the point.

"First impressions count," I said, "And doubly so in court."

I was stumbling for the right words which weren't coming. I finally forced myself to speak plainly. "Would you please go home and change into an understated dress, with no jewelry, not even earrings, and no scarves or high heels. Something you would wear to church."

As soon as I finished speaking, I sensed I had embarrassed her and began a jumbled apology, repeating what I'd said about first impressions and the likely make-up of the jury panel.

She cut me off with a firm shake of her head. "I understand your concern. I should have thought of it myself."

After Janet left, I had two hours to review my notes about who I wanted to be on the jury. The only other trial I'd had in San Jose had been a few years earlier, and the thirty or forty people sent up from the jury commissioner's office were typical for a mostly urban county.

Before the war, Santa Clara County was largely rural, dominated by farms, orchards and even a well-regarded wine industry. The post war era saw an explosion in growth. The demographics had dramatically changed from mostly rural and agricultural to urban and industrial with the high tech industries of Silicon Valley dominating the economy. San Jose, the county seat, had a population larger than San Francisco.

I went downstairs for a soda and ate my lunch on a bench near the rose garden the judges had planted and maintained. It was a fragrant place to study my notes before returning to the courtroom. Janet arrived at one-fifteen. My eyes immediately went to her outfit. She tilted her head slightly, and in what seemed like slow motion, her right hand moved to the side of her dress, delicately lifting it outwards six or eight inches before releasing it to drift back to her side. She then arched her eyebrows in a satisfied now? expression.

She had changed into an understated navy print dress. It was perfect for court. She looked elegant, and I said so. Her response was a gracious smile, expressing far better than words that she was not upset.

I had explained the jury selection process previously, and gave her a quick summary. "The potential jurors will be questioned, initially by the judge, and then by Baum and me, about their qualifications to serve as jurors in this case. The judge will ask us to stand and introduce our clients, and I will ask you to rise."

I did not mention the judge would also summarize the negligence allegations in the complaint. I wanted the panel members to observe Janet's reaction when the words 'negligence' and her husband's name were used in the same sentence.

There was something else of importance to tell her: "Janet, do your best not to react to anything the Angs say on the witness stand, and avoid running into them in the hallway or the elevators. I suggest you use the ladies room on the third floor." She nodded her head in agreement.

At one-thirty the panel was brought into the courtroom. This was going to be the last relaxed moment I would have for the next three weeks, and I savored this final bit of calm before the impending storm began.

They were led in by a clerk from the jury assembly room on the first floor who handed a list of their names to Judge Leahy's clerk. On her way out, she stopped at the door to bid them farewell, as if they were a group of youngsters about to board the bus for summer camp.

While they were filing in, I went to the side of the courtroom to unobtrusively make some quick assessments about the ratio of men to women, their age range, and identify anyone who, by appearance or demeanor, differentiated themselves from the group as a whole. Something struck me as odd about the panel, drawn as it was from a mostly urban county; the complete absence of minorities. There was not a single Black, Hispanic, Asian or other minority group person among them. The mean age seemed around fifty.

Baum had stood as well to observe the panel. His tall trim build gave him the distinguished professional look of a confident, successful lawyer. His suit bespoke thousand dollar custom made tailoring, in sharp contrast to my 'off the rack' appearance. I noted Baum, Blake and I were attired in the uniform every lawyer wears on the first day of a trial: 'sincere blue' suits.

Judge Leahy had informed us earlier of the procedure he wanted us to follow regarding jury selection. He would ask the standard questions approved by the judicial council, and then turn the questioning over to us. He put no restrictions on the scope of our inquiries other than to keep our questioning pointed and relevant to the special issues of the case. This was a good sign. Nothing is worse than a judge who is constantly intermeddling in a trial, trying to micro manage every aspect of the proceedings.

Before their appointment to the bench, most judges had been trial lawyers themselves. In every trial there will be occasions where the lawyers question witnesses differently from the way the judge would have done if he were still trying cases. Although the rules allow the judges to question witnesses, most restrain themselves from doing so, making the assumption that the lawyers have their reasons for not asking certain questions. If Judge Leahy continued to stay out of the proceedings throughout the trial, I could ask for little more.

The clerk knocked on the door to chambers and went inside with the list. She emerged in a few moments, and in a tone immediately silencing the courtroom said, "All rise, Department Six of the Superior Court of California, in and for the County of Santa Clara, is now in session, the Honorable David W. Leahy, judge presiding."

She paused as the judge moved at a fast pace from chambers to the bench and seated himself. When he was settled in, she completed her cry.

"Please be seated and come to order, court is now in session." All attention was now on the judge.

"Good afternoon, Ladies and Gentlemen. I hope you have not been waiting too long in the assembly room." There was a murmur of "good afternoon" in response.

"Call the next case," the judge said in an instructing tone.

The clerk turned to face the massed panel members, slowly reading the entire caption and docket number into the record. She asked the panel to rise, and raise their right hands.

"Do you, and each of you, solemnly swear that you will well and truly answer the questions asked of you concerning your qualifications to act as trial jurors of this case, so help you God?" After their murmurs of "Yes," the clerk asked them to be seated.

The selection process had begun, and for the next hour the judge would be the center of their entire attention.

He introduced himself. "My name is David Leahy, and I will be the judge presiding in this case."

Not referring to himself as Judge Leahy was a nice touch, making an immediate positive impression with the panel.

His pleasant speaking voice carried well as he read a brief statement of the case, giving the names of the parties, and the date and place of the incident. As I anticipated, Janet noticeably stiffened when the judge summarized the allegations of negligence in the complaint.

He informed them the case would take about three weeks to try, ending on Friday, December 12, if all went as scheduled.

"The attorneys in the case are David Baum and Martin Blake of San Francisco for the plaintiffs, and Jay Jacobs, also of San Francisco, for the defendant."

Coming next was the always ego deflating question. "Have any of you heard of, or otherwise been acquainted with, any of the parties or their attorneys?"

No one had ever raised their hand to say they knew, or even heard of me.

As the judge was about to go to the next question, a lady in the back put her hand up hesitantly, and looked briefly in my direction. I studied her face closely, but could make no connection. Had I defended her in a small case that settled quickly? Or perhaps she was a witness I'd interviewed in the past? I felt certain she would say, "I know Mr. Jacobs," and take offense at my obvious failure to recognize her. The judge indicated she should continue.

In a very low voice, she said, "I remember thinking at the time," gesturing toward Janet, whom she had been looking at and not me, ". . . how awful it must be for that poor woman to lose her husband, and her son too."

This was a good point for us . . . if the others heard the last part of her remark. Her soft voice had trailed off, and the judge had already begun speaking about the next topic on his list before she finished. It did not appear that he heard the end of her statement.

The judge was continuing. "During the trial, the following witnesses may be called to testify on behalf of the parties." Reaching for the sheets we had given him of our potential witnesses, he read their names without stating which side might call them. No one indicated knowing any of the people on our lists.

When the judge asked for a show of hands of those who felt they could not serve, a scattering of hands were raised. He listened attentively, and excused two people who said they were caregivers. He also excused a man taking pain medication, and a non-driver with no access to public transportation.

The judge cleared his throat, signaling for the panel's close attention.

"Ladies and Gentlemen, I will now ask the clerk to pick eighteen names at random out of the drum on her desk. When you hear your name, please take the seat in the jury box in the order that your name is called. The bailiff will assist you."

The first twelve people called for questioning would sit in the jury box. The next six would sit in the front row of the spectator area. If any of the people seated in the jury box were excused, they would be replaced by one of the six people in the first row.

The clerk gave four or five vigorous turns to the drum, opened the cover, and began pulling out slips of paper, one by one. After eighteen names were called, the judge announced he would ask questions concerning their qualifications to serve as jurors in the case.

"Does anyone believe a case of this nature should not be brought into court for determination by a jury? Do any of you have any belief or feeling toward any of the parties, attorneys or witnesses that might be regarded as a bias or prejudice for or against any of them? Do you have any interest, financial or otherwise, in the outcome of this case?" There were no affirmative responses.

"At this time the lawyers will ask questions of you."

A pivotal part of the trial, the voir dire process, was about to begin. This was the lawyers' opportunity to ask questions of the panel members. 'Voir dire' is a French phrase. Roughly translated, it means 'to speak the truth' about the questions put to them to determine if they are biased, prejudiced, or in some other way favor one side in a particular case. The stated purpose of voir dire is to determine whether a person can be fair and impartial. The lawyer's real objective during voir dire is to discover any biases the panel members may have, but not for the reason lay people would expect. Jurors without biases are not who lawyers want ... they want biased jurors, and go to great lengths to get them. If a lawyer intuits a panel member has a bias that might make the person favorably disposed toward his client, the lawyer will do everything he can to have that person seated on the jury. Conversely, if a lawyer senses any of the panelists are inclined toward the other side, he will make an even greater effort to get them excused.

The judge declared a short break which I used to study my notes. When we were back in session, the judge briefly explained the voir dire process to the panel, saying that we—Baum and I—would now be asking them questions.

Baum rose, thanked the judge, introduced himself and Blake again, and asked if he might identify his clients. The judge nodded his approval. He first introduced Mrs. Ang, then Dwight and Kathleen Ang, identifying them as two of her five children. He walked to the lectern, placing his seating chart, and pleasantly wished the panel good afternoon.

In a conversational tone, he explained that his purpose in asking questions was to learn a little bit about them, making it sound like he needed their assistance and would appreciate their help. A few heads nodded.

As Baum questioned them about their occupations, families, and home lives, the group of eighteen began to take on a more human dimension. Many of his questions had invitational prefaces: 'how do you feel about,' or 'please elaborate on that,' prompting the panel members to express their feelings in greater detail, allowing Baum to have a dialogue with them.

While Baum was proceeding with his questioning, Blake was busy making notes. As the panelists answered questions, much of their true feelings were communicated nonverbally by facial expressions, gestures and posture. With their attention focused on Baum, Blake was able to carefully study them, unobserved.

Baum asked, "If you find, under the law and the facts, that the Angs are entitled to a verdict, would any of you have any hesitation about compensating them for the damages they have suffered?" Everyone agreed with this obvious proposition. He then asked if there was an upper limit any of them might have, perhaps one or two million dollars, beyond which they would not go regardless of what the evidence was on the subject of damages. None had any such upper limit. Baum was subtly conditioning them to think in the terms of big numbers.

He thanked the panel for their candor and attention. Turning to the judge, he indicated he had no further questions for the moment.

It was a polished, low key performance. By the time he finished, Baum had established a positive rapport with the panel. None of his inquiries caused offense, and his efforts to educate them about his case were done so subtly the panel members were probably unaware it was even taking place. As anticipated, the judge declared a short break. I reviewed the notes I made of Baum's examination. One area Baum had not extensively covered was their experience with boating, giving me an opportunity for individual questioning which would not be repetitive.

Upon returning to the bench, the judge looked at me and said, "You may inquire."

I admonished myself to go slowly, and be nonjudgmental about anything they said. I walked to the lectern with my seating chart and outline.

"Thank you, Your Honor," and turned to the panel.

"Ladies and Gentlemen, my name is Jay Jacobs. In this case which has affected so many families, I am representing Mrs. Dowd." I had Janet stand and introduced her to the panel.

"Mrs. Dowd's husband, Francis Dowd, was the owner of a boat named the *Aloha* that he took out fishing on March 9th, two years ago. Five men were onboard that morning. Mr. Dowd, of course," I gestured to Janet, "as well as their son, Gerald, who was nineteen and home from college on spring break. Also onboard were Mr. Dowd's brother-in-law, John Kennedy, as well as Werner Buntmann who worked with Mr. Dowd at Raytheon, and Mr. Andy Ang who did contract work for Raytheon."

I outlined that the boat left Sausalito and was never seen again. There were no survivors, and no eyewitnesses had been found. I concluded my summary by saying there had been a great deal of conjecture about what may have occurred, but no one knew for sure what happened to the *Aloha*.

The first thing on my outline was to find out who owned a boat.

My voir dire strategy was to get anyone with boating experience off the jury. People who were past or present boat owners, as well as those who had been fare paying passengers on party boats, or guests on someone else's boat, posed a risk I didn't want to take. Of critical importance was to make certain I did not end up with just one person with boating experience on the jury. If there was only one person with boat knowledge, when they began their deliberations at the end of the case, that person would try to impose his views concerning safe boat handling on the other jurors, regardless of his real qualifications with boats. Having just one person with boating experience on the jury would be as dangerous as trying an auto accident case with only one person who knew how to drive.

When I asked who owned a boat or had experience with boating, my stomach wrenched. Four people stated they had a boat now, or owned one in the past. Four others had either been out on party boats, or were guests on friends' boats out on the ocean.

We were not finished with our questioning by four-fifteen and Judge Leahy ended the session for the day. Before sending them home, he carefully admonished the panel not to discuss the case with anyone, and to return in the morning at nine-thirty.

I asked Janet to be in court by nine-fifteen. She had to be anxious, but was keeping vigilant sentry duty over her emotions.

After everyone left, the judge informed us he was going to end the next day's session at noon, which meant our opening statements were put off till the following week.

I walked to the parking lot in a grey drizzle. If I had to get wet, I wished it would really rain.

Heading back to San Francisco, I began scrolling through the panel's responses to the questions Baum and I asked. I knew he would have a definite plan about who he wanted on the jury, and one of my evening tasks would be to get a sense of who those people were. It took more than an hour to drive home, and I barely finished my review of the panel by the time I arrived.

As soon as I came up the steps, Marsha asked what happened with the motion.

"We won the motion," I said, and let her know jury selection had started, and that we would probably be finished by noon the next day.

She looked at me quizzically.

"You were so worried last night. You don't look too happy about winning," her eyes running over my face.

"I am relieved," I said.

Her expression remained in place.

"Please tell me what happened," she said, patting the sofa for me to sit down beside her.

"I won the motion to have a jury trial, but I lost a lot too."

She waited while I sorted through the full effect of what happened.

"Failing to check the correct box on the form, and then not noticing the mistake for months, has made me look unprepared and unprofessional. How inept can you be when you can't even fill out a one page form correctly? Believe me, honey, he's not impressed.

"And there's something else that's a lot worse." I broke off, sorting through my thoughts. "In effect, Baum has told the judge . . . 'We would be happy to have you decide the case, but Jacobs doesn't trust you . . . he wants a jury.'"

Marsha looked askance. "He won't think that."

I shook my head. "Maybe not consciously, but how can it not affect him subconsciously, and don't forget the judge has almost unlimited discretion in deciding what evidence the jury gets to hear, and in the rulings he makes on motions throughout the trial."

The more I thought about it, visions of a Pyrrhic victory came to mind.

After dinner, I spread out my seating chart on the dining table and got to work. It was immediately apparent I would have to accept a lot of people I didn't want. Eight people identified themselves as having some degree of boating experience, and each side is limited to six peremptory challenges to excuse people they don't want. It was going to be impossible to excuse everyone with boating experience.

There are two kinds of challenges. Challenges for cause and peremptory challenges. Challenges for cause are typically granted by a judge, at the request of one of the lawyers, either because a panelist knows one of the parties, or a witness, or has an obvious bias. There is no limit to the number of challenges for cause that a lawyer can request from the judge. With a peremptory challenge, a lawyer can excuse a panel member without having to explain why he wants that person off the jury, but each side is limited to six peremptory challenges.

A quick look at my notes told me I could excuse the four people who were past or present boat owners, but I was going to have to accept some people who had been fishing on party boats, or were guests on someone's boat out on the ocean. Getting the boat owners off would use four of my six peremptory challenges. I would have to use the two remaining very carefully.

Awake before the alarm went off, I went to the park for a half hour run. I kept telling myself this trial is the most important thing in Janet's life, and she would have no chance if I didn't restore my self-confidence. Against what should have been my better judgment, I got us into this mess, and now I had to get us out.

Janet arrived as I finished unpacking my files, and we discussed the panel. At nine-thirty the clerk called out, "All rise. Department Six of the Superior Court of the State of California is now in session, the Honorable David Leahy, judge presiding." Waiting until he was settled in, she continued, "Please be seated and come to order."

"Good morning, Ladies and Gentlemen," he said, and looked briefly at his notes.

"Mr. Jacobs, I believe we finished with you yesterday. Do you have any further questions?"

Standing so I was once again directly behind Janet, I began. "Good morning, Your Honor. I do, if I may proceed."

He nodded.

I focused my remaining inquiries on those with boating experience and informed the judge I had completed my questioning.

The judge turned to the panel and explained that the attorneys would now have an opportunity to exercise our challenges. He gestured toward Baum to begin.

Baum exercised his first challenge on a man who felt, from what he'd read in the papers, that verdicts were getting too high, but said he would not let that thought affect his thinking. Baum was apparently unconvinced and excused him.

My first challenge was a man I could not get to look at me. His eye contact had been consistent with Baum, but none at all with me. His answers to my questions were cryptic and, when he did speak, his gaze was always somewhere else. He owned a boat and intimated fishing out on the ocean was too risky. Even when I exercised my challenge, he did not look my way.

Baum then challenged a man who was a group head at a high tech company. I had a lot of concerns about him myself, and when it turned out he was a boat owner, I put him on my 'must excuse' list. By excusing him, Baum saved me a challenge.

My next challenge was a woman who had been a school teacher. In the past, teachers had proved to be very poor choices to leave on a jury. They habitually see jury deliberations as a classroom, with themselves in charge. She frequently had her hand up, giving long answers to Baum's and my questions. She clearly wanted to serve, and very likely would have nominated herself for the job as jury foreman. She was very displeased when I asked the judge to excuse her, giving me an acerbic look as she left the courtroom.

Baum then challenged a business executive in his middle years with an advancing stomach. He said nothing offensive when he was questioned, but I was not surprised Baum challenged him. The affinity between this man and Dowd as executives probably made him too risky for Baum.

My next challenge was a young man in his twenties who still lived at home. He described himself as a part time student, which sounded more like a euphemism for being voluntarily unemployed. My main concern was that his family owned a boat which he used on occasion.

The challenge was back to Baum. He and Blake huddled in a whispered conference referring to their respective notes, and then fell silent. Baum stood, announcing plaintiffs passed.

The voir dire chess game had started, putting me in a predicament I had not anticipated would happen so quickly. The panelists who replaced the three people I challenged, and Baum's three challenges, were part of the original group of eighteen who had been extensively questioned. If I made any further challenges, the clerk would reach into the drum and call someone who had not been questioned at all. I had doubts about some of the twelve people presently in the jury box, but there were a number of panelists seated in the spectator area who had not yet been called that gave me greater concerns.

Unfortunately, one person who was on my 'must excuse' list remained in the box. If he had not been a boat owner, I would have had no concerns about him. Nothing he said made me feel uneasy, but I couldn't risk leaving him on the jury. I stood, and asked the judge to excuse him. I steadied myself as the clerk reached into the drum and called the name of his replacement. It was one of the few women in their middle years remaining in the panel.

She beamed on hearing her name, walking swiftly to the jury box, and sat on the edge of her chair as Judge Leahy questioned her. I liked her demeanor, and there was nothing alarming about her answers to the preliminary questions the judge asked. My attention drifted from her responses to the questions the judge was asking, and studied my seating chart. There were a few people in the box I had concerns about, but the four boat owners on my 'must excuse' list were gone; three from my challenges and one Baum excused. I had two challenges remaining, which tactically meant I only had one left. An old adage instructs: 'When you use up your final challenge, the replacement you get will be worse than the person you excused.'

The challenge was back to Baum who once again conferred with Blake, giving me time to reflect on the people I had concerns about. Involuntarily, I turned to look at the people remaining in the spectator area, and made up my mind.

Their whispering stopped, and I turned back. Baum studied his notes in silence, and finally announced that plaintiffs passed.

The judge looked to me inquisitively. I asked if I might have a moment, and leaned toward Janet, asking her how the panel looked. She responded, "Fine."

"Your Honor, Mrs. Dowd is pleased with the jury as constituted."

It was done. With two consecutive passes, we had our jury.

The judge ordered that the panel be sworn in. As I watched the jurors taking the oath, it came to me that other than superficially, I knew little about them, and nothing *of* them. How they would interpret the evidence and deduce the truth would be driven by their collective life experiences, and about those things I had nothing more than a few insights and gut instincts. The most that could be hoped for was they would not be so swayed by sympathy for Mrs. Ang they would be unable to hear Janet's defense of her husband's actions.

The judge turned toward the jury, asking them to give particular attention to what he was about to say.

"Ladies and Gentlemen, your selection as the jury to decide this matter is the first stage of the case. The next step, when we reconvene next week, will be the opening statement of the plaintiffs followed by the opening statement of the defendant. The plaintiffs will then put on their evidence. After the plaintiffs present their witnesses, the defense will present its evidence. You will then hear closing arguments from both sides, after which I will give you instructions on the law you will apply. At that point you will retire to the jury room, select your foreman, begin deliberations, and reach a verdict."

The judge was now ready to conclude with the admonition he would give them throughout the trial.

"Ladies and Gentlemen, you are not to discuss the case with anyone, including each other, or allow anyone to discuss the case with you. You are not to form or express an opinion on any aspect of the case until the matter is finally submitted to you. You are to make no independent investigation on any aspect of the case, visit the scene, or do research work on any subject that might come up at trial."

He paused, looking at them one at a time. "You are to decide the case solely on the evidence you hear in court, and nothing else."

He wished them a Happy Thanksgiving, reminding them to assemble in the jury room at nine-thirty on Thursday of the following week.

As the jury members left the courtroom, there was a noticeable sense of purpose about them. I hoped the events of the last two days would steep into their psyches over the long break, and they would return fully aware of the importance their verdict was going to have on the two widows before them.

Being out of session for so long would not be easy for Janet. I was glad all of her remaining family, with the exception of one daughter who lived on the East Coast, would gather at her home for the holiday. We said our goodbyes, and I wished her Happy Thanksgiving.

On the way back to the office, I reflected on something Dad told me a number of years earlier. I'd asked how he was going to try a certain case he was about to begin. His response, "I don't know yet," came as a surprise. Seeing my reaction, he went on. "I won't know until the jury is selected. Whoever ends up sitting in the jury box will determine how I try the case." I had not forgotten the significance of that observation and how applicable it was going to be in this case.

The most striking thing about the composition of the jury was their level of education: all had completed high school, and most were college graduates with a few of them holding advanced degrees. There were eight women and four men, a slightly higher ratio of women than most juries in an urban county. The mean age was around fifty, no one was under thirty.

With no boat owners among them, when the jurors thought about the ocean, they would vacillate between landlubbers' romanticized fascinations and their instinctive fears of it.

It occurred to me how Janet would live the rest of her life with an aspect of overwhelming importance to her—the reputation of her husband— now in the hands of these twelve strangers.

Arriving at the office, I spoke with everyone and took care of a few pressing matters on my other cases. We all wished each other a Happy Thanksgiving and ended the day early.

As soon as I walked in the door, Marsha wanted to know if jury selection was completed and asked me to tell her about them. "Their educational level is higher than any jury I've had before. And I was able to achieve my main objective of getting all the boat owners off the jury.

"They're older than I would have preferred for a wrongful death case, particularly the women. The older women will have a natural affinity with Mrs. Ang, sympathizing with the difficult adjustments widowhood has suddenly thrust upon her."

Marsha asked about their backgrounds.

"There are three engineers, and two of the women are married to engineers."

"That's good," she said, "you've always said engineers take the jury instructions seriously and are good about demanding that plaintiffs prove their case."

I thought for a moment. "Ordinarily that's true, but the unusual circumstances of this case make them problematical." She looked at me questioningly as I continued. "The theme of my case, 'we don't know what happened,' is going to get a cool reception from those engineers. They will be scrutinizing the experts' testimony very carefully. Any opinions not factually supported might go unnoticed by the other jurors, but not by them."

"Who else was selected?"

"Three have law enforcement backgrounds. I usually challenge them."

Marsha looked confused, and asked why.

"Because they're so claims conscious. Other than longshoremen and cab drivers, policemen are the most likely to file compensation claims. My experience with them on juries has been very mixed, but I didn't have enough challenges left."

The extra days we would be out of session would provide additional time to go over my trial plan. But that would have to wait till Friday. Marsha had extracted a promise from me that Thanksgiving Day would be just for us. I knew what that meant: no working on the case, and no watching football.

We enjoyed the traditional Thanksgiving dinner Marsha prepared. Afterwards, we drove to Golden Gate Highlands for a long walk on the bluff trail. It turned out to be a wonderful way to decompress.

A passing hiker told us there was an extra low tide and the beaches below us were passable. We climbed down a steep trail, and continued our walk on the beach, passing the skeletons of several old ships which had come to grief on the rocks.

Off in the distance, I could see the Lighthouse at Point Bonita. The surf pounding the Marin Headlands reminded me the *Aloha* was out there somewhere resting on the bottom. Five lives had been taken by a sea that never fully welcomes man into its realm, almost saying 'your ancestors abandoned me to live on the land millions of years ago, and you are not welcome back now.'

I spent the days before we were back in session honing my cross-examination questions, and working on my trial books. I had made computer print outs of all the discovery materials I had accumulated over the last two years, putting it in big blue binders, three inches thick, ready for use at trial. There were over a dozen of them.

Marsha helped me refine my outline, and listened as I recited my opening statement. I practiced it until I knew what I was going to say; not the exact words, but had the gist of it committed to memory.

As busy as I was over the long weekend, one thought kept intruding in my mind: I was about to enter an unknown world of trying a huge case against a very experienced litigator with the reputation of snuffing out his opponents.

# 17

**M**arsha helped me load the car. After straightening my tie, she gave me an encouraging smile and a long kiss, meant to last until I returned home that evening.

On arrival at the courthouse, the clerk informed me Baum had something to take up with the judge before the jury was brought in. A few minutes before nine-thirty, we were called into chambers. Judge Leahy did not look particularly rested after the long break. After a desultory good morning, he turned to Baum and asked what he wanted to bring up.

With an aggrieved look Baum said, "Your Honor, I am sorry it is even necessary to bring this up, but for some time we have been asking counsel to provide a copy of the statement he took from a witness named Captain Taylor McGee. Captain McGee wants a copy of the statement he gave to his investigator, and despite several requests, counsel has refused to provide a copy. We have a brief in support of this request." Blake handed it to the judge, sliding a copy across his desk to me.

I read it quickly. The brief indicated there was a Federal Rule of Civil Procedure requiring that statements be produced. No California statute or cases were cited. There was a reference to an academic treatise which suggested that accepting the Federal rule would be a good practice to adopt in California State Court matters. Commentary by some law school professor about a Federal rule hardly rose to the level of binding precedent on an action filed in a California State Court case. I was confident the judge would see it that way.

The brief also implied I had taken Captain McGee's statement in a misleading fashion. This I could not let go unchallenged.

When the judge finished reading their brief he looked at me.

"Do you have a response?"

I did not like the way this was going. The proper inquiry would have been, 'Do you wish to be heard?' It was a small point, but the judge's tone seemed to imply I was to respond to an accusation that had some merit to it, rather than argue a legal point.

I decided to respond to the accusation first.

"I do, Your Honor. First, let me say that Captain McGee voluntarily gave his statement to my investigator, in my presence. On completion, he read his statement carefully, and made several corrections before signing it. He did not make a condition of giving his statement that he be provided a copy."

Baum interrupted me: "He wants a copy now." Blake added, "I have asked counsel several times to provide a copy of the statement, and he has refused."

"Is it correct that Mr. Blake asked you for a copy of the statement, and you have refused to give him one?" the judge asked.

I was now even more concerned about the direction the argument was taking.

I replied, "Of course I refused to give him a copy of the statement. He called me several times about it. After the second call, I did some research to assure myself that my position was correct. As they admit in their brief . . . there is no California authority, none whatsoever, requiring me to do so. In fact, the rule in California is plainly to the contrary."

I paused to frame my words carefully. "This statement is protected by the attorney work product privilege. To hold otherwise would mean an attorney could just sit back, let his opponent do all the work and then say, 'give me your work product.' My opponents discovered Captain McGee, and know his whereabouts. If they want a statement from him, they can get one for themselves."

Baum and Blake were ready to start arguing again, but the judge held his hand up. Looking at me, he said, "But it is Captain McGee who wants the statement."

Turning to Baum, he asked, "Is it correct, that Captain McGee wants a copy of his statement?" They replied simultaneously, "Yes."

I had to stop this farcical charade. Judge Leahy had to know that it was Baum, not Captain McGee, who wanted the statement. And the reason why Baum wanted the statement would have to be equally obvious to the judge. There was no doubt in my mind that Baum and Blake had met with McGee and gone over all the questions they were going to ask him on the witness stand. Baum wanted the statement to prevent me from using it to impeach Captain McGee if he said anything different on the witness stand from what was in his statement.

Trying to stay focused, I responded. "Your Honor, they are not McGee's lawyers as far as I know. If they are . . . well, let's find out."

I turned to Baum. "Are you actually representing to the court that you are Captain McGee's lawyer?"

Judge Leahy reasserted himself into the argument. "Mr. Jacobs, please address your remarks to me."

"Your Honor, I apologize, but I am upset, and with good cause." I picked up the brief and began reading the part that was so offensive: "The purpose of defense counsel obtaining a statement from the witness, as opposed to taking his deposition, was undoubtedly to obtain materials for the purposes of impeachment. In circumstances where the testimony of the lay witness could be recorded in a misleading fashion, the witness, therefore, needs the protection of reviewing his statement in advance of his testimony."

I took a moment to let the judge consider what I'd read to him before continuing.

"Captain McGee's statement was taken in my presence, and in no way was he 'misled,' as is insinuated by counsel. If he didn't want to give me his statement, he didn't have to. And if he felt he was being taken advantage of, he could have terminated giving his statement, or refused to sign it if it was inaccurate."

In an acerbic tone, the judge asked, "Submitted?"

I had only a moment to collect my thoughts. If I said 'yes,' he would allow no further argument. I looked at the judge. "I have this to say, and I will be finished."

Pausing to frame my next words carefully, and to cool down as well, I said, "Your Honor, I submit to you, plaintiffs' counsel is trying to get you to do something that you have no authority to do."

This was dangerous ground to tread on; no judge wants to be told what he can or cannot do.

Making an effort to keep my tone as respectful as possible, I continued: "They have cited no case and no statute as authority for you to force me to produce this clearly privileged document. Surely it is incumbent upon an attorney requesting an order from the court to cite some legal basis for doing so. There has to be something more than just 'I say so.'"

Giving me a look only an iceberg would welcome, the judge repeated his earlier question. "Submitted?"

I said, "Yes."

Without giving the matter a moment of further thought, he turned to me. "Give them a copy of the statement."

I was incredulous. "Your Honor, I object to your order that I give a copy of this clearly privileged document to plaintiffs' counsel."

I was certain there was no legal authority for his order, but failure to make a record of my objections would eliminate any chance to successfully make an appeal on the point. I was about to demand that the court reporter be brought in and make a record. Before I made the request, which would have only further antagonized the judge, I remembered when unloading my bags in the courtroom that I had not brought the file containing Captain McGee's statement with me.

"Your Honor, I did not anticipate Captain McGee would be called as a witness today, and I don't have his statement with me."

Before the judge could respond, Baum cut in, "I never said I was not calling McGee as my first witness." His tone, almost a bark, startled even the judge, who asked, "Are you calling Captain McGee today?"

Baum was about to speak when Blake leaned over, whispering to him. After a brief exchange Baum looked up. "He will be our first witness."

The judge looked immensely relieved at this turn of events. Since I did not have the statement with me, his ruling that I provide them with a copy was now moot.

Looking at both of us, he said, "Is there anything else either side wishes to bring to my attention before we begin?"

"No," we all replied.

Standing up, the judge said he would take five minutes and then proceed with opening statements.

As we headed for the door, the judge casually added, "I am ordering that you inform each other who your witnesses will be for the next day." I was still seething about his ruling, and did not pay much attention.

I joined Janet at the table. She appeared composed, but I knew her well enough to know whatever her actual feelings were, they were being kept well in check.

I said we'd be starting momentarily, and reminded her I would introduce her again in my opening remarks to the jury. She was anxious and I wanted to say something reassuring, but nothing that would remotely do so came to mind.

Shortly, the bailiff opened the door to the hallway that led to the jury room. As the jurors filed in, the somber look on their faces reflected their awareness that this case involved the death of five men, and what they were going to decide would matter to a lot of people.

In a moment the judge appeared, his black robe flowing about him. The clerk began her incantation as he ascended the bench.

"All rise, Department Six of the Superior Court of the State of California, in and for the County of Santa Clara, is now in session, the Honorable David Leahy, Judge Presiding."

Once he was settled into his chair, she completed the opening ritual. "Please be seated and come to order."

There was a moment of shuffling as everyone settled themselves, quickly refocusing on the judge.

"Good morning, everyone. I trust you had a fine Thanksgiving holiday, and hope none of you were inconvenienced by our delay in resuming."

After saying that opening statements would be next, he turned to face the jury, his voice taking on a cautionary tone the jurors picked up on immediately.

"The comments made by the attorneys during opening statements are not evidence. Their remarks are only what they expect the evidence to be. The only evidence in the case will come from witnesses on the stand, and any documents or other exhibits admitted into evidence; not the remarks of counsel."

He then nodded at Baum who was seated at the end of his table closest to the jury box. He rose, walking slowly to the well of the court.

"May it please the court, counsel, and Ladies and Gentlemen. At this time, I would like to give you an overview of the case, which will help you better follow the evidence you will hear. Some of the evidence may come in out of order, but the case itself is not difficult to understand."

He began chronologically. "Before sunrise on March 9th two years ago, Francis Dowd took his little boat out on the ocean to go fishing. The boat left the Sausalito marina and was never seen or heard from again."

He looked over the jury box, assuring himself they were fully engaged before continuing. "There were no survivors and no witnesses to what happened, and only bits and pieces of wreckage were ever recovered. In addition to Francis Dowd, four others were onboard that morning, including Andy Ang, the deceased husband of Mrs. Ang," gesturing to her in the first row behind their table.

"Sitting next to her are two of her five children: her son Dwight, and her daughter Kathleen. Her three other children are in Manila and unable to attend the trial.

"Mr. and Mrs. Ang were married for more than thirty years. The family resided in Manila where Mr. Ang owned and operated a company that did business with Raytheon." Baum stated the reason Andy Ang had come to the United States was to negotiate a new contract with Raytheon, which was accomplished, and mentioned the invitation from Francis Dowd to go fishing on the *Aloha*.

He had Blake place a nautical chart on the easel in front of the jury, and traced the course Dowd planned to take from the Sausalito marina to the fishing grounds in the Duxbury area.

"You will hear evidence from an eyewitness that there were large breaking waves in the channel leading to the Duxbury area," Baum said, pointing to the chart.

"You will also hear evidence that a few months before this incident, Mr. Dowd's boat, the *Aloha*, had been burglarized. All the safety equipment and navigational gear was taken," and added they would hear conflicting accounts about whether it had been replaced.

Moving to a new subject, "I want to make it clear that Mrs. Dowd is not a defendant in this case. The defendant in this case is the Estate of Francis Dowd. The only reason Mrs. Dowd's name appears in the pleadings is because she is the executor of the Estate." He then added a self-serving reference to the contingent nature of attorney's fees by saying, "Some attorneys just want their commissions, but I really believe in my client's case."

I had only a moment to consider making an objection to this reference to attorney's fees, but elected not to do so. An objection at side bar would have been sustained, but the only remedy would have been for the judge to admonish the jury to ignore Baum's remark, which would only draw further attention to it.

Baum began summarizing. "After you have heard all of the evidence, you will find that the only conclusion which is consistent with the facts is this: Mr. Dowd took the *Aloha* into Bonita Channel when the presence of large waves made it unsafe to do so, and as a result the boat was capsized and sank."

He thanked the jury, and nodded to the judge before resuming his seat. It was a perfectly choreographed opening statement. In a case that was going to be laden with a great deal of circumstantial evidence, Baum already had them thinking about what might have happened.

After a ten minute break, which compounded the nervousness I was already feeling, the judge returned to the bench and nodded to me. I moved toward the well of the courtroom.

"Thank you, Your Honor." I nodded toward the bench and then turned to the jury box. "Ladies and Gentlemen of the jury, I will be representing Mrs. Dowd in this matter. Her husband, Francis Dowd, was the owner of the *Aloha*.

"I would ask you to keep in mind that throughout the trial the plaintiffs have the advantage of going first. Just as they gave their opening statement first, they get to call all of their witnesses first as well. Please keep in mind that there are two sides to every story, but you will have to wait until all of plaintiffs' witnesses have testified . . . a week or more of testimony . . . before you will be allowed to hear our side."

I then launched into our basic theme.

"What happened that morning remains a mystery, and while there has been much speculation, guessing and theorizing about what happened, no one . . . really . . . knows."

Continuing, I said we would offer evidence of three possible explanations for the loss of the boat: that it had been struck by a rogue wave; run over by a large ship coming out of San Francisco; or, the *Aloha* hit a semi submerged log, referred to by mariners as a dead head, causing it to sink. I added that the most likely explanation was being capsized by an unpredictable rogue wave.

Baum said something in his opening statement about the *Aloha* that I needed to correct right then.

I went to my brown court bag where I kept a number of items that always seemed to have a use at trial, including a compass, a protractor, a magnifying glass, and marking pens in assorted colors. One of the items was a fifty foot tape measure which I retrieved, and walked back towards the jury box.

"Counsel referred to my client's vessel as 'a little boat,' but that's not what the evidence will be. The testimony you will hear is that the *Aloha* was a full-size fishing boat, thirty-four feet long. I would like to show you just how long that is, if I may, Your Honor."

I asked the bailiff to hold the end of the measuring tape while I walked back down the aisle dividing the spectator area toward the rear of the courtroom. I unrolled the tape to the thirty-four foot mark and held it up.

"This, Ladies and Gentlemen, is thirty-four feet, the length of Mr. Dowd's boat. As you can see, the *Aloha* was not 'a little boat,' but a big, full-size, thirty-four footer, designed and built to be taken out on the ocean. And there's something else the evidence will show: the *Aloha* was well maintained and properly equipped for ocean fishing." I began rewinding the tape. After a few twists, I stopped and rolled it back out. Placing my thumb at the thirty-four foot mark I walked over to their table, holding the tape close to Baum's face until he acknowledged the measurement with a curt nod. I doubted he would be referring to the *Aloha* as a "little boat" again.

A quick glance told me I had covered what was on my outline. It was time for a short summary before I sat down.

"The allegations made in the complaint are only what the plaintiffs say occurred. After you have heard all of the evidence and the instructions on the law from the judge, it will be up to you twelve ladies and gentlemen of the jury to determine whether these allegations of negligence made against Francis Dowd are in fact true.

"I believe after you have heard all of the evidence, you will find that the plaintiffs' allegations are not proven."

I thanked them for their attention and returned to my seat.

One of the instructions the judge would give the jury at the end of the case concerned who had the burden of proof. He would tell the jury that Baum had the burden of proving that Francis Dowd was negligent. But in the minds of the jurors I would have an unspoken burden to meet, just as surely as if it were a formal legal duty, to convince those twelve people that whatever happened on March 9th was not due to Francis Dowd's negligence. Their attitude was going to be: 'you say your client was not at fault—prove it.'

Returning to the bench after a short break, the judge resumed. "We will hear the plaintiffs' case first." He looked to Baum, "Call your first witness."

Baum had risen. "Your Honor, we call Captain Taylor McGee," and turned toward the rear of the courtroom. In a moment the door opened, and Blake, who had been sent to get him, reappeared with the captain.

While McGee was being summoned, I searched my mind about why he was being called first. His appearance as their first witness ran contrary to a strategy followed in every case . . . always start with a strong witness, and finish with a strong witness. Captain McGee had something to say, but he hardly rose to the level of a witness strong enough to be called first. There was probably a scheduling problem and Baum had to fill in with him.

It was not until McGee was coming forward to be sworn in by the clerk that the answer came. Calling him as their first witness prevented me from contacting my office to have his statement found and brought down to the courthouse. I recalled Blake rushing out of the courtroom after the meeting in chambers, probably to find Captain McGee and inform him I did not have his statement with me. Now, without it, I would be unable to confront him in my cross-examination if he said anything on the stand that differed from what he had said in his statement.

# 18

The ritual of the first witness taking the stand is a significant moment for a jury. Sensing that their role as judges of the facts is about to begin, they are filled with eager anticipation.

Based on the extremely cool reception Captain McGee gave me when I spoke with him on his boat, I knew he was not going to be a friendly witness, but he would not likely be openly hostile either. Baum would carefully bring out of McGee that he knew none of the parties and had no interest in the outcome of the case. Any attempt to portray him as biased would backfire.

I quickly ran through what I could recall from his statement. What came to mind was his comment that waves were breaking halfway across Bonita Channel. The only helpful thing I could remember was his remark that breaking waves can come up suddenly.

He stopped briefly at the railing, surveying his new surroundings. The clerk waited for him by her desk, in the well of the court below the judge's bench, to give him the oath. Upon his "I do," she directed him to the witness stand.

The harshness of the fluorescent lighting accentuated the deep lines etched in his face from long years at sea. While taking the oath, I noticed his raised hand was so large in comparison to the rest of his body that it looked like a ham sticking out from his sleeve.

McGee had not troubled himself to dress up for court; the thought probably hadn't even occurred to him. He was wearing a well-worn pair of old slacks and a long sleeve open neck shirt. When he looked toward me, there was no sign of recognition.

Before he had spoken a word, his personality was filling the courtroom. He looked and acted like what the jury expected a captain to be.

Baum began, "Please tell the jury your name."

"Taylor McGee."

"What is your occupation?"

"I have my own fishing boat, the New Merrimac." He described it as a party boat designed to carry fare paying passengers on fishing trips out on the ocean.

"Where do you keep your boat?"

"At the commercial pier in Sausalito."

Handing him the pointer, Baum asked him to show the jury where he customarily went fishing. Stepping to the chart, he identified the principal areas for salmon: Muir Beach, Slide Ranch, the Farallon Islands, Pillar Point and Duxbury Reef. He explained the fishing fleet based in San Francisco Bay consisted of commercial fishermen, party boats such as his, and the boats owned by sport fishermen.

"The three groups customarily fish in the same general area. It all depends on where the salmon are at the moment."

Baum had initially been standing close to the lectern. Five questions later, he was back by his table, well out of the jury's line of vision, letting their entire focus of attention be on Captain McGee.

"Were you out fishing on Friday, March 9th, two years ago?"

"Yes, I was," he responded simply.

"Captain, in your own words, please tell the jury what you did from the beginning of your trip that day."

He gave himself a moment to think before answering. "I left my berth in Sausalito at 6:10, and followed the shoreline inside San Francisco Bay heading for the Golden Gate Bridge. After going under the bridge, I headed west toward Point Bonita."

Baum interrupted. "Where did you intend to go fishing that day?"

"Duxbury Reef."

Baum stepped closer. "What course did you plan on taking to get to Duxbury that morning?"

"My plan was to come around Point Bonita and then go through Bonita Channel to Duxbury." McGee replied.

"Is going through Bonita Channel the usual course you take to go to the Duxbury area?"

"Yes, it is."

"Why do you customarily take Bonita Channel to fish at Duxbury?"

"Because it's the shortest way to get there," he retorted pragmatically.

Continuing slowly, Baum asked, "Did you actually take the course you planned on, of rounding Point Bonita and then going through Bonita Channel to Duxbury?"

"No, I didn't."

Baum allowed another long pause, which had its intended effect of focusing the jury's attention before continuing.

"Did you change your plans and go fishing somewhere else?"

"No, I still went to Duxbury."

"What course did you take to get to Duxbury that morning?"

"I went out by the Main Ship Channel."

Moving to the chart, Baum affected a puzzled look, as if this was the first time he'd heard Captain McGee intended to take one course to Duxbury, and then apparently changed his mind and gone out another way.

"Captain, why did you change your plan of going through Bonita Channel, and instead went out by the Main Ship Channel?"

Baum slowly moved back to his table, letting the jury entirely focus on McGee's answer.

"When I arrived at Point Bonita and started to go around the Point, I looked up the Channel and saw waves breaking all the way across. It was too dangerous to go through, and I turned my boat around and went out through the Main Channel."

"How much farther is it to go to Duxbury via the Main Ship Channel rather than Bonita Channel?"

"Four or five additional miles at the most."

"How much extra time is involved in taking the Main Channel to Duxbury?"

"Maybe twenty minutes," McGee responded.

Baum busied himself with his notes, allowing McGee's last few answers to sink in before continuing.

"Were other boats going out fishing that morning?"

"There were two or three in front of me and about the same number behind."

"Did you notice what the boats ahead of you did when they arrived at Point Bonita?"

"They turned around and headed towards the Main Ship Channel. Seeing the boats ahead of me turning, alerted me to look up the Channel. When I got to Point Bonita, I saw the big breakers the others must have seen, and changed my course and went out by the Main Ship Channel too. The boats coming behind me did the same thing."

"Did you see any boats that went through Bonita Channel?"

He paused, shaking his head. "I don't recall seeing any boats do that."

In the statement McGee gave me, he said there were some breakers in the Channel; nothing about all the way across. But without his statement in hand, it would be impossible to impeach his testimony. I looked at the clock, cursing myself for not immediately calling the office after the meeting in chambers and having his statement brought down to me.

In rapid fire order, Baum put a string of questions to McGee. Had he seen any fishing boats in distress that morning? . . . No. Had he seen any flares or distress signals of any kind? . . . No. Had he heard an emergency call for help on his radio? . . . No. Had any of the other fishing boat captains told him at some later date that they had seen any distress signals, or heard radio calls for help? . . . No. Did any of them say anything about a big ship running down a fishing boat, or sighting any deadheads that day? . . . No!

Turning to another area, Baum asked if he kept a log book. McGee said he did and held it up. I had not noticed he'd brought it with him. He was asked to read the entries for March 9. There were notations about the number of passengers he had onboard, where he went fishing and the number of fish caught, an entry about big breakers, and taking the Main Ship Channel to Duxbury.

Baum asked, "Captain, describe in your own words the breaking waves you saw in Bonita Channel that morning?"

"They were white-capped waves, with their tops breaking over."

"Can you give an estimate of their height?"

He thought for a moment, "Ten to twelve feet high, some higher."

Baum paused. "Is it difficult to describe the size and location of the big breaking waves you saw in Bonita Channel that morning?"

"Yes, it is."

Baum reached for a photograph and asked the clerk to mark it for identification. He then walked over to my table handing it to me.

It was an 8 by 12-inch black and white aerial photo, shot at a wide angle, showing a mass of breakers all across Bonita Channel. There were a few smooth swells, but for the most part the entire Channel was filled with an angry mass of breaking, white-capped waves.

The thing a lawyer fears most in a trial are surprises. I felt my stomach twisting into a knot.

"Do you object to the admission of this exhibit?" Baum asked.

Without replying, I looked at the judge. "May we approach, Your Honor?"

The judge motioned us forward, gesturing to the side of the bench away from the jury box.

The photograph, which I had not seen before, would be a disaster if admitted into evidence. In the few seconds it took to walk to the bench, I tried to think of objections to make. Being caught off guard compounded the difficulty I was having in coming up with any arguments that would persuade the judge. Before any of us could speak, the judge asked to look at the photograph. His eyebrows lifted as he studied it carefully. In the silence, I kept pressing the start key in my head, trying to reboot my brain which had gone completely blank.

I was still trying to formulate an argument when the judge addressed me. "Do you object to the admission of this photograph?"

"Yes, Your Honor. Firstly, parallax distortion occurs when a scene is photographed from the air versus what the eye sees in viewing the same scene at ground level. Captain McGee's view was obviously from the bridge of his fishing boat, a few feet above sea level, and this is an aerial photograph, taken thousands of feet in the air."

The judge looked at me dubiously, knowing I was grabbing at straws. In a disjointed manner I continued. "In addition, the incident occurred at a time of darkness, and this photo was taken in broad daylight." From his skeptical look it was obvious the tide was running out with the judge; I could feel the sand moving under my feet.

Baum inserted himself. "If Captain McGee can state that the waves he observed that morning were similar to those shown in the photograph, a proper foundation will have been laid for its admission into evidence."

Gesturing to me, Baum continued: "Counsel's comments go to the weight, not the admissibility of the evidence."

Blake added: "It is for the jury to decide what weight, if any, they choose to give the photograph."

The judge tilted back in his chair, weighing our arguments. Leaning forward he said, "If the witness states that this is a picture of Bonita Channel, and it depicts the condition of the waves he saw that morning, I am going to admit it. Step back, gentlemen."

The picture was handed to McGee, and he was requested to examine it carefully.

Baum then asked, "Does this photograph show Bonita Channel in the area around Point Bonita?"

"Yes, it does."

"Is this photograph a reasonable depiction of the waves you saw when you came around Point Bonita and looked up the Channel?"

"Yes," he replied.

Turning to the judge Baum stated, "We request that this photograph be admitted into evidence."

The judge looked to me. I repeated my objections.

Without hesitating a moment, the judge ruled. "It will be admitted into evidence as the next exhibit in order."

Baum waited until the clerk attached an exhibit sticker to the photograph before continuing. "May this exhibit be passed to the jury, so they may see it at this time?" The judge assented, and the photograph slowly made its way through the jury box.

Each juror studied it intently, absorbing every detail before reluctantly passing it to the next person. Some reacted with near gasps; there was one audible "Jesus." Mostly their expressions registered surprise, even astonishment, at the size and sheer number of breaking waves filling Bonita Channel. When the picture was passed from the back to the front row, the jurors in the back tier leaned forward for one last glimpse. None looked without some reaction to the picture. It seemed an eternity for the picture to circulate through the jury box.

When the last juror handed it back, Baum commented it was close to noon, and asked Judge Leahy if it would be a convenient time to break for lunch before he began a new area of questioning. The judge agreed, and admonished the jury not to discuss the case amongst themselves. We would resume at one-thirty.

As the jury filed out, I noticed Baum staring at me, well aware he had done a lot of damage with the photograph. Like a magician, Baum very adroitly used misdirection to camouflage the real reason for calling McGee to the stand, waiting until the end of his questioning to introduce the picture, when it would have maximum effect on the jurors.

There was no way to put a positive spin on the photograph: it was a real blow. If they believed Dowd took the *Aloha* into Bonita Channel at a time when it was filled with waves the size as shown in the photo, it would be a disaster. I hoped my face was not giving away what I was feeling.

There was a small room down the hallway from Department Six used for attorney client conferences. Since the courtroom was closed over the lunch recess, I went there to work. I opened my briefcase with the files I needed, and the yellow pad with the few cryptic notes I made of Baum's examination of McGee.

The photograph neatly hemmed me in. My own expert, Captain Seymour, had said the most likely cause of the disappearance of the *Aloha* was being capsized by large breaking waves, and Bonita Channel the most likely location. The photo showed waves of the size Captain Seymour had said in his deposition were big enough to sink the *Aloha*. Left unanswered, the photograph would be difficult, if not impossible, to rebut.

No wonder Baum had called Captain McGee as his first witness.

Time was short to formulate a strategy on how to deal with Captain McGee's testimony. Thankfully there are only a few tactical choices available in deciding how to cross-examine witnesses whose testimony has hurt your case: attack the witnesses' credibility, attack the accuracy of their recollections, call into question their ability to have actually seen what they claim, or expose any biases they may have.

When I spoke to McGee on his boat, he mentioned that breakers can come up suddenly in Bonita Channel. Baum had not asked about that, and I might get McGee to repeat what he told me on his boat. I wrote the question down on my pad, and started to think of a way to broach the subject without getting his guard up. After a moment of thought, I ripped the sheet from the pad and threw it in the wastepaper basket. Of all the rules applying to cross-examination, one is so cardinal in nature that it is practically written in stone: never ask a witness a question unless you know in advance how they are going to answer.

The only thing I could come up with that had any chance for success on cross-examination was the time issue. McGee testified he left the dock at ten minutes after six. The *Aloha* was a faster boat and sailed at six. Questions about the time might not make him suspicious his testimony was being challenged. Trying to attack anything else he said was not going to work. Without his statement, I couldn't directly confront his testimony in court, and any attempt I made to do so would only entrench him in the positions he had taken earlier. McGee's testimony, as bad as it had been, was not the main concern. It was the photograph. The impact the picture made on the jury wasn't worth a thousand words, it was more like ten thousand, and I had no idea how to neutralize it.

A few minutes before one-thirty, the jury was brought back in. The clerk knocked on the door to chambers, calling the courtroom to order as the judge took the bench. Captain McGee had already resumed his seat in the witness box.

The judge turned to him. "Captain McGee, do you understand you are still under oath?" McGee acknowledged he understood.

Turning to Baum the judge said, "You may continue your examination."

Baum stood, announcing he had no further questions.

The judge asked, "Do you wish to cross-examine?"

I rose and moved toward the lectern, noting McGee was sitting more erectly than in the morning.

He had almost certainly been spoken to by Baum and Blake over the lunch break. They probably gave him the same pep talk I would give a witness who was about to be cross-examined: reassure him that he had done well on direct, stick with his testimony, and not get rattled or lose his composure.

After putting my notes on the lectern, I turned toward the witness box. "Good afternoon, Captain."

It was not a question, and he did not respond. The forward tilt to his body indicated he was on high alert, the look of a man not about to be anybody's prey.

The first order of business was to see if he had been turned into an actively hostile witness. Some preliminary questions would give me an indication where I stood with him. I began with the only viable issue I had: the time issue.

"Did you note the time in your log book when you passed under the Golden Gate Bridge or any other landmarks on your way out that morning?"

"No."

"Can you remember now, two and a half years later, when you passed those landmarks?"

His face remained impassive as he mulled over the question. Whatever he was weighing about how to answer, he opted for the safe response.

"I can't recall."

"Do you recall when you rounded Point Bonita?"

"No."

I felt some minor sense of relief. His answer would at least let me argue that he and Dowd arrived at Point Bonita at different times. McGee's boat was an old one with a diesel engine, and probably not very fast. Good size swells were running that morning, and for the comfort of his passengers he probably hadn't been moving at full speed. It was time to delve into something else.

I would be going out on a limb from now on, and the farther out I got the more likely it was to break.

Regaining eye contact, I asked, "Did you take this picture?"

"No," he replied, staring at me in an irritated, uncomprehending manner.

McGee had used little facial expression in response to Baum's questions, and up to this point none with mine. His expression now was clearly communicating: 'of course I didn't take the picture.'

"Were you present when this picture was taken?" I continued.

"No."

"Do you know when it was taken?"

"No."

"Is this your photograph?"

"No."

"Who provided the picture?"

He paused a moment, then pointed to Baum and Blake.

"The lawyers," he said.

This line of questioning was getting me nowhere. From the corner of my eye, I could see the jurors squirming. It was perfectly obvious McGee had not taken the photograph and they were annoyed with the questions. Despite being on the path of disregarding the golden rule of cross-examination that every first-year law student knows—never ask questions you don't know how the witness is going to respond to—I blundered on.

"Captain McGee, did you know Francis Dowd?"

He hesitated, longer than with the other questions.

"I've *heard* about him," he finally responded.

There was something decidedly off with his answer. It wasn't what he said ... by themselves the words had little meaning. It was entirely his tone. The way he said, "I've *heard* about him," was similar to the tone used when one woman, speaking in a very deprecating way about another, uses the phrase, 'Oh, *that* woman.' There was no mistaking that whatever he'd heard about Dowd was decidedly negative.

The chance that Captain McGee, as a member of the professional fishing fleet whose boat was berthed in an entirely different marina, would have heard anything about Francis Dowd, a sport fisherman, was virtually nil. My instincts were telling me that someone had run the poison pen game on Captain McGee.

He'd *heard* about Dowd all right and, unless I was dead wrong, I knew the source of that information. More importantly, I knew the effect it had on him. The professional captains have very jaundiced views of recreational boat owners, and for good reasons. In their many years fishing out on the ocean, McGee and the other captains would have seen repeated instances of amateur sport fishermen getting themselves into trouble because of poor judgment, lack of skill, and—worst of all—chance taking.

I had been salmon fishing on twenty or thirty occasions, a tiny fraction of the times the professional captains like McGee had been out. But even in my limited experience, I had seen boats, built for the calm waters of an inland lake, ten or more miles from shore. In other instances, small boats designed to carry two people had twice that many onboard with no life jackets. The worst lapse was drinking. It was easy to pick out the boats where this was happening. The boaters' boisterous voices easily carried over the water, often leaving a trail of beer cans floating in their wake. There didn't seem to be a correlation between the size of a boat and the skill of the operators. Even big boats, the size of the *Aloha*, had their share of chance taking cowboy skippers. In his many years as a professional fisherman, Captain McGee was bound to have seen dozens of incidents like these. His answer, "I've *heard* about him," goaded me into taking my cross-examination in a new direction.

What I was about to embark on required the photograph. The time it took to get it from the evidence box on the clerk's desk gave me a few seconds to think. I cautioned myself one final time. I would be questioning him in an area I had no idea how he would answer, going one question at a time, letting his answers guide me to the next question.

"Captain McGee, have you heard Mr. Dowd owned his boat, the *Aloha*, for seven years?"

He looked at me with the watchfulness of a stalked animal before responding.

"No," he replied.

"Have you heard he had taken the *Aloha* out on the ocean fifteen to twenty times a year for the past seven years?"

"No."

"Were you told that in those one hundred or more trips there were no mishaps of any kind?"

His "No" this time was a little slower in coming. Hoping I wasn't deceiving myself, I thought I heard a barely discernible note of unease in his voice, encouraging me to go on.

My instincts told me to increase the pace in order to keep him from anticipating my questions, but I couldn't risk a poorly framed one that would give Baum the slightest chance to object and break up the tempo I had established.

I moved closer to the witness stand.

"Captain McGee, were you informed that Mr. Dowd served four years in the Navy?"

"No," he answered. I hoped the jury had not missed what I felt was a slight edge of respect as he answered this question about the Navy.

"Were you told by anyone that Francis Dowd served those four years at sea on submarines?"

"No."

On impulse, even though his answers would be anticlimactic, I decided to switch the form of my questions so all of his answers would be in the affirmative. What I wanted the jury to do was concentrate their attention on his face. I would be doing so as well, letting his facial expressions, which had become more and more telling, be my guide whether to continue my questioning.

"May I approach the witness, Your Honor?" The judge nodded.

"Captain, at the time you looked up Bonita Channel, and made your decision to change course and go out the Main Channel, the wave conditions were similar to what's shown in this photograph, is that correct?" I held the picture up.

After a moment of thought, he replied: "Yes."

Bringing the photo down, I looked at it, stalling to give myself a moment to frame the next question. "Captain McGee, taking a boat the size of the *Aloha* through wave conditions like those shown in this photograph, that wouldn't just be careless or negligent . . . that would have been the act of a madman, wouldn't it?"

He said nothing initially, and then began nodding his head, so slowly at first it was barely discernible, becoming more pronounced as he finally began to speak.

"Yes, it would be."

As the answer faded away in the courtroom, McGee's face, so weathered by the sun and wind, showed emotion for the first time.

Working to keep my tone completely neutral, I asked in a lowered voice, "Captain McGee, from what you've just learned for the first time, here in court about Francis Dowd, taking his boat through waters that look like this," I held the photo up to him, "doesn't sound like something he would do, does it?"

It was a rambling, clearly objectionable question, but there was silence, the entire courtroom riveted on the captain. As the moments passed I anticipated an objection, but Baum and Blake made no move, not even whispering.

He finally spoke, "No, I don't suppose he would. . . . No."

His words rippled through the courtroom, and for the first time since I had begun my cross-examination, he wasn't staring back in a wary, guarded way.

"You know, Captain, I don't think he would either," I said.

He looked at me, sorting through my words. Concluding it wasn't a question, he made no reply.

The jury had been staring at him intently, and I hoped they noticed when I said, "I don't think he would either," that Captain McGee nodded his head in agreement; his facial expression stating his thoughts far better than any words he might have spoken.

"Thank you, Captain."

I turned to the judge.

"No more questions, Your Honor."

There was no redirect examination by Baum, and he was excused.

Along with everyone else, I watched Captain McGee as he strode to the door, pulled it open, and departed. When the door closed shut, I headed for my table.

I had taken only a few steps before noticing I still had the photograph in my hand, and walked back towards the clerk's desk. Just before placing it in the evidence box I had a second thought. I walked over to plaintiffs' table and placed the photograph face up in front of Baum.

I had not stepped on a land mine—and even felt I'd gained something from my last few questions. But that didn't change the fact that the photograph, which had so powerfully impacted the jurors, was in evidence and would be available to them in the jury room. The cold reality was: the impact of oral testimony diminishes over time, but a photograph remains vividly fixed in jurors' minds.

Popular wisdom has it that 'seeing is believing,' but I'd never heard anyone say 'hearing is.'

# 19

Judge Leahy gave the courtroom a few moments to recompose before ordering that the next witness be called.

Baum stood. "If it pleases the court, plaintiffs call Michael Wrisley," and sent Blake to the hallway to retrieve him.

Most witnesses stop as they come through the door to get their bearings. Not Wrisley. He strode in like he owned the place, moving confidently to the clerk to be sworn in. Without waiting to be asked, he raised his hand for the oath, responding "I do" in a loud voice. The clerk's gesture to the witness box was unnecessary; he was halfway there. After settling in, he turned to the judge and nodded, did the same to the jury, and with a nod to Baum indicated he could begin.

After having him state his name, Baum asked his occupation.

"I am a journalist," Wrisley said, and outlined that he worked for a weekly sailing newspaper called Latitude 38.

"How long have you been with them?"

He gave the number of years, and answered other questions about the location of the paper's offices, and its circulation.

Basic questions of this nature are intended to make a witness comfortable with being on the witness stand. They seemed to be having the opposite effect on Wrisley who was straining at the leash for substantive questioning to begin.

"Mr. Wrisley, did there come a time when you became aware of the loss of a boat named the *Aloha*?"

His already erect posture straightened further.

"Yes, I did."

"What were the circumstances?"

"My paper asked me to do an in-depth article about the loss of the *Aloha* and other boats from the same storm."

Only by moving quickly was Baum able to get in another question. "As a part of your research, did you contact the United States Coast Guard?"

Wrisley responded that he had spoken with Officer Dennis George at the Fort Point Coast Guard Station. George informed him an investigation had begun, and showed Wrisley debris that washed ashore on Ocean Beach in San Francisco which might have come from the *Aloha*.

"Mr. Wrisley, did you take photographs of this wreckage?"

"I did."

Baum handed him some photographs. "Are these the photographs you took?"

Wrisley looked at them briefly, and confirmed they were.

Baum asked the judge if the five photos could be marked for identification as plaintiffs' next exhibit, casually adding, "Counsel has seen these photographs."

I had seen photographs taken by the Coast Guard, but none by Wrisley who had been identified in answers to interrogatories as someone who photographed debris allegedly from the *Aloha*.

I arranged to have copies made of the Coast Guard's photographs, and had a fire investigator carefully examine them. He informed me there was no indication that either a fire or an explosion had occurred. This was a considerable relief. Any sign of an explosion might have been the type of *prima facie* evidence allowing Baum to bring the *Marine Sulphur Queen* case to Judge Leahy's attention.

Baum handed me the five photographs. Four were snap shots of white fiberglass debris; the fifth picture showed a galley tabletop. They looked innocent enough, but the McGee photograph of breaking waves in Bonita Channel was very much in my mind, and I put myself on alert for another photographic ambush. After examining the photos, I handed them back to Baum. Since he had not offered the pictures into evidence, I could only wait to see what developed.

"Mr. Wrisley, what was your purpose in taking these pictures?"

He turned to the jury. "They were taken as a part of the investigation I was making for the article I was working on."

"How many other wrecks have you investigated?"

"Oh, many," he replied expansively.

Wrisley, who Baum was now referring to as an investigative reporter, could not have missed that he was the center of attention in the courtroom. My senses told me he was eager to testify about something vastly more important than merely providing the foundation for the admission of the photographs, and readied myself for another photographic ace to emerge from Baum's well-tailored sleeve.

"Could you tell the jury what observations you made concerning the debris you inspected?"

"Some of the boat's fiberglass material had become detached from the frame-work of the hull."

"What caused the separation of this material?"

I was out of my chair in an instant, charging toward the witness stand. Pointing my finger at Wrisley, I spoke loudly, "Just one moment Mr. Witness, I have an objection to make. And you will wait until the judge has made his ruling before you start answering."

Wrisley, who had already turned towards the jury, jerked his head back to me, his face brimming with resentment. When I was satisfied he would not blurt out the answer he was so obviously primed to give, I turned toward the bench to find Judge Leahy glaring at me. Like most judges, he did not like having witnesses given instructions by anyone other than himself, and was plainly not pleased.

"Your Honor, may we approach?"

With an impatient gesture, he motioned us forward.

At side bar, I said, "There are a number of objections I have to these photographs coming into evidence, and to this line of questioning as well."

After glancing at the clock, the judge whispered, "I am going to excuse the jury, and then hear your objections."

Argument on my objections could easily have been made at side bar. I suspected the real reason for sending the jurors out was that Judge Leahy did not want another melee the jury could overhear, similar to what had taken place over the McGee photograph. As the bailiff led the jurors out of the courtroom, I resolved to keep my voice down and my emotions in check.

"Your Honor," I said, "Mr. Wrisley is a reporter, apparently called to lay a foundation for some photographs he took. Now, he is being asked to render an expert opinion on the forces necessary to cause pieces of hull material to separate. That is a task for a physicist, a naval architect, or a maritime accident reconstruction specialist. . . ."

Before I could continue, the judge cut in, "Perhaps the witness has sufficient training or experience to state an opinion on how the pieces came apart."

"Even if by some stretch of the imagination he is qualified to render an expert opinion, I still object on the ground that he was not listed as an expert witness."

The judge leaned back in his chair to think. He then looked toward

Baum and Blake, making a quick upward movement with his chin—a mannerism we were getting used to, meaning 'your turn.'

Blake spoke: "This witness has investigated many accidents involving all types of boats, and examined numerous pieces of wreckage to determine the cause of an accident. The jury should be allowed to hear his testimony based on his extensive experience examining debris from many wrecks, and give an opinion on how the pieces came apart."

My instincts were telling me they were trying to lay a foundation for Wrisley to testify that an explosion might have caused the pieces to separate, bringing in the *Sulphur Queen* case.

The judge looked at me to respond.

"Regardless of what his qualifications might be, he is being asked to render an expert opinion, and his name is not on their list of expert witnesses. I further request that none of the photographs be admitted into evidence. Their only purpose will be to assert in closing argument that powerful forces were exerted on the *Aloha* to cause pieces of hull material to be torn from their fittings."

Turning back to Blake, the judge asked, "Is it correct that Mr. Wrisley's name was not disclosed as an expert witness?"

Blake acknowledged that was true and started to speak, but the judge held his hand up, palm out, like a traffic cop—another of his mannerisms we had become familiar with. This one meant 'stop talking.'

After a pause, he leaned forward. "Submitted, gentlemen?"

"Yes," we said.

The judge took a moment to formulate his ruling before speaking.

"I will not allow this witness to express an opinion based on his examination of the debris. He is not listed as an expert."

Turning to the photographs, the judge looked toward Baum and Blake. "Are you offering all of them into evidence?"

"Yes," both responded.

The judge turned to me.

I said, "Four of these photos show white fiberglass material that can be found on any beach, but there is no proof whatsoever that any of it came from the *Aloha*. The photograph of the wood table top may be from the *Aloha*, but has not been identified as such."

As I was about to continue the judge held his hand up. Turning to the clerk, he asked for the photographs, looking through them one at a time, and then compared a few of them together. Putting them aside, he said, "Only the photograph showing the table top will be admitted."

I wasn't happy about the table picture, but my principal objective, preventing Wrisley from giving expert opinions about explosions or otherwise, had been accomplished.

The judge ordered that the jury be brought back in.

Wrisley remained in the witness box during the arguments, listening intently. When the judge ruled that he would not be allowed to testify as an expert, he appeared shocked, staring at me with ill-disguised enmity. It seemed obvious then that Wrisley had been carefully groomed to testify extensively about the cause of the loss of the *Aloha*.

Baum's last question, "What caused the separation of this material," had been left hanging in the air. It would now go unanswered.

Baum asked Wrisley a few questions about the one photograph that had been admitted into evidence, and concluded his direct examination. The judge asked if I wanted to cross-examine.

I did not want to risk asking any question that might give Wrisley the slightest excuse to start testifying about the cause of the loss of the *Aloha*, and confined myself to a few inquiries about when and where the picture was taken, and sat down. He was then excused.

Wrisley had fervently wanted to render expert opinions. As he strode past my table on his way out of the courtroom, he shot me an irate glare.

The judge ordered that the next witness be called.

Blake had followed Wrisley out of the courtroom, and returned in a few moments with Scott Noble, their expert on wave formation. Noble dropped his well-worn briefcase to the floor, and after taking the oath stepped to the witness box.

My concern about Noble was not that he would be a wily, hard to pin down witness. His earnest manner and almost professorial demeanor presented different difficulties. The jury was bound to respond favorably to his unassuming style. They would also find his substantial professional qualifications, and specialized experience in oceanography, gave ample credence to his opinions.

Blake remained standing near the lectern waiting until Noble finished arranging his files. Prior to this moment, only Baum had spoken for the plaintiffs.

Blake began by asking Noble to state his name, the name of his firm, his educational background, and an overview of the professional associations and the technical papers he had written. After finishing with his credentials, Blake asked him about his work in ocean engineering.

The jury followed with interest as he outlined the considerable breadth of his professional experience. He was then asked to tell the jury what he had been asked to do in this case.

"I was asked to assess the weather situation, and the condition of the waves in the vicinity of the San Francisco Bar and Bonita Channel on the date of the incident."

Blake let that linger a moment.

"Please tell the jury what you did to make your analysis."

Noble began a long recital. "I reviewed a copy of the official Coast Guard investigation report. I also analyzed data from a wave recording buoy maintained by NOAA," which he informed the jury was the National Oceanographic and Atmospheric Administration. "I obtained and examined further data about waves from other sources, and records from the National Weather Service. I also reviewed information produced during the discovery stage of this case."

Blake put a large illustration Noble had made of a breaking wave on the easel, and asked him to step down and explain what causes a smooth rolling swell to turn into a breaking wave. The jury showed obvious interest as Noble explained from a technical point of view how an incoming swell can turn into a breaking wave as it nears the shore, a phenomena the jurors had seen many times for themselves at the local beaches.

Noble's tutorial on the basics of wave formation had been the hors d'oeuvres. Blake then turned his questioning to the main course . . . the wave conditions existing on the morning the *Aloha* disappeared. This was the testimony the jury had been waiting to hear. They were obviously impressed with Noble's credentials, and leaned forward attentively to hear his opinions.

Noble turned to face the jury box. "My analysis of the data recorded for March 9th from the buoy operated by NOAA indicates the swells coming in that morning were quite large, in both their height and length. They were also unusually long period waves."

Blake asked him to explain the oceanographic term 'long period waves' and its significance to the case.

Noble turned toward the jury, informing them that waves were measured in three ways: their height, their length and by their 'wave period,' which he explained was the amount of time it takes for a wave to pass a fixed point.

Referring to his file, Noble continued: "The wave period that morning was in excess of twenty seconds which is an unusually long period."

Asked how unusual, Noble replied, "Waves in excess of twenty seconds occur only two or three times a year."

He was then asked to state his opinion about what happened to the waves as they approached the area around the San Francisco Bar that morning.

"In my opinion, because of their length, their height, and their speed, the incoming swells very likely turned into breaking waves in the area around the Bar."

Blake then asked about the height of waves on March 9.

Noble found a document in his file, turned to the jury, and began reading from it aloud. "The average height of the top thirty-three percent of the waves that morning was eleven feet. The top ten percent of the waves averaged fourteen feet, and the top one percent were eighteen feet high."

I made a quick note on my pad that I would have to deal with this reference to eighteen foot waves when I cross-examined him.

Noble was then asked what happened to the swells when they reached the shallow water around the Bar.

His face adopted a professorial look as he began a careful critique.

"The sudden decrease in water depth on the Bar caused dramatic changes to the height and also the shape of the incoming waves, changing them from smooth, undulating swells into waves with steeply sided fronts. The height of the swells increased as well."

Blake pointed to the Potatopatch area on the chart, and asked whether the incoming swells would have turned into breaking waves when they reached that location.

Noble replied, "The data indicate some of the swells recorded that morning would definitely have turned into breakers in that area." Stepping to the chart he pointed out to the jurors that the Potatopatch was very close to the western edge of Bonita Channel.

"In your opinion, would waves breaking on the Bar that morning have been capable of capsizing a boat the size of the *Aloha?*"

"Yes, in my opinion, they would," adding he had a drawing to illustrate the point. An artist's rendition was placed on the easel showing a large wave with a steeply sloped front, and its crest breaking over. A boat was depicted in the wave's trough, about to be overwhelmed. The jurors stared at the picture almost in disbelief at the sheer size and power of the wave. Taking note of their reaction, Blake busied himself with his notes to give the jury ample time to absorb the dramatic impact of the illustration.

In the next series of questions, Noble stated that the height and unusual length of the waves that morning were such that breaking waves would have been occurring not only on the Bar but in Bonita Channel as well.

Noble was then handed the McGee photograph and asked to examine it carefully. After doing so, he was asked, "Are the waves shown in this photograph what you would have anticipated seeing that morning?"

"Yes. The waves shown here are of the size and type I would have expected that morning."

"In your opinion, would it have been unsafe to go through Bonita Channel in a boat the size of the *Aloha* in those conditions?"

"It would have been very dangerous to do so," shaking his head slowly.

Blake reviewed his notes and said he had no further questions. The judge declared a short break and left the bench.

After I had taken Noble's deposition, I made a copy of the transcript and sent it to Rae Strange, asking for his comments. Strange called a few days later, identifying areas where his opinions differed from Noble's, which for the most part amounted to minor professional differences. Toward the end of our conversation, he mentioned that Noble had only obtained the wave data from the NOAA buoy. In contrast, Strange obtained the data from all three of the available buoys. He had also compared and analyzed the data, and then prepared a detailed summary.

Blake had taken Strange's deposition. A copy of the summary Strange had compiled was given to Blake during the deposition, and it had obviously been passed on to Noble.

On the witness stand, Noble did something very unusual in responding to Blake's questions: he had repeatedly used Strange's summary, not to discredit the data Strange had assembled, but to support his own conclusions. Ordinarily, expert witnesses rely on their own data exclusively while testifying. The only time the other side's data is even mentioned is to demonstrate that the opposing party's expert did not have the correct data to work with, or had improperly interpreted it.

Back in session, the judge looked at me. "Cross-examination?" I nodded.

Walking toward the lectern I kept repeating to myself, 'you don't win your case by cross-examining the other side's experts.' The jury had reacted so positively to Noble and his opinions. I planned on limiting myself to the points in my notes and sit down.

I noticed that some of Noble's answers to Blake's questions varied slightly from the responses he had given in his deposition. I began my cross-examination by asking about those changes. Unruffled, Noble candidly admitted he had changed some of his opinions. He then pulled out Strange's summary, citing it as the basis for modifying some of the positions he'd stated in his deposition. I wasn't expecting that answer and quickly moved to another topic.

"Mr. Noble, the elapsed time between the waves that morning was quite unusual, is that correct?"

"The wave period was in excess of twenty seconds, which only occurs two or three times a year."

"This unusually long time period between the waves that morning would have made it more difficult for a boat operator to estimate their height, would it not?"

He shook his head. "In deep water out on the ocean that might be true, but I believe the *Aloha* was in much shallower water, somewhere in the vicinity of the Bar when it sank." He quickly added, "What made the conditions in Bonita Channel so dangerous that morning was not the long period waves, but the presence of breakers in the Channel." Once again, he held up Rae Strange's summary as support for his answer.

I asked whether he had worked for the Corps of Engineers before joining his current firm. He replied that he had.

"Did you make any attempt to obtain the wave data for March 9th from the Corps of Engineers?"

"I reviewed a copy of the data from the Corps of Engineers buoy that was attached to the Coast Guard report."

"But that's not the actual data, is it? What's attached to the Coast Guard report is just a summary, isn't that correct?"

He admitted it was.

"So you didn't obtain the Corps of Engineers raw data and analyze it; you relied on the summary attached to the report?"

"That's true, but the summary attached to the Coast Guard report was accurate."

I had him backed into a corner, and pounced.

"How do you know that, if you didn't analyze the data yourself?"

"In my experience, the Coast Guard is thorough in their investigations, and checks the accuracy of any information they use before including it in their official reports." He paused for a moment. "And besides that, I read the analysis your expert Rae Strange made of the Corps of Engineers raw data. And he confirmed that the summary attached to the Coast Guard report was correct."

This was the third or fourth time Noble had used Strange's summary to bolster his answers. This time the jurors were unable to restrain their smiles, knowing I had stepped into a large and widening hole of my own making. In addition to the application of the laws of evidence, there are moments in every trial when Murphy's Law comes into play—and this was one of them. I struggled to maintain my composure, knowing my face was giving away the embarrassment I was feeling. I had to do something, and quick, to defuse the effect Noble was having on the jury, by using Strange's summary against me.

"Mr. Noble, the data from these three buoys is reliable and useful, correct?"

"Certainly."

"Having this data is essential in order to determine the height of the waves in the area around the Bar that morning?"

"Yes."

"This data is a matter of public record, available to anyone?"

"Yes, it is."

I then asked, "Did you contact the Scripps Institute or the United States Army Corps of Engineers to obtain the data from their buoys that you just stated is reliable, useful and available?"

"No."

"If you ran into any difficulties in interpreting the Corps of Engineers data, you could have called them up, since you used to work for them, isn't that correct?"

He agreed, quickly adding, "But I worked for the Corps of Engineers up in Oregon, and was unaware they had a buoy in this area."

I was astonished. The Corps of Engineers maintains buoys near the mouth of every major river in the United States, and are responsible for dredging out the Main Ship Channel leading into San Francisco Bay.

I had a few more questions, but letting the jury ponder why Noble didn't know the answer to that question seemed like a good place to stop.

"Nothing further, Your Honor."

I was glad to get Noble off the stand. He had been so carefully prepared, there was little left on the table to cross-examine him about the vivid picture he painted of the size and power of the waves in Bonita Channel that morning. As I resumed my seat, I was still smarting at the way Noble effectively used the summary that Rae Strange had so painstakingly prepared to support his own opinions.

The judge asked Baum to call his next witness.

"We call Kathleen Ang, Your Honor."

Witnesses are excluded from being in the courtroom before they are called to the stand to prevent them from being influenced by the testimony of others. But this rule does not apply to the parties in a lawsuit. Baum introduced Kathleen and her brother Dwight on the first day of trial. She had been in court every day, providing ample time for the jury to make preliminary impressions. Kathleen was twenty-five, with the same fine boned features and flawless porcelain complexion of her mother.

After being given the oath, Kathleen took her seat on the stand looking first at her mother, then toward Baum signaling her readiness.

He began by establishing that she was Andy Ang's daughter, and then had Kathleen outline her own and her siblings' education and work experience. All had been to college and were working in their respective fields with the exception of her youngest brother Glenn who was still in school. When asked about their family activities, she said they had a tradition of taking vacations together which continued even while they were in college when she and her brothers and sisters had many competing outside interests. As busy as her father had been with his work, he always found time to help with their studies, encouraged them with their extracurricular activities, and attended their sporting events when he could. The message being very compellingly conveyed by Kathleen's testimony was that the Angs were a strong knit family where education was prized and hard work expected.

Baum handed me a professionally done photo portrait of Mr. Ang. He was neither smiling nor taciturn, just calmly gazing at you through the lens of the camera: a gentleman of quiet dignity and respectability.

There was no objection I could make to this picture which was bound to have an emotional impact on the jury. I handed it back without comment.

After the photograph was marked as an exhibit, it was handed to Kathleen in the witness box.

Baum must have told her the photograph would be introduced into evidence through her, but she looked at the picture as if she had never seen it before, her head bent down, staring at it.

"Kathleen, is this a photograph of your father?"

Baum's voice seemed to startle her, causing her head to snap up. It was immediately apparent she was struggling for control. After a moment to compose herself, she replied in a barely audible voice.

"Yes."

Baum asked for permission to circulate the photograph to the jury. When it had gone through the jury box, he announced he had no further questions.

The judge turned to me.

"Do you wish to cross-examine?"

I stood, remaining at the table next to Janet, and turned to face Kathleen. The old saw, 'never cross-examine a witness unless you have something to gain,' applied in spades to her.

"Miss Ang, I am sorry for your loss. I know all of the families touched by this terrible accident have suffered greatly. I have no questions. Thank you."

Judge Leahy leaned toward the witness box.

"You are excused," he said gently.

Kathleen rose gracefully, and with her gaze fixed on her mother, walked unsteadily through the well of the court, resuming her seat by her side.

Her presence on the stand acted as a poignant reminder to the jury of the ongoing loss the Angs suffered by her father's death. Kathleen had painted a very touching portrait of her father as a kind and loving man, and impressed the jurors as the sort of daughter any parent would be proud to have.

If you don't connect emotionally, you don't connect at all. Kathleen very clearly had.

Baum remained standing. "If it pleases the court, our next witness is Dwight Ang."

Squaring his shoulders, Dwight walked purposefully toward the clerk, answering the oath confidently. From my brief look at the photograph of Mr. Ang, I could see little resemblance between Dwight and his father.

Baum asked him to state his name, where he lived and confirm that he was Andy Ang's eldest son. From the corner of my eye, I noticed Janet flinch. The words "eldest son" must have triggered a reflexive and painful thought about Gerald.

"Please tell the jury about your education, where you are employed, and what you do."

Dwight stated that he had a degree in physics from the University of California, and worked as a physicist for the Raytheon Company at their Mountain View facility.

The engineers on the jury showed an obvious interest in the physics degree. All the jurors seemed surprised he was employed by Raytheon, at the same facility Dowd managed.

Baum began his substantive questioning by asking Dwight if he was aware of his father's plans for the future. Dwight described discussions he'd had with his father about wanting to continue his relationship with Raytheon, and his desire to pursue other business opportunities as well.

This was an area I had to be on alert, and pushed my chair back, ready to object if he started testifying in specifics. It had been claimed in discovery that Mr. Ang planned to expand his operations, but no details had been given. As long as Dwight's testimony was limited to broad generalities about his father's hopes to 'expand his business,' the judge would permit it.

"Were you aware of the purpose of your father's trip to the United States?"

"He told me he was coming to renegotiate his contract with Raytheon."

Baum turned to family related questions.

"Dwight, please tell the jury what prompted you to pursue a degree in physics?"

"As a business man in the high tech industry, my father was interested in the fields of engineering and physics. During high school he took an interest in my science classes and encouraged my interest in obtaining a degree in physics here in the United States. My younger brother Glenn is in college now, pursuing a degree in mathematics and computer science."

"While you were still living at home, please describe what activities the family engaged in."

"Father helped all of us with our homework and school projects." He paused. "Although his business activities occupied him constantly, he always found time to help us with personal problems too."

By the time Baum's direct examination was completed, the jury had a clear picture of Andy Ang as a hardworking, successful entrepreneur who took great pride in his children and their accomplishments.

The judge looked to me, asking if I had any cross-examination. I stood quickly.

"Thank you, Your Honor."

I had a few areas of inquiry for Dwight, but he was obviously worked up emotionally, and I would have to tread cautiously.

"Your father had been out fishing on the *Aloha* several times before?

"Yes."

"On each occasion, he told you he'd caught some fish and had a good time?"

"Yes."

"Your father never told you Mr. Dowd had been reckless or careless, or done anything that caused him to be concerned for his safety, did he?"

"No."

"Did you speak with Mrs. Dowd on the evening of the incident?" I sensed Janet stiffening in her chair.

"Yes, I did." He paused, swallowing hard a few times before continuing.

"I planned to have dinner with my father that evening, and when I didn't hear from him I called to ask if she had heard from them. Mrs. Dowd told me she had not, and had become concerned. She contacted the Coast Guard just before I called her. They told her there were no reports of any boats in trouble, but would look into the matter and call her back."

"What happened next?"

"Mrs. Dowd invited me to come to her house and wait while the Coast Guard tried to contact the *Aloha* by radio, and make inquiries about whether anyone reported seeing a disabled boat."

Dwight said he accepted the invitation. When he arrived at the home, other people were there as well. I was ready with my next question, but he wanted to go on.

"As time went on, the news was not encouraging. The Coast Guard called back to say they had been unable to reach the *Aloha* by radio, and no reports had been received about boats in trouble. They told her a search would be made, but it could not begin until daylight."

I wanted to resume my questions, and at the same time did not want to risk offending Dwight or the jury by cutting him off while he was speaking with such obvious feeling. He then stated something I was unaware of.

"Mrs. Dowd offered to have me stay the night at her home, in one of the spare bedrooms, so I could be there if the Coast Guard called with any news. And I stayed there that night."

I doubted he could add much more. I looked at the judge and said I had no further questions.

There was an extended whispered conversation between Baum and Blake. Baum then stood and said he had no redirect questions. Dwight was excused. He was the last witness of the afternoon.

The judge admonished the jury not to discuss the case with anyone, including among themselves, and adjourned the trial to the next day.

Much of the testimony by Dwight and Kathleen about the loss of their father had been upsetting for Janet. As we said our goodbyes, I could see the pain pulsing in her face.

After strapping my court bags onto my cart, I was ready to leave, and remembered I had not been informed who plaintiffs would call as witnesses the following morning, as the judge ordered.

I walked over to Baum who was speaking with Dwight.

"Excuse me, who will you be calling tomorrow?"

Without taking his glance from Dwight, Baum said, "Talk to Martin," and continued his conversation.

This did not suit me. Baum was lead counsel for the plaintiffs, and he, not Blake, should be dealing with me. I had been dismissed without even the courtesy of Baum deigning to look in my direction.

Blake, who had heard the exchange, continued busying himself packing their bags. It was quickly apparent that his intent was to finish before acknowledging me. Speaking in a tone louder than I intended, I said, "Well, who are your witnesses tomorrow?"

Blake looked up as if he were unaware I had been standing there, and finally said, "Jane Ang, Captain Going, and Stan Karp."

"Anyone else?" I asked. He shook his head, and returned to packing their bags.

I knew better than to let this 'one-upsmanship' upset me, but I didn't like the attitude of either one of them.

I never subscribed to my father's credo: 'the other lawyer is not your opponent, he is your enemy.' I saw no reason for not attempting to get along with my opponents, and at a minimum to at least be civil. I noticed from the first day they were determined not to respond to my greetings of 'good morning,' and dropped that attempt at civility.

It was quarter to five. Before leaving, I called the office to deal with a few matters requiring my attention, and then walked to the parking lot. The freeway was clogged with rush hour traffic, and it was past six by the time I arrived home.

Marsha was waiting for me as I came up the steps and asked how the day had gone. I outlined the opening statements and the jury's reaction to them. She asked me to be more specific. "Any facial expressions or body language?"

"Not until Baum gave the names of the Angs' five children . . . that seemed to touch the jurors. Mostly, they listened to the rest of his opening, and mine as well, without giving much away."

"How is the judge?"

"Good, so far. He's not interfering, letting us try the case without micro managing everything."

After supper I went to the office downstairs to work. By the time I finished preparing for the next day, Marsha was asleep.

# 20

At nine-thirty, we were ready for a new day of testimony. After ascending the bench, the judge greeted the jury and gestured to Baum.

"If it pleases the court, our next witness is Stanley Karp."

The jury looked inquisitively as Karp stepped forward to be sworn. There was little resemblance between him and his predecessors on the stand. This was a boat case and there was nothing even remotely nautical about Karp. If it had been a personal injury case, the jury would have assumed he was the treating physician. His well defined facial features were practically accessories to the dark pin stripe suit and perfectly matched tie he chose for his court appearance.

After settling himself in the witness box, he calmly surveyed the courtroom, beginning with the jury, then the judge, ending with counsel and the parties.

Baum asked him to state his name for the record.

Clearing his throat he responded, "Stanislaus Karp."

Baum took Karp through preliminary questions, confirming he was employed by Raytheon, and had him outline the highlights of his career with the company. He said Dowd was his immediate superior, and they worked well together. He described Dowd as hard working, very loyal, and expected the same from his staff in return.

Baum turned to specifics. "Mr. Karp, do you have any responsibilities concerning contract negotiations with the vendors doing business with Raytheon?"

"Yes."

"Do those responsibilities include negotiations with their overseas contractors?"

"They do."

The reason for his appearance on the witness stand was now apparent.

"Did Mr. Dowd ask you to do anything concerning Mr. Ang?"

"I was asked to negotiate a new contract with Mr. Ang on behalf of Raytheon."

"Did you do so?"

"Yes," elaborating that the negotiations had taken two days, and an agreement on a new contract was reached on March 8th, the day before the *Aloha* tragedy.

Baum asked him to outline the compensation aspects of the contract relating to the management services Mr. Ang was to provide.

Karp indicated Mr. Ang was to receive a basic compensation fee, expense allowances, and additional sums as Raytheon's facility in Manila was expanded. The total was approximately $150,000 annually. Baum placed a large pad on the easel, and had Karp step down from the witness stand, handing him a marking pen. Karp was asked to write down the details of the compensation package.

There was a pause as Baum let those numbers sink in with the jury before handing him over to me. I had a few things I wanted to flesh out.

The judge indicated I should proceed.

"Mr. Karp what was your relationship with Francis Dowd?"

"Francis Dowd was a vice president of the company, overseeing our West Coast operations, including the facility here in Mt. View with 1,500 employees. We produce proprietary semi-conductor chips, and assemble various electronic products for our own use, and for sale to others. He had responsibilities over other Raytheon facilities here on the West Coast, and various overseas contract manufacturing operations as well."

"Thank you, Mr. Karp." I turned to the judge and said I had nothing further.

Baum had no redirect examination and Karp was excused.

After nodding to the judge, he rose from his chair. The jury watched until the door closed, cutting off their last glimpse of Stanislaus Karp.

Baum announced that Captain Jack Going would be the next witness. I felt my irritation level rising. Going was the pilot on the only ship coming in or out of San Francisco at the time the fishing boats were heading out on March 9, and I was annoyed with myself for not being the first person to contact him. It would have been easy to do. The business section of the *San Francisco Chronicle* ran a daily column entitled "Ship Arrivals and Sailings." Listed under 'Arrivals' were the names of the inbound ships, the port they were coming from and the pier where they would dock. 'Sailings' gave the date the ships were due to depart and what port they were bound for. Someone working for plaintiffs must have contacted the San Francisco Pilots Association, learned that Captain Going was piloting the only ship in the area at the time of the incident, and contacted him.

When he was identified as a witness in answers to interrogatories, I called the Association several times trying to reach him. After my third call was not returned I got the picture . . . he'd probably been advised not to talk to me.

As he stood in the well taking the oath, his trim build and erect bearing projected the image of a captain. He quickly seated himself.

After stating his name, Baum asked him to outline his occupation.

"I pilot large ships in and out of San Francisco Bay,"

"On the morning of March 9th, two years ago, were you piloting a vessel?"

"Yes, I was. I had been assigned to take out a container ship named the *Queensway Bridge*," adding that the vessel was a modern ship owned by the Kawasaki Shipping Company of Kobe, a well-known and highly regarded Japanese ship line. She was outbound for Japan fully loaded with containers. He identified the terminal where the ship was docked, described the undocking process, and the course he had taken piloting the ship through San Francisco Bay.

Baum handed him the pointer and had him step down to the chart.

"Please tell the jury the position of the ship you were piloting as it approached the Golden Gate Bridge, and show the course you took through Golden Gate Channel toward Point Bonita."

After he identified the traffic lanes the big ships use while going through Golden Gate Channel, Baum asked, "Did you keep the *Queensway Bridge* within those traffic lanes at all times?"

"Absolutely, and I maintained a moderate speed, with no radical course changes."

Baum asked whether there were any unusual conditions that morning.

Going responded no fog was present and there were no other large ships, either inbound or outbound, but he had noticed a number of small craft. He elaborated, "From past experience, I knew the fishing fleet customarily leaves at 0600, and I was alert for them."

"How many fishing boats did you see?"

"As the *Queensway* passed Point Bonita, I became aware of fishing boats ahead of me in the Main Ship Channel, which was somewhat unusual. The more likely place to see them would have been in Bonita Channel."

Baum slowed his tempo, subtly signaling the jurors that an important point was coming.

"Captain, can you estimate how many boats you saw ahead of you in the Main Channel as you passed by Point Bonita?"

"I can't remember the exact number, but at least two or three. The boats were over where they were supposed to be, hugging the right side of the Main Channel, well out of the way. If any had been in mid channel, I would have blasted the ship's horn to let them know a large ship was overtaking them and to move to the side of the Channel. My practice is to keep a close eye on all fishing boats until I am well past them."

Asked to comment on the *Queensway Bridge* and its officers and crew, Going turned toward the jury and repeated the *Queensway* was a big modern ship owned by a large and highly respected Japanese shipping company, Kawasaki Ship Line out of Kobe. It was well maintained with a competent captain and crew. The ship's captain was on the bridge from the time they left the dock until Captain Going left the ship at the end of the Main Ship Channel. In addition to the ship's captain on the bridge, there was the officer of the watch, a helmsman, and at least one lookout.

Baum then asked whether he'd seen any fishing boats close to the *Queensway Bridge*. Going replied he had seen none close by, nor had the ship's officers or lookouts. He added the ship's radar was operating and regularly monitored.

"As you were taking the ship out, did you notice the conditions existing on the Bar?"

"There were breaking waves on the Bar, concentrated in the area around the Potatopatch. I remember the conditions that morning because there were a number of breaking waves in Bonita Channel as well."

Baum handed him the McGee photograph, pointedly asking him to study it carefully.

"Are the waves depicted in this photograph the same approximate size and type you observed in Bonita Channel that morning?"

"Yes, they are."

After letting that answer sink in, Baum changed topics and asked Going to explain what a 'dead head' was.

"It's a large piece of wood, such as a stump or a log, floating at or just below the surface. They are an occasional problem even for large ships, damaging their propeller blades or the rudder. I always keep an eye out for them, and advised the *Queensway*'s captain to have the lookouts stay alert for dead heads as well, and report any sightings to the bridge immediately."

"Did you see any dead heads that day?"

"No."

"Were any reported to you."

"None."

Baum asked how he could remember this information about dead heads two years after the fact. I had just written a note to cross-examine him about that point.

"Dead heads are mostly a seasonal phenomenon. Sighting one in early March would have been unusual, and I would have likely remembered it."

Moving to a new topic, Baum asked, "Please explain what a 'run down' is."

A dark look came over his face as he began his answer.

"A run down occurs when a large ship hits and runs over a small craft such as a fishing boat, or a sail boat."

Baum spoke slowly, leaving a lot of air space between each word.

"Captain, do you have any knowledge of an impact between the *Queensway Bridge* and a fishing boat that morning?"

"No," Going answered emphatically.

"Was any such event reported to you by the officers or crew of the *Queensway Bridge*?"

"None, whatsoever."

Baum stated he was finished with his questioning and turned him over to me. His direct testimony had been strong, leaving me limited areas for cross-examination. My senses told me Captain Going wanted to make sure the jury did not think a run down had occurred while he was piloting the ship.

I decided to meet the issue head on and began with a series of questions about run downs. As I anticipated, he was adamant no such event had occurred. As my inquiries went on, the jury became restless with the persistence of my questioning. But my audience for this aspect of my cross-examination was not the jury, but Judge Leahy. The jurors had no idea that Baum and I would be arguing an important point of law to the judge at the conclusion of the evidence portion of the trial. And it was critical that I make an elaborate record now, through Captain Going's testimony about run downs, to support the argument I would be making to the judge.

I had a few more questions before I turned to a new area.

Prior to the trial, I had looked up the *Queensway Bridge* in Lloyd's Register of Shipping, and made notes of its dimensions. Looking up from my notes, I asked, "Captain Going, do you recall that the length of the *Queensway* was seven hundred feet?"

He thought for a moment. "That sounds about right."

"You stated the vessel was fully loaded with containers, is that correct?"

"Yes."

"The ship's deck would have been stacked four or five high with containers?"

"That's correct."

"Those stacked containers created a visual blind spot in front of the bow?"

His answer was slow in coming, but he did not attempt to evade the question.

"Yes, there was a blind spot."

"How long was that blind spot?"

"I would estimate probably six hundred feet."

This was twice the distance I had guessed, and commented, "Six hundred feet, that's the length of three city blocks isn't it?"

"That sounds about right."

Normally, I would have paused to let his very helpful response about the length of the blind spot resonate with the jury. But I feared Captain Going might sense he had given me a gift and start modifying his answer. I quickly changed subjects before he could.

"Are you aware of the run down incident which took place less than six months ago between a large oil tanker, the *Golden Gate*, and a fishing boat named the *Jack Jr.*?"

"I'm aware of it," he said, eyeing me carefully.

"Captain, your testimony is: no run down incident took place between the *Queensway Bridge* and a fishing boat that morning?"

"That's correct," he said, quickly adding, ". . . and the ship's captain, the officers on watch, as well as the helmsmen and lookouts were there too, and none of them reported the ship hitting anything."

His denial gave me an opening. Maybe.

"Captain Going, are you aware that the Coast Guard thoroughly investigated the incident involving the run down of the *Jack Jr.*?"

"Yes."

"Are you also aware that the Coast Guard interviewed the entire crew onboard the *Golden Gate*, and no one was aware of the fact that their ship ran down and sank the *Jack Jr.*?"

There was a long pause before he answered, his angry stare reflecting his displeasure with the question.

"That's true," he finally grunted.

Any further questions even remotely suggesting that the ship he was piloting might have run down the *Aloha* were going to be met with outright hostility that might blow up in my face. I turned to the judge.

"Nothing further, Your Honor," and he was excused.

As I watched him leave the stand, I hoped Judge Leahy would find Captain Going's responses to my questions about the *Jack Jr.* persuasive when we made our arguments to him about the instructions he would give the jury on the law they were to apply in reaching their verdict.

The judge's voice snapped me back to the present.

"Call your next witness."

Baum announced Mrs. Ang was next.

From the first day she sat in the front row, immediately behind Baum and Blake, flanked on either side by Dwight and Kathleen, attentively watching the proceedings.

The jurors watched carefully as she stepped forward to take the oath. Janet was watching as well, her face an expressionless mask. I noticed Mrs. Ang's was the same.

The women on the jury would find little to fault in Mrs. Ang's appearance. From the first day of trial every outfit she had worn was tasteful, and there was nothing ostentatious about her jewelry.

The similarities between these two women were remarkable. Each had five children, two boys and three girls, approximately the same ages. Their husbands were self-made men who had come far in life on their own merits. No family or social connections had eased the paths of either of them to success.

There was one very substantive difference: Jane Ang's eldest son was at her side. . . . Janet's son was entombed at the bottom of the ocean.

As she settled into the witness box, I recalled my first meeting with Janet and the compassion she had for Jane Ang and her children resulting from Andy's death; and how abruptly that empathy ended when I explained there would be no payment to Mrs. Ang unless Fran was found negligent.

I could feel the coolness emanating from Janet now as she waited to hear the testimony of her husband's accuser.

Baum began. "Please state your name."

"Ong Le Chin Ang," she replied, and with an engaging smile continued, ". . . my American friends find the name Jane a little easier."

The jury reciprocated her smile, warming to her already. If Mrs. Ang was at ease, they were prepared to be as well. If she became tearful, the jury would doubtless be sympathetic, and in the unlikely event she became angry, they would probably be understanding.

Baum took her through an extensive examination of her background. Although her voice was not a large one, she spoke with perfect diction in

American accented English. The slight, almost musical lilt to her voice made it pleasant to hear.

She testified about being born in southern China, emigrating first to Hong Kong, and eventually arriving in Manila. Maintaining tight composure, she described the early years of her marriage to Andy, and her education in the Philippines. After graduating from college she went to medical school, but added that she had never practiced medicine. She and Andy wanted a family, and rearing their children took precedence over a medical career.

"Mrs. Ang, would you give us the names of your children."

Gesturing, she said, "Dwight and Kathleen are here. My three other children are Eleonore, Beatrice, and Glenn. The youngest is Glenn who still lives at home."

She outlined the remarkable success all her children had achieved academically. The justifiable pride she and Andy had in their accomplishments shone in her face.

Two photographs of the entire family were admitted into evidence, and passed to the jurors who examined them carefully. They were a handsome family who looked like the overachievers she described.

Baum turned to the present state of her husband's business affairs.

"Please tell the jury the current status of your husband's company?"

Her expression changed from proud parent and mother to a business face. After Andy's death she became the president of the company, and with the assistance of a professional manager was involved in overseeing its operations. Before that time, she had no direct participation.

"Mrs. Ang, before his death, did your husband discuss his future plans with you?"

"He discussed business matters with me, and I was aware of his plans for the future."

"How frequent were these conversations?"

She was unsure of the frequency, but outlined a credible scenario of a husband discussing business matters with his wife, and his desire to expand his operations into different and more remunerative areas.

"Did your husband's plans include doing business in China?"

"They did."

"Had an agreement been reached with any Chinese company?"

"Yes."

Baum gave something to the clerk, asking that it be marked for identification. When this was done, he handed me a copy of a document on the letterhead of a state owned electronics corporation in China. From a quick reading, it appeared to be a memorialization of a contract whereby Mr.

Ang's company would build and operate a plant in China for the manufacture of high-tech electronic components.

I was completely taken aback. I had sent a number of interrogatories to the Angs seeking information about Mr. Ang's company, including his future plans. The answers had always been in generalities. I also asked for copies of documents that supported any claims the Angs were making for lost income. None had been produced.

Like the McGee photograph, this document was a complete surprise. I read through it again, trying to think of arguments to make, and little was coming that would be persuasive. I handed the document back to Baum, and looked at the judge,

"May we approach, Your Honor?"

He waved us forward. Before I spoke, the judge leaned down, asking me, "Will this take long?"

"I'm afraid it will, Your Honor. Five or ten minutes at the least."

The judge sighed and dismissed the jury temporarily. As the jurors filed out, I looked at the clock; it was quarter to twelve. I had the distinct feeling Baum was planning to do the same thing with this document that he had done with the McGee photograph. Get it admitted into evidence, circulate it through the jury box, and then have Mrs. Ang testify about how remunerative the contract would be, substantially increasing the monetary losses the Angs were claiming.

Since we were not going to be in session in the afternoon, the result would be that the jury would go home for the weekend with Mrs. Ang's testimony about the profitability of this contract ringing in their ears.

The judge looked at me to begin.

"Your Honor, would it assist the court if you reviewed the document first?"

He read it through carefully, and then a second time, before asking me to state my objections. I said I had a number of objections, not only to the document coming into evidence, but also allowing Mrs. Ang to testify about it. From the expression on the judge's face, the prospect of multiple objections was not welcome. The admission of the document was rapidly developing into a morass of legal complexities only the Borgia's of Renaissance Florence would have welcomed.

Fearing he might want argument right then, when I hadn't even begun to marshal my thoughts, I spoke quickly. "Your Honor, would you consider deferring your ruling on the admissibility of this document until we have had an opportunity to brief the matter for you?"

The judge looked towards Baum and Blake who were busily whispering. Baum looked up. "We will brief the matter if the court prefers."

The judge looked at the clock, deep in thought. The sound of his fingers tapping became quite noticeable in the silence as he reflected.

"I'll let you brief the matter, and hear arguments Monday morning about the admission of this document. Submit your briefs no later than nine o'clock."

He then ordered the bailiff to bring the jury back in.

He admonished them not to discuss the case with anyone, wished them a nice weekend, adding a reminder that court would resume Monday morning at nine-thirty. They were then excused.

Janet looked at me, wanting to know what was happening.

I described the contract to her and said Jane Ang would doubtlessly testify it would have been a very profitable arrangement, substantially increasing the Angs' claimed damages. I told her I wouldn't know if I could prevent the contract from being admitted into evidence until I had done a substantial amount of research work.

A worried look passed over her face. "It looks like you will have a busy weekend." I wondered if she knew that lawyers seldom get a full night's rest during a trial. We said our goodbyes, and I began to put my files away. I was concentrating on the task and hadn't noticed Blake coming up behind me.

"We will continue with Mrs. Ang on Monday, and then Captain Sheppard. He will be our last witness."

He then asked, "Who will you be calling Monday afternoon, if we finish then?"

I had not expected them to rest their case before Tuesday at the earliest, and not given much thought about who our first witnesses would be.

Silently I went through my list, and it was clear I'd not made up my mind. Blake was giving me the same appraising look I had become accustomed to from Baum.

I told him I hadn't decided yet, but I would call his office in the morning—Saturday—and let him know.

We stood staring at each other.

He finally said, "If you will call before noon tomorrow, that will be satisfactory," and pushed his cart toward the door. While Blake and I had been speaking, I noticed Baum leaving the courtroom.

I finished putting everything on the luggage carrier and headed for the door. I was the last person out. Using my shoulder to hold the door open, I pushed the top heavy cart into the empty corridor.

Turning toward the elevators, I noticed a solitary figure standing at the end of the hallway. His back was turned, but I recognized the slender figure of Baum. He was making a phone call. The acoustics in the empty hallway amplified his voice, making his words clearly audible. He was saying,

"It's all over with now; it's just a matter of how much."

His reference could only have been to the trial. I felt like the wind had been knocked out of me. What he said kept ringing in my ears as I walked to the parking lot.

On the freeway, traffic was moving fast. The heavy congestion made it impossible to think about anything except driving. Once the traffic was moving at a consistent speed, Baum's words returned in sharp focus, accompanied by the thought I'd been unable to suppress since the trial began. . . . I had taken this case to trial out of a misguided sense of wanting to help Janet, and instead I'd set her up for consequences that were going to devastate her if the jury decided Fran was negligent. This thought kept whirling in my head like a dervish, and I began having the same trouble breathing that I experienced when I ran too fast up the steep hill by our house at the end of my morning run. If I had been running, I would have stopped to catch my breath and let my heart rate slow. I felt a sudden need to pull the car over. Just ahead was a rest stop. Pulling in, I parked the car. My chest felt tight, constricted. In the men's room, I splashed cold water on my face repeatedly until I cooled down. Emerging into the fresh air, I walked back and forth, taking deep breaths until I felt able to resume driving.

An hour later, I arrived at the office, immediately going upstairs to the library to begin the research work on preventing the China contract from being admitted into evidence. Several hours passed, and all I accomplished was a rough outline of the points I needed to cover.

I had hoped doing the research work would keep my mind off Baum's remark, but my concentration lasted no more than a few minutes before his words, "It's all over with now; it's just a matter of how much," returned. Hammering in my head was what the effect would be on Janet if the case was lost.

It had taken days to get over the panic that seized me when I learned Baum would try the case. Now, I'd slipped back into that same fear gripped state. I went home at five o'clock deeply discouraged.

Marsha wanted to know how the day had gone. I begged off getting into a conversation saying I had to work on something important, went to our office downstairs and closed the door. I stared blankly into the darkened garden, the reality of the situation enveloping me. I had spent months assuring Allstate we had a chance at trial, and not to settle the case, but that was when Blake was my opponent. The stark truth was . . .

after I learned Baum was going to try the case, if a way had presented itself to get out of going to trial, I would have seized it. But that opportunity was long gone. The reality was the *S.S. Settlement* had sailed, and I wasn't onboard. As I sat staring out the window, a growing sense of impending disaster gripped me. My confidence had evaporated.

Marsha's voice, calling downstairs that supper was ready, jolted me. I trudged up the steps to the dining room, slumping into a chair. A moment later she came in with our plates and stopped, confused.

"Honey, you're in the wrong place."

I looked up uncomprehendingly.

"You're in the wrong place," she repeated, looking at me closely. "You're sitting in my place," she said, gently pointing to my unoccupied chair, ". . . you should be here."

It then became clear: I had taken her place instead of my own.

"It doesn't matter," I mumbled.

"Of course it matters," she replied, pointing again. "You sit here, at the head of the table."

For a moment I wanted to unburden myself about what happened, tell her the case was over and I had ruined Janet's life, but I couldn't bring myself to do it.

"Something's terribly wrong," she said, in a voice I had never heard from her before, the keening sound of piano wire wound to the breaking point. "What happened today?!"

I said nothing and finally got up, moving slowly to my customary place at the head of the table, hardly noticing that she held my chair out for me. She then seated herself.

My appetite gone, I stared at my food.

Imploringly, she said, "Jay, please tell me—"

I shook my head, cutting her off. "Not now," I said, and then in a lower, almost pleading tone, ". . . not now."

Marsha has a well-honed sense of knowing when things are not right, despite any protestations to the contrary from me, and an equally well developed sense of nurturing that is not easily put off. I wanted to tell her what Baum had said, and admit it was probably true. I had taken this case to trial against an opponent I couldn't stop. And worst of all, Janet, who had put her faith and her trust in me, was going to be destroyed too.

After dessert, Marsha cleared the table so I could work upstairs. She was about to speak again, her worried look making it clear what the subject would be. I shook my head, and she went to our bedroom to read.

In the reflection of the dining room window, I saw a man overwhelmed with fear staring back at me. Blake would have been a good opponent, but not someone I would have lost sleep over. Baum was different: one of the dozen or so trial lawyers at the top of the plaintiffs' bar that other lawyers refer to as a 'Prince of Darkness,' the ones who bury their opponents.

I got us into this mess, and there was no place to run and no place to hide. My survival, and more importantly Janet's, depended on me focusing on what I had to do. Right now I was the enemy more than Baum.

Janet could have embraced the idea of settlement, but she had not taken that easy way out. Keeping her husband's honor intact meant everything to her.

I raged at myself. I was her lawyer, and I had a duty to her. That duty was not to 'try as hard as I could,' or 'do the best I can,' but 'to win her case.' It wasn't going to happen unless I got my confidence back. I had to face up to the fact that what I needed was a major transfusion of Janet's courage.

An hour later, Marsha came back to the dining room in her nightgown. Leaning down she said, "You have all weekend to prepare your brief, and I'll help you with it. But right now it's time for bed."

"It's only nine-thirty," I protested, ". . . I have to work on this."

Kissing the top of my head, she took the pen from my hand, closing the notebook.

"No, no, sweetheart, its bed time now," leading me by the hand.

A half hour later, I was asleep in her arms.

I woke up refreshed, had my run in the park, and after breakfast got right to work. I had promised Blake to call before noon with the names of our witnesses for Monday afternoon, and ran the list through my head. Our two experts were out. I would put one of them on during the middle of our evidence, and the other as the last witness for a strong finish. I gradually narrowed the list down, and added Janet's name as a backup in case one of the other witnesses failed to show up.

Before noon, I called Blake's number. A male voice answered, saying Blake was out, and asked, "Is this Jay Jacobs?"

"Yes, it is," I replied.

"This is Dave Baum."

I had not recognized his voice. When he identified himself, I couldn't get any words to form. My only thought was what he'd said the day before.

I finally gathered myself enough to say that Blake wanted a list of who we would call Monday if there was time available.

Baum confirmed: "I expect to finish by noon Monday."

I said I had our list of witnesses ready, and he asked for a moment to find a piece of paper.

I read the list I had prepared, "Janet Dowd, Karen Burns, Rod Thiessen, Jim Phelan, and Bob Hodges."

Baum wrote the names down without comment and read them back to me.

I added, "I might not get to all of them, depending on when you finish."

He must have been studying the list, and asked, "Who is Jim Phelan?"

"He is a fisherman who was out that day," I replied.

There was a pause, and Baum asked, "May I know what he is going to say?"

I was not going to let myself get drawn into giving an explanation on the thrust of each of our witnesses' testimony, but the question needed an answer of some kind, and with a forced laugh I said, "Sure, if you show up Monday."

It was a remark I'd heard a boxer say in response to a reporter's question whether he had any concerns about his opponent in an upcoming fight. The boxer had replied, "the only thing I'm worried about is he won't show up."

Baum did not find the remark amusing, responding "ah . . . ha."

Before the conversation could continue, I said, "Well, I'll see you Monday," ending the phone call.

It occurred to me if the testimony went in quicker than expected on Monday, I would have to put Rae Strange and Captain Seymour on the stand Tuesday.

I immediately called Strange, apologized for the short notice, and explained I would have to meet with him Monday evening in my office for final preparation, and call him as a witness sometime Tuesday. He said he would arrange to catch a flight from Santa Barbara in time to be in my office Monday evening by six o'clock. Captain Seymour lived in the Bay Area and had greater scheduling flexibility. I arranged to meet with him Sunday for final trial preparation, and he agreed to make himself available either Tuesday or Wednesday for testimony.

Earlier in the week, Strange sent an exhibit he wanted to use at trial. It contained a summary of the data he obtained from the three wave recording buoys. Unfortunately, the numbers were too small for the jury to see at a distance. It would have to be redone. Marsha said she would make a new exhibit with numbers three inches high so they could be read easily at a distance by the jurors. Getting her keys, she said she was off to the art supply store for a large piece of foam board and stencils.

Marsha mentioned several times wanting to come to the trial. I wanted her to come, but not until all of the witnesses she interviewed had testified, in the event I had to call her as a witness if their testimony on the stand varied from what they had told her.

I turned my attention to preparing an outline for my cross-examination of plaintiffs' last witness, their boat handling expert, Captain Sheppard. He would be adding weight to Baum's theory that Francis Dowd had attempted to go through Bonita Channel when it was unsafe to do so. I reminded myself that cases are not won by cross-examination of the other side's expert witnesses. The best that can be hoped for is to limit the damage they do.

The way the evidence was coming in, I was becoming concerned about an instruction Judge Leahy would give the jury about the law they were to apply regarding negligence. He would instruct the jury that Francis Dowd had a legal duty to acquaint himself with the dangers involved in taking his boat out to Duxbury. And one of those dangers was that boat operators should not set a course too close to the edge of Bonita Channel, particularly in the area around Potatopatch Shoal. This was what happened to the boat where three men had been washed overboard the year prior to the *Aloha* incident, and had been prominently mentioned in the "Graveyard of Ships" article published in the *Chronicle* one week after the *Aloha* went down. I felt certain Baum would argue going too close to the Channel's edge was a danger Dowd should have known about. Even if no one on the plaintiffs' team was aware of the "Graveyard" article, they would have learned about the danger from some other source. It was hardly a secret.

Captain Sheppard was not a fisherman, and didn't have the depth of experience of the local fishing boat captains, but he would have friends and acquaintances in the fishing fleet. During the course of his preparation on the case, Sheppard would have contacted one of them to help him prepare. I had forgotten about the involvement of plaintiffs' investigator Hal Lipset. He had been combing the waterfront talking to dozens of fishermen. An obvious thing Lipset would have done after he found out the person he was interviewing had no specific information about the *Aloha* incident, would be to roll out a chart and ask the person to show him what hazards a boat operator might encounter on a trip out to Duxbury. The danger of navigating too close to the buoy line was bound to have been mentioned by one of the fishermen he interviewed.

Over the weekend I had done more research work about the possible application of the rule in the *Marine Sulphur Queen* case to this incident. It hadn't taken long to confirm there was no California case involving a boating accident with no survivors, no witnesses, and no boat. I had the sinking feeling if the *Queen* case were brought to Judge Leahy's attention, there would be little I could do to convince him it did not apply, particularly since he had been so willing to apply a federal rule when it was demonstrably not applicable regarding McGee's statement.

During my research, I noted the *Sulphur Queen* case had been mentioned in a number of scholarly legal journals. This meant that in addition to the risk of losing the case if Judge Leahy applied the *Sulphur Queen* rule, it would also establish a precedent in California law. As a precedent it would be extensively reported in the law journals with my name prominently mentioned as losing counsel.

# 21

Traffic was moderate all the way to the courthouse on Monday morning. I arrived before nine o'clock, the first one there. I asked the clerk if the judge had arrived, and she said he was in chambers. I handed her my brief, asking if she would please deliver it to him. She gave me a knowing smile, aware that I wanted the judge to read my brief first. When the clerk opened the door to chambers, I saw Judge Leahy at his desk in shirtsleeves, absorbed in reading what appeared to be a volume of Witkin's *Commentaries on California Law*. I hoped it was the volume concerning contracts.

Janet came in and we exchanged 'good mornings.' As she took her seat at my side, I noticed crescents of tiredness under her eyes that no makeup could hide.

Baum, Blake, and the Angs arrived shortly afterwards. After reading our briefs in chambers, the judge called us in to outline the protocol he would follow: Mrs. Ang would go back on the stand for further testimony related to the admission of the contract, without the jury present. We would make our arguments on the record next, and he would then rule on its admissibility.

Mrs. Ang resumed her place on the stand. Baum had her testify that Andy had learned China was offering lucrative business arrangements to attract the capital and expertise of overseas Chinese businessmen, such as himself, to build and operate high tech facilities. He had gone to China and negotiated just such an arrangement.

She was shown the document and said it stated the agreement Andy told her had been reached, and how confident he was that it would be an advantageous and very profitable arrangement. Only his untimely death had prevented the venture from going forward.

The judge said he would now hear our arguments on its admissibility, and asked me to proceed.

Based on his previously demonstrated preference of getting to legal points quickly, and stating them precisely, I pared my argument down to the key issues he would have to decide.

"Your Honor, I have three objections to bring to your attention. The first is the 'best evidence rule.' This document is obviously a copy, and no explanation has been given about what happened to the original."

The exceptions to the 'best evidence rule' are so numerous I did not expect the judge to give this argument much weight. When I asked if he wanted any further argument on this point, his response was to look at the wall clock. I quickly moved on.

"Our second objection concerns authentication. Mrs. Ang stated she was not present when this document was signed. She does not know the man who signed it, and is unfamiliar with his signature. So there is no way to know if he in fact signed this document."

"Our third objection is the issue of authorization."

He looked at me quizzically. I clarified, "Not, authentication, which I just discussed; I refer to an entirely different issue, the matter of *authorization*."

I had never argued this objection before or heard anyone else making it. He looked skeptical, but said nothing as I continued.

"We do not know whether this man is authorized under Chinese law, or the by-laws of this company, to enter into this purported contractual agreement."

The judge interrupted. "But it says right here on the document that he is the president of the company."

I shook my head. "But that doesn't make it so, which is just my point." I cleared my throat. "Here are just a few of the unknowns: is he, in fact, the president? Is this his signature? And most importantly, we don't know if he was authorized to enter into this contract. For example, in the United States before a company undertakes a large loan with a bank, or sells an important asset like a piece of land or a factory, the company's board of directors must *authorize* the transaction."

Judge Leahy was a labor lawyer before coming on the bench, and I had an example ready I knew he would be familiar with.

"Your Honor, say a company reached an understanding on a new labor contract with the business agent of a union. It would not be valid at that time because a business agent is not *authorized* to bind the union.

That would have to wait until the members voted to accept the contract." The judge nodded his head.

After summarizing my arguments, I asked if he had any questions. The judge shook his head, and looked at Baum.

Baum disposed of the 'best evidence rule' objection first. He then concentrated on the key point in his position: the document clearly stated a contractual agreement had been reached between Mr. Ang and the Chinese company. The judge then asked, "Submitted, gentlemen?"

We replied, "Yes."

Judge Leahy tipped his chair back, rocking it gently, deep in thought, sorting through our arguments. When he finished, he brought his body forward so abruptly the big chair squeaked loudly in protest. Pausing, he framed his words for the record.

"I'm not going to admit this document." My immense relief was short lived, as he quickly added, "At this time."

Looking at Baum, he said, "Until such time as this document is admitted into evidence, there shall be no reference to it by any witness other than a foundational witness, and you will alert the court before any such witness begins testifying." Baum agreed.

"Is there anything else before we call the jury in?" His face clearly stating the answer he wanted to hear.

We shook our heads. He looked at the clock, declared a ten minute recess, and left the bench.

Janet turned to me expectantly with a puzzled look. I was confused myself.

"Well they won't get the contract in, at least not now," I told her.

The judge had been persuaded a legally sufficient foundation for admitting the document had not been laid, and at the same time he had all but said: if they brought in a witness to authenticate it, he would admit the contract. I envisioned urgent phone calls being made to China, arranging for whoever signed the contract to be flown in to lay the foundation necessary for its admission. It suddenly dawned on me: I had not asked Mrs. Ang if the manager accompanied Mr. Ang to China. If the manager had, he would be familiar with the negotiations ... and he was in Manila. Arrangements could easily be made to have him here in twenty-four hours. I noticed that Dwight had left the courtroom hurriedly.

I began wondering if persuading the judge to keep the document out had been a major tactical error, if the result was going to be that a live witness would be flown in, dramatically authenticating the contract, and then testify that its level of profitability would amount to hundreds of thousands of dollars annually.

The issue of the contract had to be put aside for now. The judge would resume the bench in ten minutes, and I needed to prepare for the next witness.

The tried and true trial strategy—always save your best witness for last—came to mind. They were following that old saw by positioning their boat handling expert, Captain Peter Sheppard, as their final witness.

After taking his deposition, I knew Sheppard was going to make a good impression as a knowledgeable and competent boat handler that the jury would like . . . I did myself.

During the break, Captain Sheppard came into the courtroom to confer with Baum and Blake. He was wearing a tweed jacket that looked as if he had owned it for years, settling around his body so both he and the jacket were comfortable with each other. He had the look of a boat captain about him, and a very English one at that. When he caught my eye, he gave a short business like nod.

Before the jury came back in, he was sent to the hallway for the dramatic effect his entrance would make.

When called, Sheppard strode decisively into the well of the court, standing erect as the clerk gave him the oath. The jury perked up as soon as he stated his name. He spoke in an earthy, unrefined English accent, in sharp contrast to Blake's highly ornamented English. His voice filled the courtroom; no one would have to strain to hear him.

After he settled into the witness box, Blake had him state his name and then describe his occupation.

"For the past twenty years, my experience has been with small craft. For ten years, I have acted as a professional captain making long distance deliveries of small craft, both sail and motor, for owners who don't have the time, or lack the experience, to take their boats long distances out on the ocean."

"What percentage of your work involves motor craft?"

"I would estimate half motor, half sail."

"Are you based right here in the San Francisco area?"

"I am."

"Where do you typically make your deliveries?"

He cocked his head. "Anywhere up and down the Pacific Coast from Canada to Mexico, even Hawaii on occasion. Local deliveries I do myself. Anything involving either overnight or long distances, I hire a crew to assist me."

He was asked to state the size and type of motor craft he had operated. The boats ranged from twenty up to a hundred feet in length which required hiring a crew of three or four, depending on the distances involved.

"Based on your training and years of experience handling small craft on the ocean, do you feel able to render an opinion on the safe operation and handling of a motor boat thirty-three feet long?"

"Yes, I do."

"In your opinion, what are the most common reasons for losses involving motor craft on the ocean?"

"Maritime losses can be separated into two basic categories: either equipment failures or incidents attributable to operator error." With a note of sadness in his voice, he continued: "In my experience, most maritime tragedies involving small craft are avoidable."

"Under what weather conditions have you handled the boat deliveries you mentioned?"

"Regardless of their size, I never take a boat out on the ocean if I feel the weather conditions make it unsafe to do so. On a few occasions I have been out when the weather conditions deteriorated unexpectedly. When that happened I changed my course, or took refuge in a safe harbor if one was close by. In my experience, extreme weather conditions seldom come up without some warning."

He paused thoughtfully, "Many owners, particularly those who take their boats out only sporadically, are insufficiently aware of the problems that can suddenly come up out on the ocean and don't know how to react when a dangerous situation arises." The innuendo inferred by this question and Sheppard's answer was not lost on the jury: perhaps Dowd was one of the large number of 'cowboy skippers' who frequently got themselves into trouble out on the ocean from a combination of bravado, lack of knowledge, and inexperience. This was damning testimony, but there was no way I could keep it out.

The questioning turned from the general to the specific.

"Captain, what hazards exist for boaters in the San Francisco area?"

With a long sigh he responded. "It seems practically every navigational danger known to man exists in the waters around San Francisco. For starters, the entrance to the harbor out by the Golden Gate is very narrow, and the shore on both sides is lined with nearly vertical rocky bluffs. Strong winds can come up quickly and unpredictably. Powerful tides and currents exist which are exacerbated by the seasonal outflows of the Sacramento River system. The frequent fog conditions in and around San Francisco add to the navigational difficulties."

The questioning turned to the conditions around the San Francisco Bar. Blake had him step down to the chart, pointing out the parameters of the crescent shaped Bar. He then had Sheppard identify Bonita Channel, and the various buoys, lights and other navigational aids used to mark it.

"Captain, please tell the jury what you base your opinions and conclusions upon concerning the loss of the *Aloha*."

Sheppard said he had reviewed certain reference works such as the United States Coast Pilot, various tide and current tables, the navigation charts for the Bay Area, and the Coast Guard investigation report. As the documents were mentioned, Blake had him explain what they were and how they assisted him in reaching his conclusions. During this long recital Sheppard never looked at his notes, impressing the jury with his grasp of the facts.

"Captain Sheppard, what particular training and experience have you had in small boat handling that has assisted you in forming your opinions in this case?"

He turned to the jury, speaking to them in a personal way.

"I have been in and out of San Francisco on dozens of occasions on sail and motor boats, ranging in size from small cabin cruisers to large, ocean going yachts. I have been through Bonita Channel approximately fifty times."

Blake summarized the highlights of Scott Noble's testimony about the size and height of the waves that existed on March 9. He then asked, "Captain Sheppard, on the morning this tragedy occurred, what decisions did the boat captains have to make concerning the safe operation of their boats in the vicinity of Point Bonita?"

In responding, Sheppard took Noble's technical explanations about the sea and weather conditions, and in plain language began drawing a vivid picture of the navigational choices the boat operators faced on March 9. It was a tutorial on what a prudent mariner should have done to analyze the information available, and what actions should have been taken under the circumstances existing that morning, very effectively portraying the sea as a living character participating in these events.

The seminal question was then put to him. "Captain Sheppard, based on your education, training, and many years of experience at sea on small craft, do you have an opinion about what caused the loss of the *Aloha*?"

Sheppard drew himself up, signaling the importance of the question. The jurors leaned forward in rapt attention, waiting.

"In my opinion, the *Aloha* was capsized and sank while attempting to go through Bonita Channel at a time when the presence of large breaking waves made it unsafe to do so."

Blake gave a considerable pause, letting the answer sink in before continuing.

"Have you reviewed anything which supports this opinion?"

He mentioned the McGee photograph, commenting that it showed the size of the waves existing in the Channel that morning.

Handing him the photo, Blake asked, "Can you estimate the size of the waves shown in this photograph?"

He looked at the photo carefully, his eyebrows knitted in concentration.

"I can't say definitively, other than they are obviously quite large."

Before completing his answer he looked at the jurors, letting his tone underline his words. "Unquestionably, a boat the size of the *Aloha* should not have attempted to go through in such conditions," shaking his head, more in sadness than censure.

"Is there any other information you base your opinion on that dangerous wave conditions existed in Bonita Channel that morning?"

He was already nodding. "Yes, I read a summary of the data concerning the height of the waves recorded from two a.m. to eight a.m. on the morning in question. The data indicates large swells were present in the area around the San Francisco Bar at that time."

"What data are you referring to?"

"I am referring to the data included in the Coast Guard report," holding it up.

Blake collected the document from Captain Sheppard, brought it to my table and handed it to me.

The copy of the report I obtained was a single document of six or seven pages. Blake handed me two documents. The first document was the Coast Guard's report concerning the *Aloha*. The second was a typewritten page with the words "Investigating Officer's Note" at the top. Attached to it was the wave data Captain Sheppard referred to.

While I was going through the report, Blake remained standing in front of me, his hand outstretched in an attempt to hurry me through my review of the pages. Ignoring this ploy, I examined each page carefully to see if any notes had been made in the margins which might be useful in cross-examination. When I finished looking through each page, I handed them back. It was a clean copy.

Turning to the judge, Blake asked that they be marked for identification and refocused his attention on Sheppard.

"Captain, have you reviewed a transcript of the small craft warning that was broadcast by the National Weather Service at 0800 on March 9?"

"I have," and he began elaborating about the consequences that frequently occur when small craft warnings are ignored by boat operators.

Blake looked at his notes and asked, "In your opinion, would it have been unwise for a vessel operator to take a boat the size of the *Aloha* into the open ocean after the small craft warning had been broadcast?"

"Leaving the protected waters of San Francisco Bay after 0800 would have been very unwise. If a mariner had not arrived at Point Bonita by the time of the broadcast, he should have returned to port."

"Captain, do you have an opinion about what time the *Aloha* left its berth in Sausalito?"

"I believe the *Aloha* left much later than six o'clock."

"What do you base that on?"

"The party boat fleet left at approximately six a.m., and no one on any of the party boats reported seeing the *Aloha*, and no one reported seeing any distress flares shot up. This leads me to conclude that the *Aloha* left as late as seven-thirty."

"Captain, is it correct to state: if Francis Dowd left Sausalito at seven-thirty, the small craft warning would have been issued well before the *Aloha* arrived at Point Bonita?"

"Yes."

"In your opinion, should he have heeded the small craft warning and returned to port?"

"Very definitely, he should have returned to port." He stopped to consider his words, and then stated emphatically, "And even if he had not heard the broadcast, the wave conditions themselves were a clear warning that the conditions in Bonita Channel were dangerous, and Mr. Dowd should not have attempted to go through."

Every trial has tide changes, the momentum shifting from one side to the other. This was one of those moments. Everyone in the jury box was tangibly reacting to the vivid picture Captain Sheppard was painting of the menace and raw power of the waves existing that morning.

Blake gave a moment to let the Captain's answer steep in their minds before continuing.

"Captain Sheppard, would the *Aloha* have been unseaworthy if she sailed without a radio?"

"In my opinion, yes."

"Do you have an opinion whether the *Aloha* had a radio onboard?"

"I don't know, but there seems to be considerable doubt if one was onboard."

"What do you base that opinion on?"

"The Coast Guard did not pick up any radio calls for help that day, nor did any of the fishing boat captains. There is also the fact that the *Aloha*'s radar set was stolen. A replacement radar had been purchased, and it was initially thought to have been put on the *Aloha*, but it was subsequently learned that it had not been installed. These factors lead me to believe that perhaps the replacement for the radio stolen from the *Aloha* had not been installed either."

"Captain, have you considered the explanations put forward by the defense to explain away the loss of the *Aloha*?"

"I have," he replied with a look of disregard.

What have you concluded?"

He rubbed his chin contemplatively, and then began speaking with assurance.

"In my opinion, the only explanation which is supported by the evidence is this: the *Aloha* attempted to go through Bonita Channel when it was dangerous to do so, and was sunk by the large waves existing in the Channel at that time."

Blake announced he had no more questions and began gathering his notes scattered on the lectern. In the midst of doing so, he unexpectedly looked at the judge and requested that the Coast Guard report be admitted into evidence.

The request caught me by surprise. The Coast Guard report, despite the fact that it was quite long and unusually comprehensive, was really nothing more than an accident report, similar in form to the reports made by the California Highway Patrol for motor vehicle accidents. California has a statute expressly forbidding the admission of police reports into evidence unless there has been a stipulation by all counsel to admit the report.

I was in a dilemma. If I objected, Blake might call Dennis George, the Coast Guard officer in charge of the investigation to testify. His deposition had not been taken, and I was uncertain what he might say in court.

I shuffled through some notes, giving myself a few extra seconds to decide whether to object to its admission. It was a coin toss; the sort of debate that could take hours to decide. An impatient voice intruded.

"Mr. Jacobs?" It was the judge.

I swallowed hard, muttering that I had no objection.

The judge looked at the clock and announced there would be a short recess before I began my cross-examination of Captain Sheppard. I hurried through my outline, crossing out most of the notes referring to Bonita Channel. There would be no benefit in having Sheppard repeat his already damaging testimony about the dangerous conditions in the Channel.

After the jury was seated, the judge came back on the bench. He looked to me, "Do you wish to cross-examine?"

Thanking the judge, I moved to the lectern and asked the captain if he was ready to begin. He nodded.

"Captain Sheppard, how many times have you been through Bonita Channel?"

"I would say at least fifty times."

"Is Bonita Channel ever used by large ships?"

"No, its use is strictly for small craft," adding emphatically, ". . . but only if the wave conditions existing at the time make it safe to do so."

"Is it ever safe to take small craft directly over the Bar itself?"

"Again, that depends on the conditions existing at the time. If the waves are small, in the range of three or four feet on a nice summer day, it would be safe to take a boat directly over the Bar. I have done so myself and felt comfortable under conditions such as that."

"Captain, have you ever taken a boat the size of the *Aloha* through Bonita Channel when there were breakers on the Bar, but the Channel itself was clear?"

He leaned back, thinking, before answering.

"Probably a third of the times that I have been through Bonita Channel there were breaking waves on the Bar, and the Channel was clear." Before I could ask my next question, he quickly added, "But those were not the conditions existing on March 9th. One of the captains out that morning reported waves were breaking not just on the Bar, but across Bonita Channel as well." I noticed some of the jurors looking at me, gauging my reaction to this answer.

I moved to a new area of inquiry.

"Captain, are you aware that Mr. Dowd had been in the Navy, and what his duties were?"

"I'm not sure."

"Does the submarine corps refresh your memory?"

"I recall reading that somewhere."

"Are you aware that the submarine corps is the elite of the Navy's seagoing fleet, and over half of those accepted to submarine school do not complete the program?"

He said he was not aware of that, but in a respectful tone acknowledged, "Serving on a submarine must have been exacting duty."

I asked a few more questions about the difficulties of submarine duty, and then looked at my notes.

It was tempting to get into the time issue with him, but he had stated his opinions about when the *Aloha* left the marina quite firmly. He was not going to change his views, and it wasn't going to help our case to have the jury hear his very damaging testimony on that subject all over again.

There were a few other areas I could inquire about, but he had been so well prepared it was not worth the risk of asking anything else.

Turning to the judge, I said, "No more questions for this witness, Your Honor."

There was a limited amount of redirect examination by Blake and he was excused.

After giving a respectful nod first to the judge, and then the jury, Captain Sheppard left the stand.

As I anticipated, he had been an effective 'strong finish' witness for plaintiffs. His knowledge and experience made him a very credible witness, and his demeanor added a convincing flourish to his testimony.

Baum brought a few procedural matters to the judge's attention: a copy of the death certificate regarding Mr. Ang was admitted by stipulation, and the China contract was re-offered into evidence. Repeating his earlier ruling, the judge said it would not be admitted over my renewed objection, once again adding, "At this time."

Drawing himself up, Baum confidently stated, "Plaintiffs rest, Your Honor."

I braced myself, anticipating that this would be the time Baum would ask for a hearing outside of the presence of the jury requesting that the rule in the *Marine Sulphur Queen* be applied in our case. To my great relief he did not, but that did not mean he could not raise the issue before our experts began testifying.

Gesturing toward me, the judge informed the jury they would hear from the defense next, and declared a short break.

# 22

While the stipulated matters were being read into the record, my secretary entered the courtroom. She gestured in the direction of the hallway, and mouthed, "They're here."

My first two witnesses would be Thiessen and Burns, who had refused to appear voluntarily. As I walked toward the hallway, my mind went to the scene that ensued when Marsha subpoenaed them. Among the array of things they stated about why they would not testify was a lack of transportation to San Jose. Rather than risk having them not show up, I arranged to have them driven. Bracing myself for an extremely unfriendly reception, I opened the door. If they were still angry to the point that they might be out of control on the witness stand, I would have no choice but to speak with the judge in chambers and request that he admonish them. No matter what their mood might be, I would have to stay composed.

As I approached, their faces froze in glacial stares, manifestly unhappy about being in court. I began a jumbled apology for causing them to lose time from their work. They were uninterested in hearing it and interrupted me simultaneously, demanding to know if their testimony was still necessary. I said it was, adding hurriedly that my examination would be brief, no more than fifteen minutes.

Hoping it would moderate their anger, I acknowledged what I sensed was the real reason behind their reluctance to testify.

"I know your sailboat is your home, and I respect that. I'm also aware that living on your boat is contrary to the marina's rules."

It was immediately apparent this was the raw nerve. They were about to start ventilating, and I continued before they could.

"If this case were being tried in Marin County, you would have real reason to be concerned, but San Jose is seventy miles away, in a different county. No one here is going to know it might be against the rules for you to be living on your boat, and inform the marina."

They exchanged quick glances, seemingly mollified. I made a hurried assessment. They did not seem overtly hostile, at least not on the surface. Reluctantly, I decided to put them on the stand, telling myself if things blew up, I could call Marsha and have her read her notes.

Before making the decision final, there was one thing I did have to know. In discovery I had revealed their names as potential witnesses, but since Thiessen and Burns refused to meet with me after being subpoenaed, I had no idea whether they had been contacted by the plaintiffs' side.

As casually as I could make it sound, I asked, "Has anyone other than my investigator come around asking questions about the *Aloha*?" adding, ". . . investigators don't always identify themselves as such."

"No," they said quickly.

I had no choice but to accept their answer, and at the same time remind myself that Baum's investigator, Hal Lipset, had turned up Captain McGee whose boat was docked at the Sausalito commercial pier less than a mile away. It would have been logical for Lipset to do what Marsha had done of canvassing the part of the marina where the *Aloha* was tied up. If he had, he could not have missed finding Thiessen and Burns since they were there every day.

There was no time now to go through the questions I had for them before we went into the courtroom . . . I would be finding out what they had to say at the same time the jury did.

I decided to put Thiessen on first, and explained to Ms. Burns that court rules prohibited her from being in the courtroom while he was testifying. The bailiff came to the door, asking me if I was ready. I turned, looking intently at Thiessen. He stood stock still, glaring for a long worrying moment before finally nodding. We entered the courtroom. I had him sit in the last row of the spectator section until we were back in session.

The door to chambers opened and the judge quickly seated himself as the clerk called the courtroom to order. The judge looked at me to proceed.

"Thank you, Your Honor. The first witness for the defense is Rodney Thiessen."

The clerk motioned him forward for the oath, and then directed him to the witness box. He settled in, looking around to get his bearings.

I had him state his name, putting off asking where he lived until he was more at ease with being on the stand. I proceeded with a series of comfort questions about what he did for a living, where he worked, how long he had been with his firm and briefly describe his duties and responsibilities. When he seemed comfortable, I then asked what is normally the second question I put to a witness, and held my breath.

"Mr. Thiessen, where do you live?"

"I live in the Sausalito marina."

"How long have you lived there?"

He thought a moment, "Over five years."

"You told us you work in San Francisco. How do you get to work every day?"

"I take the ferry from the Sausalito terminal to San Francisco."

"What time do you have to be at work?"

"Seven o'clock every morning."

The critical part was next. "Mr. Thiessen, do you have a regular practice you follow to get to work by seven o'clock?"

"Yes, I do."

"Please tell the jury what your routine is."

"I get up, fix a light breakfast, and then take what I'll be wearing that day with me, and walk to the head of the dock where there is a washroom equipped with lockers, wash basins, and showers. After I dress for the day, I walk to the Ferry Terminal."

"Do you return to your boat after you finish getting dressed?"

"No."

I looked at my notes to give myself a moment to frame the next question.

"Turning your attention to the date of Friday, March 9th, two years ago, did you follow your usual custom and practice about when you got up, had breakfast, and went down the dock to the shower room?"

"Yes, I did."

"Were you previously acquainted with a man named Francis Dowd, the owner of a thirty-four foot power boat the *Aloha*?"

"Yes."

To make the point again, I asked, "So that morning would not have been the first time you ever saw Mr. Dowd?"

"No."

"About how many times prior to that date had you seen Mr. Dowd?"

He paused to reflect. "A dozen times, probably more."

"So you had previously introduced yourself to him, knew what boat he owned, and where it was berthed?"

"Yes."

My questions were getting too long. The jury was hearing too much from me and not enough from him. It was time to get into substance.

There was another, and significantly more important reason to pick up the pace. I didn't want him on the witness stand any longer than necessary, fearing he might revert to his former hostile attitude.

"Mr. Thiessen, what berth did Mr. Dowd's boat, the *Aloha*, occupy?"

He didn't know, and I framed a substitute question.

"Can you tell us the location of his berth in relationship to yours?"

"His boat was four or five berths away."

"How wide is the dock?" He looked around to find something he could point to. Not finding anything, he estimated the width was six to eight feet wide.

I had one last foundation question to put to him.

"Mr. Thiessen, when you walk down the dock toward the changing room, do you have to pass the berth where Mr. Dowd's boat, the *Aloha*, was kept?"

"Yes, I do."

To make sure the jury did not miss the point, I asked, "So Mr. Dowd's boat was closer to the shore?"

"Yes."

"Calling your attention to Friday, March 9th, did you see Mr. Dowd that morning?"

"I did."

We were almost past the point where Thiessen could hurt me if he wanted to. Steeling myself, I continued.

"Where did you see him that morning?"

"Mr. Dowd was standing at the end of his berth, right by his boat."

"Did you say anything to him?"

He thought for a moment. "I said 'Hello.'"

"Are you certain it was Mr. Dowd?"

"It was definitely him . . ." he paused, "and his son was there too."

"Were other people there besides them?"

He lapsed into thought before answering.

"There were three or four men, I'm not too sure how many. I remember Mr. Dowd and his son because I knew them, but there were some other men too."

I put the next question gingerly. "What did they seem to be doing?

He replied promptly, "There were fishing poles, a bait chest, and some tackle boxes. It looked like they were going fishing."

"Did you stop to speak to them?"

He shook his head. "No, I had no time for that. We exchanged a 'hello' and 'good morning,' as I passed by on my way to the shower room."

"How far apart were you when you passed Mr. Dowd and the others?"

"Three or four feet. I knew what he and his son looked like, and it was definitely them."

It was time for the definitive question.

"Mr. Thiessen, do you know what time it was when you passed Mr. Dowd on your way to the shower area that morning?"

He thought for a moment before answering, "A little before six o'clock."

"Do you know when the *Aloha* left the marina that morning?"

"Karen told me—"

He got no further. Baum was instantly on his feet with an objection of hearsay which the judge promptly sustained.

I was tempted to ask a few more questions, but the additional details I wanted to clear up with Thiessen were not worth the risk of opening up unwanted areas for Baum to cross-examine him about.

I thanked him and said I had nothing further.

"Cross-examination," intoned the judge. Baum got to his feet quickly, firing questions in a fast staccato.

"How well did you know Francis Dowd?"

"Not well."

"You have no personal knowledge of when the *Aloha* left the marina that morning, do you?"

"No."

"You can't say for certain what time it was when you passed Mr. Dowd's berth that morning, can you?"

Thiessen hesitated. "I can't say for certain. I just did what I usually do to get to work on time every day."

There was a whispered conference between Baum and Blake, and then "No more questions." I had no redirect, and Thiessen was excused.

A lot of thoughts streamed through my mind about his testimony. The most prominent was a huge sense of relief.

The judge's voice interrupted my thoughts.

"Call your next witness."

I went to the hallway for Ms. Burns. She stood immediately, a color wheel of feelings swirling over her face. Most notably she was acutely anxious, which gave me considerable relief. Witnesses who are enthusiastic about testifying invariably have an agenda in mind other than just answering questions. The uncertainty reflected in Ms. Burns face was reassuring, particularly since her expression could easily have been one of hostility based on her reaction when Marsha served her with the subpoena.

I said we were ready for her, and held the door open. I stood back watching the jurors as she headed toward the clerk. Ms. Burns was dressed discreetly with no jewelry or makeup. She was a pretty woman with no need for either. The men in the jury box would initially react positively. The women were likely to be more tentative in forming their impressions. If she conducted herself decorously, they would like her. If not, she would receive a more hostile reception from the eight women.

After taking the oath and being seated, I had her give her name, and began a series of non-substantive 'comfort questions' to ease her into being on the witness stand. The amount of time varies greatly between witnesses about when they are ready for questioning to begin in earnest. I let their body language tell me.

Ms. Burns came to comfort level quicker than most witnesses. My level of comfort, however, was plummeting with each answer she gave.

After interviewing her, Marsha told me she had the impression that Ms. Burns was very bright. I was beginning to hope she was not one of those highly intelligent Mensa types who answer questions too quickly, without giving themselves a moment to think before starting to speak.

Burns was tired of comfort questions, and ready to proceed. The jury already knew about the sailboat, the dimensions of the dock, and the shower room from Thiessen. They wanted to know why she was on the stand.

Hoping the reluctance I felt wasn't outwardly manifesting itself, I began.

"On March 9th, two years ago, were you living on a sailboat located at slip 835 in Sausalito?"

"I was," she replied, promptly volunteering, "I lived there with Rodney Thiessen," adding for how long.

I quickly asked if she was working in San Francisco at that time. She was, stating who she worked for and the location of their office.

As a follow up I asked if she had a set time to be at work. She did, and volunteered when it was.

"How did you get to work?"

"I would take the ferry from the Sausalito terminal over to San Francisco," adding how long it took to walk from the terminal in San Francisco to her office.

Every question I had asked so far could easily have been answered 'yes' or 'no,' but she had volunteered additional information in every response. It was apparent that Ms. Burns was not going to be easily reined in.

"Did you have a custom and practice about what time you got up and made preparations to go to work?"

"Yes, I did." Before she could continue, I cut her off. We were at a critical juncture and the additional details she was providing were opening too many areas for Baum to cross-examine her about. Minor inconsistencies were bound to crop up between her testimony and Thiessen's that Baum could use to destroy the credibility of both of them.

I then asked when she got up every morning. She stated the time and confirmed it was the same every morning.

"Ms. Burns, did Rodney get up before you did?"

"Yes. Rod had to be at work earlier than me. He went to the shower area before I did, and caught an earlier ferry."

"What time did you customarily leave your boat to go to the shower area?"

Without a pause to reflect, she answered, "Between six and six-fifteen," elaborating that she would go to the shower room, dress for work, and walk from there to the ferry terminal.

"That morning, Ms. Burns, what time did you leave your boat to go to the shower area?"

This question was critical. For the first time, there was a notable gap between the question and her response. I began wishing fervently for a string of rosary beads in my pocket; if I did, they would have been spinning.

"I can't say for sure when I left the boat that morning, other than I always leave between six and six-fifteen, never later than six-fifteen ... ," she paused deep in thought, "but usually closer to six than six fifteen, and definitely not later than that."

"Prior to the day in question, did you know a man named Francis Dowd, the owner of a boat named the *Aloha*?"

"Yes, his boat was a few slips from ours; I knew he owned the *Aloha*."

Cautiously, "When you passed Mr. Dowd's berth, close to six o'clock that morning, did you see Mr. Dowd or anyone else?"

"No," she answered simply.

Moving quickly, I asked, "Was the *Aloha* in its slip?"

Shaking her head, "When I passed by no one was there, and the *Aloha* was gone."

Fortified by that answer, I decided to try a question I wanted to ask Thiessen, and had opted not to.

"Ms. Burns, the events you've just told us about occurred over two years ago. How can you remember these seemingly insignificant details now?"

Even with careful witness preparation, questions of this nature are a risk, mostly because the answers sound contrived. As soon as I finished, I realized I'd left myself wide open for a very unwanted response.

Her expression changed distinctly. For the first time, the enormity of the incident seemed to break over her.

When she began to speak, her voice softened. "We heard on the news that a boat with five men onboard was missing. In a later broadcast, the name of the boat was mentioned. Since we knew Mr. Dowd and the boat, we discussed the matter quite a bit. Rod mentioned seeing Mr. Dowd, his son, and some other men on the dock when he walked past, and it was obvious they were going fishing with all their gear. I told him the slip was empty when I went by. In subsequent broadcasts, or maybe from the papers, we learned a search had been made, but no one was found. It was presumed . . . that they . . . had all drowned."

This last bit of testimony was plainly difficult for her. By the time Ms. Burns finished her answer, she was speaking almost in a little girl voice the jurors were straining to hear.

In the silence after she completed her response, someone in the back was sniffling.

Emulating her lowered voice, I paraphrased her testimony into a question.

"Ms. Burns, you learned from Rodney that when he walked past Mr. Dowd's slip, about ten minutes before six o'clock, Mr. Dowd and his son and some other men were there. And when you walked by, sometime right after six, no one was there and the *Aloha* was gone. Is that correct?

She nodded in response, teetering at the brink of tears.

I gestured that she needed to give a verbal answer. In a barely audible voice, she managed to get out, "Yes."

It had been some time since I'd heard a witness put such powerful emotion into their voice as she did with that simple one word response.

It was clearly time to stop.

I turned to the judge, and in the same lowered voice said I had nothing further.

Baum did not elect to cross-examine her, and she was excused by the judge. Head bowed, she left the courtroom.

Hopefully, Thiessen's and Burns' testimony put to rest the issue of when the *Aloha* left the marina. If the jury believed Dowd left around six o'clock, he would have been well past Point Bonita by the time the small craft warning was broadcast.

The judge asked me to call my next witness.

In the hallway I found Captain Phelan sitting stiffly erect on one of the benches, an unread newspaper at his side. He responded with a curt nod when I told him he was next.

Phelan had on a red plaid Pendleton shirt and black fishermen's jeans, faded almost gray from many washings. Inexplicably, his work boots were brilliantly polished. The bright red in the shirt accentuated the florid coloring in his face. He looked like he had just come from his boat.

I expected some manifestation of dissatisfaction about being in court, but whatever his feelings were he kept them to himself. I inquired if he had any questions. He shook his head. At the door he stepped past me, pausing for a moment to take in the courtroom.

The clerk was standing in the well. Sensing he should go to her, he approached at a purposeful pace. She gave him the oath which he acknowledged distinctly. The jury watched intently, assessing his appearance. After pulling his chair to the front of the witness box, he folded his hands on the desk top, ready to begin.

"Please state your name."

He responded firmly, "James D. Phelan."

"Where do you live?"

"San Francisco."

"Do you own a fishing boat?" He did, but unlike his predecessor on the stand, Ms. Burns, who would have immediately volunteered the boat's name, he confined his answer to a simple, "Yes."

"Where do you keep your boat?"

"Fisherman's Wharf, San Francisco."

From the moment Captain Phelan sat down, there had been an increasing patter of whispering from behind me. The noise of pages rapidly being flipped began to intrude as well. The jury was becoming distracted.

"Turning your attention to Friday, March 9th, two years ago, did you take your boat out salmon fishing that day?"

There was a sharp scrape of chairs being pushed backwards. I turned to see Baum and Blake propelling themselves out of their seats, speaking at the top of their voices, "Side bar, Your Honor."

Without waiting for the judge's consent to do so, both were charging toward the bench. Brushing past me, they were already speaking by the time I arrived, telling the judge, "If this witness was out fishing that day, there has been no notice of him."

Turning to me, Blake harshly demanded, "Who is he?"

Before I could answer, Baum interjected, "There is no mention of his name anywhere in discovery." Blake chorused, "And no notice of him as a witness."

I cut in before they could continue.

"Your Honor, pursuant to your order that we notify each other about our witnesses, I rang their office Saturday and told Mr. Baum who I would be calling. I specifically stated Mr. Phelan would testify today. He asked who Phelan was, and although I was under no obligation to do so, I told him, 'He is a fisherman who was out that day.' Those were my exact words: 'He is a fisherman who was out that day.'"

The two of them exchanged glances. Baum had the look of a musician whose instrument had suddenly gone out of tune. Apparently, he failed to mention that detail of my call to Blake.

The judge looked at Baum inquiringly, and he acknowledged that I had called on Saturday.

He asked me to continue.

"Your Honor, I did include Mr. Phelan's name on our list of witnesses which you read to the jury."

Noticing the sheet of paper with my witnesses laying on the bench, I reached over, pointing to the middle of the list.

"Here's his name, Your Honor, Jim Phelan."

Instead of looking where my finger pointed, the judge was glaring at me. His expression made it clear that I had seriously offended him. The transgression apparently was the intrusion of my arm over the bench. It seemed appropriate to point out Phelan's name on the list, but the judge was acting like I'd put my feet up on his desk in chambers. The withdrawal of my hand had the desired effect, and the judge turned his attention to my witness list. Finding Phelan's name halfway down, he held the sheet out to them.

Disregarding the proffered list, Blake started up again.

"There is no mention of Phelan in any of the defendant's answers to our many sets of interrogatories inquiring about witnesses."

Turning to me, his angry voice escalating rapidly, Blake repeated, "Who is he!?"

Ignoring him, I said, "Your Honor, may I explain?" He nodded.

"I learned of Mr. Phelan's existence only in the last few weeks, well after the close of discovery. I want to represent to the court that this was not a situation where I knew of his existence as a witness, and waited until after discovery was closed to go out and talk to him."

I asked the judge if he wanted me to elaborate. He nodded.

"I chartered a fishing boat to take me out past Point Bonita to familiarize myself with the areas in question. On the way back to the marina, the boat's captain mentioned that the Department of Fish & Game has regulations requiring the party boat fishermen to file reports specifying where they went fishing each time they go out. I contacted the State and through them learned Mr. Phelan had been out on March 9. Discovery was closed, and under the rules I am under no obligation to amend my interrogatory answers." The judge turned to them, "Was there any agreement to keep discovery open?"

They shook their heads, and said, "No."

Blake then reiterated I had an obligation to inform them that a witness had been located, and they were unfairly prejudiced by his surprise appearance. It was at the tip of my tongue to say they were hardly in a position to complain about surprises or undisclosed information after the McGee photograph, their attempt to turn Wrisley into an expert witness, and springing the China contract on me.

What goes around always seems to come around in a trial. The 'surprisors' had become the 'surprisees,' and now, with the shoe on the other foot, they were very angry.

By then Blake and Baum were speaking at the same time, their voices rising to a point the jury had to be hearing what they said.

The judge, who had been rapidly shifting in his chair, practically barked, "That's enough. Step back."

We headed for our tables in silence.

The jurors, who had been leaning forward to overhear what was going on at the bench, sat back instantly, not wanting to be seen eavesdropping.

Turning toward them, he said, "Ladies and Gentlemen, there is something I need to take up with counsel, and must ask that you return to the jury room. We will resolve this matter as quickly as possible."

Their curiosity had been piqued, and the jury clearly wanted to remain in the courtroom. In response to being asked to leave, they shuffled out as slowly as possible, like children being sent to their rooms.

When the last of them filed through the door, the judge stated, "Let the record reflect the jury has left the courtroom."

Unbidden by the judge, Baum and Blake renewed their arguments, stating I had an obligation to inform them about this witness. They were angry and I was becoming so myself. Fortunately their strident demeanor acted as a timely warning. I reminded myself: a lawyer who allows himself to succumb to anger is an indulgence his client cannot afford. Captain Phelan was far too important to our case for me to get heated and lose my focus.

Reasserting his authority, the judge sternly ordered us to sit down, his face flashing a storm warning that we were sailing very close to the limit of what he was going to put up with.

During all the disruption that had taken place at side bar, the only person in court who seemed unaffected by the controversy swirling around him was Captain Phelan. He remained fixed in his position in the witness box, his hands folded one on top of the other on the desk top as if he were a school boy.

The judge paused, waiting for the courtroom to become silent. Before he began to speak I stood, quickly saying, "Your Honor, I can clear this up for the court, if I may," and turned toward Captain Phelan to ask the few questions it would take to clarify the circumstances surrounding when and how I learned of his existence.

Brimming with ire, the judge pointed a quivering finger in my direction, ordering me to sit down, stating he would ask the questions. It was a stinging rebuke, and I felt the blood surging to my face. I sensed that if the judge was not completely satisfied I had complied with the discovery rules concerning when and how I learned about Captain Phelan, he was going to rule that Phelan could not testify. I sank into my chair.

Turning back toward the witness stand, Judge Leahy said, in a tenor markedly different from the one he had just used with me, "Mr. Phelan, would you please tell me when you were first contacted by Mr. Jacobs?"

A puzzled expression came over Captain Phelan's face, looking at the judge in the same manner he had with me in his parlor.

Finally, he responded: "Mr. Jacobs never contacted me."

Judge Leahy had been on the bench for years, and heard hundreds of people testify in his courtroom. He was fully aware that witnesses frequently suffer from a state of nerves about being on the stand. Taking Captain Phelan's nonsensical answer in stride, he tried again.

"When did someone from Mr. Jacobs' office first contact you?"

Captain Phelan replied promptly, "No one from his office contacted me."

Still calm, the judge asked, "Did an investigator contact you either by phone, by mail, or any other means, not necessarily in person?"

Phelan shook his head, "No."

I listened to his responses, dumbfounded. It was obvious to everyone that I had been in contact with him. I began wondering if he was deliberately trying to get himself excused.

The judge was now practically twitching in his chair. The 'weight shifting' danger sign I had been warned about made it acutely clear to me, but apparently not to Phelan, that his patience was waning. The amount of time Judge Leahy would put up with a witness trying to be cute with him was rapidly coming to an end. I had to stop this train wreck from unfolding and got to my feet again.

"Your Honor, if I may, I can clear up—"

The judge's head whipped around. The angry flush on his face made it abundantly clear: one more word from me, and Phelan would be excused. I had no choice but to sit back down.

Returning his attention to the witness stand, Judge Leahy spoke, his voice so saturated with impatience that Captain Phelan could not possibly misinterpret the judge was at the end of his tether: "Mr. Phelan, I want to make sure I understand you. Are you saying neither Mr. Jacobs, nor anyone from his office, nor an investigator, contacted you? Is that what you are saying?"

In a tone hinting he wasn't brimming with patience either, Captain Phelan replied, "He never contacted me."

A monastic silence enveloped the courtroom. The judge stared at him, trying to decide if there was any point in making further inquiries, or if he should let Baum request that Phelan not be permitted to testify.

For the first time since the judge began his questioning, Captain Phelan elaborated on an answer. Speaking evenly, he said, "It was Fish & Game that contacted me."

Judge Leahy stared at him incredulously, struggling to comprehend what Phelan had just said.

A long silence ensued before the judge began to speak, slowly, haltingly.

"Fish & Game . . . they told you . . . to come?"

Captain Phelan shot the judge the same glare he gave me when we met in his house. I had to watch in silence as this nightmare of miscommunication continued, not daring to once again intrude.

"That's right, Fish & Game. They sent me a letter and said to contact Mr. Jacobs if I wanted to."

The judge had lost control of the examination and knew it. Taking in a deep breath, he continued: "You wouldn't happen to have that letter with you, by chance?"

I half expected him to produce it, but he said he did not.

The judge straightened himself up, and at least partly recomposed, went on.

"You received a letter from Fish & Game?"

"Yes."

"And they said to contact Mr. Jacobs," hastily adding, ". . . if you wanted to?"

"Yes."

"What else was in the letter?"

"They said their records indicated I had been out fishing that day and gave me his name and phone number."

Dryly, the judge said, "I gather then . . . it was you . . . who contacted him. Is that it?"

"Right." Captain Phelan silently kept his gaze fixed on the judge. The aggravated look on his face left little doubt what his thoughts were: 'I've said this five times now; it's a pretty simple point to grasp. What the hell's going on here!'

What was coming next was going to be critical, and I fervently hoped that Captain Phelan maintained the same sharp attention to the judge's questions he had demonstrated so far.

The judge continued: "When did you receive this letter from the Department of Fish & Game?"

When Phelan did not answer, I silently cursed myself for failing to discuss this point with him, but it never occurred to me the letter would turn into the issue it had become. When the Captain finally spoke, his words dribbled out slowly. "Well, I'm not too sure, let me see, this is December 8th. . . ." His voice trailed off, deep in thought, staring fixedly at his gnarled fisherman's hands.

Speaking softly, in order not to intrude too abruptly into Phelan's thoughts, the judge asked, "Did you receive the letter before October 27th of this year?"

This was the date discovery closed, but that date would not be known to Phelan, and the gentle manner in which the judge spoke did not alert him of the date's vital importance.

"Let's see," Phelan murmured, almost to himself, "I spoke with Mr. Jacobs on . . ." and lapsed into silence. In a movement so quick it startled everyone, he jerked his head toward the calendar hanging on the wall behind the clerk's desk. After studying it carefully, he looked back to the judge,

"I called him two weeks ago. I'm not sure of the exact date, but it was well after October 27th."

Judge Leahy leaned back, slowly kneading his neck, silently sorting through the labyrinthine testimony he had just heard. The expression on his face alternated between head shaking and arching his eyebrows. As the seconds ticked by, my heart pounded faster than a sewing machine.

Looking up, the judge finally spoke, "I am satisfied that any knowledge of the existence of this witness, or the first contact with him, was made after the close of discovery. Accordingly, I am going to allow him to testify."

Clearing his throat, he said, "Bailiff, bring the jury back in."

After the storm which had just taken place in the courtroom, it surprised me the judge did not declare a break to let everyone, himself included, collect themselves.

In marked contrast to their foot-dragging exit ten minutes earlier, the jurors eagerly resumed their seats. As they filed through the doorway, the first thing every one of them did was look at the witness box to see if Captain Phelan still occupied it. They came to order quickly, giving the judge the silence they knew, by then, he would require before speaking. After apologizing for the delay, he informed the jury the issues had been resolved. Looking at me he said, "You may continue."

Returning to the lectern, I thanked the judge and recommenced.

"Captain Phelan, turning your attention once again to Friday, March 9th, did you take your boat out fishing that day?"

"Yes."

"Did you have a particular destination in mind?"

"Duxbury Reef. The salmon had been biting in that area and I planned on going back there."

"What time did you leave your berth at Fisherman's Wharf in San Francisco?"

Without hesitating, he replied: "Six o'clock sharp."

"Do you have a custom and habit about what time you leave?"

"Yes. We always leave at six o'clock."

This was an answer I had not expected, prompting me to do a little fishing myself.

"You said 'We,' captain. Who were you referring to?"

"All the party boat skippers leave at six o'clock and most of the private sport fishermen too." After a pause, he added, "I think it was crab season too, and if it was, the crab boats would be leaving at that time as well."

I asked whether he had a customary course he took going out to Duxbury. When he replied that he did, I put a chart on the easel, handed him the pointer, and asked him to step down from the witness stand. I noticed the judge leaving the bench to follow along, and I moved the chart to more directly face the jury.

When everyone was ready, I asked, "Captain, would you trace the usual and customary course you take to get to Duxbury, and please call off the important locations along the way."

He began slowly and methodically. The important landmarks rolled off his tongue as he began from his berth at Fisherman's Wharf, putting the jury in the wheelhouse with him as he took his boat past Alcatraz, under the Golden Gate Bridge, and through Golden Gate Channel. At each step he pointed to the chart, adding commentary on why he took certain actions, and identified the buoys and other navigation aids he used in setting his course. When he came to Point Bonita, I had him indicate the location of the lighthouse, and he continued tracing his course through Bonita Channel ending his narrative at Duxbury.

When he was back on the stand, I asked, "Captain, do you keep a log for each trip you make?"

"Yes, I do."

"Please tell the jury what your entries were for March 9th."

He pulled a piece of paper from his shirt pocket and turned toward the jury.

"I copied the entries I made in my log for that day. The entries were '5/9,' and 'Breakers on the Bar, Duxbury.'"

"Please explain to the jury what they mean."

"'5/9' means I had five passengers and we caught nine fish. The entry 'Breakers on the Bar' means there were waves breaking on the Bar, and 'Duxbury' was where I went fishing that day."

"Captain, a moment ago you described the usual course you took to go to Duxbury by coming around Point Bonita, and then going through Bonita Channel to Duxbury, do you recall that?"

"Yes."

"Is that the course you took on March 9th to get to Duxbury?"

"Yes, it was. I went under the bridge, through the Golden Gate, came around Point Bonita, and then went through the Channel out to Duxbury."

There was a hole in his answer that had to be corrected. I silently prayed he wasn't going to hammer me.

"Captain, you just said 'the Channel,' did you mean Bonita Channel?"

"Right, I went through Bonita Channel."

Greatly relieved, I went on. "Back then, did you have a custom and practice you followed about checking the conditions in Bonita Channel for dangerous waves or other unsafe conditions before you started to go through?" The question was too lengthy, but each facet was necessary to avoid objections.

"Yes, I did. Before going through, I look up the Channel to see if it's safe. If it's okay, I go through."

"On the day in question, did you check Bonita Channel for any dangerous conditions before starting through?"

"Yes, I did."

"What time did you arrive at Point Bonita?"

He gave this some thought. "Around six-thirty."

"Was it still dark out?"

"Yes, but there was enough light to see that the Channel was safe."

"Did you have any difficulties handling your boat while you were going through Bonita Channel that morning?"

"No."

"In the twenty plus years you have been fishing, how many times would you estimate you've been through Bonita Channel?"

He took a moment to do some rough calculations in his head.

"I'd say a thousand times, probably more. At least that many."

"Do you feel your twenty plus years of experience, and those thousand or more trips, makes you thoroughly familiar with the wave conditions that exist in the Bonita Channel area?"

"Yes."

While he was answering, I glanced at the wall clock. I had a time problem. There were a number of other questions I wanted to put to him, but doing so posed the risk that the judge might declare a mid-afternoon break if I asked them, giving Baum and Blake fifteen minutes to prepare their cross-examination. I made my decision.

"Thank you, Captain Phelan. You have been very helpful. No more questions."

Fortuitously, the judge did not declare a recess. The cross-examination questions began, coming in short machine gun blasts.

"Did you meet with defense counsel before coming to court?"

"Yes."

"What was discussed?"

"Mr. Jacobs wanted to know if I'd been out fishing that day, and if I saw the boat that was lost."

"How many other boats were fishing that day at Duxbury?"

He responded, "Quite a few."

Told to be more definitive, he estimated, "Ten, maybe more."

"Did you see the *Aloha* that day?"

"No, he showed me a picture of the boat, but I didn't recognize her."

Phelan was asked whether he'd heard about the incident. He acknowledged that he had, it was notable because so many lives had been lost, adding it was the worst fishing boat accident he was aware of. He was also asked whether he knew Francis Dowd or heard anything about him. He had not.

He was then asked, "While you were in the Channel, did you encounter any big breaking waves?"

He shook his head, repeating what he'd said earlier.

"There were breakers on the Bar, but the Channel was okay."

If Phelan felt an innuendo was being made that he had ignored dangerous wave conditions, he did not react to it. He remained as he had from the beginning, sitting stoically, his hands never moving from their folded position on the desk top inside the witness box.

"That piece of paper you brought with you, that's not your log book is it?"

"No."

"Did anyone tell you not to bring your log book with you when you came to court?"

"No. I didn't know I had to, so I copied down the entries for that day and brought them."

Now I was sorry I had discouraged him from bringing to court his calendar/logbook. It looked so amateurish compared to Captain McGee's professional log book. When we met at his house, Captain Phelan asked whether he should bring his log book with him. I said it was up to him, but if he did, it might be marked as an exhibit and he would not get it back for some time. My thinking was a jury would expect a veteran captain to have something more sophisticated than an advertising calendar for a log book. Now its absence had become an issue affecting his credibility and mine as well. An insinuation was being made that the real reason he had not brought his log book was because I told him not to. Opponents always state in closing argument that if a document is available, and not produced in court, it contains something damaging the other side doesn't want the jury to see.

The questioning turned to the time issue.

"When did you leave Fisherman's Wharf?"

"Six o'clock sharp."

"How do you know that?"

"Because I always leave then."

"What time did you arrive at Point Bonita?"

"Around six-thirty. The light was sufficient to check Bonita Channel. There were breakers on the Bar, but the Channel itself was clear."

"Is there a difference in your mind between a swell and a breaking wave?"

"I know the difference," he responded, an edge of irritation in his voice.

"Isn't it correct there were breaking waves on the Bar *and* in the Channel as well that morning?"

"The breakers were on the Bar. The waves in the Channel were swells."

Under persistent questioning, he finally agreed there might have been scattered whitecaps breaking in the Channel. After gaining this admission, Phelan was informed of McGee's testimony: that large waves were breaking across Bonita Channel that morning, and McGee had turned his boat around and gone out to Duxbury via the Main Ship Channel. The boats in front of him and behind him had done the same. Phelan listened without reaction.

He was then told McGee also testified the wave conditions he saw in the Channel were similar to the waves shown in a photograph that had been admitted into evidence. Phelan was handed the McGee photograph and asked to examine it carefully.

He looked at the photo, studying it at length. I noticed the jury observing him carefully, watching as his eyes darted around the picture taking in every detail, but whatever his thoughts were, his face was not revealing them. It was as if Phelan were looking at a different photograph from the one the jurors reacted to so visibly.

My instincts were telling me a foundation was being laid to use the photograph as a trap, and Phelan was being led into it like an animal to a slaughterhouse. He was then told the other fisherman had come around Point Bonita at the same time he had, and the waves shown in the photograph he had just examined were what this other captain saw. For all Phelan knew, it had been established that the photo had been taken later that same day, during daylight hours.

I began envisioning sharks circling around Phelan, smelling blood. The photograph would be worse than a trap; it was going to be a convenient and very face saving way for Captain Phelan to change his testimony. All he would have to say was that after looking at the photo his memory was refreshed, and state: 'I remember now, the Channel was filled with breaking waves and I went through the Main Channel to Duxbury.' I sat in dread waiting for him to speak.

He finally finished his review of the photograph and put it aside.

In a persuading tone, he was asked, "Does looking at this photograph refresh your memory about the wave conditions in Bonita Channel that morning?"

Unaccountably, Captain Phelan picked up the photograph, studying it once again. If the jury had not already concluded his lengthy initial examination was largely a stall, they certainly would now.

Putting the photograph down for the second time, he cleared his throat in an abrasive rasp, which would have gone unnoticed if the courtroom had not been so deadly silent.

Looking up, he said, "You're not understanding this; let me explain the situation to you." He paused. "I've got a load of paying passengers onboard. If I took them through water that looked like this, do you know what would happen?"

Having framed his own question, he commenced answering it. "As soon as I get back to the dock, they're going to get off my boat and I'd never see them again." Angrily jabbing the photograph again, he continued, "I've got a business to run, I'm not going to do something like this."

The courtroom stayed fixated on the photograph until he withdrew his trembling finger, and refolded his hands in the same 'school boy' manner on the desk top. He then firmly set his jaw in the identical expression he'd displayed in his parlor after he said, "A man comes to court and you damn lawyers make a fool out of him, make you look like a liar." I could feel the heat radiating from the witness box; he was ready to ignite.

There was a whispered conversation. I held my breath, hoping there would not be another request for a side bar conference. The whispering stopped.

"Nothing further, Your Honor."

The judge shifted his glance to me. "Any redirect?"

There were loose ends to clear up. In particular, I wanted to ask whether the sea conditions can change quickly in the Channel. He would likely agree, but I hadn't discussed it with him. As much as I wanted to continue, I couldn't risk going to the well one time too many with Phelan and get torpedoed with an answer I wasn't expecting. And what I really wanted to do was get him off the stand and out of the courtroom right then and there.

I stood so quickly, I nearly lost my balance. "Nothing further, Your Honor," and turned to the witness stand. "Thank you, Captain, you have been very helpful."

He was uninterested in my thanks—what he wanted to hear came from the judge.

"Captain Phelan, you are excused."

He stood up, jammed his captain's hat under his arm and stepped out of the witness box. Like Captain McGee, he fixed his eye on the door. Moving quickly, he jerked it open and charged out. The automatic closing mechanism sighing as the door slowly closed behind him.

I filled my lungs with the first easy breath I'd had from the moment he entered the courtroom.

The judge took a few moments to collect himself before asking me to call my next witness. I headed for the hallway.

# 23

ob Hodges stood as I approached, a questioning look on his face. He could not have missed seeing Captain Phelan barreling through the door, probably cursing himself for agreeing to come to court. Ignoring his expression, I said we were ready for him and he followed me into the courtroom. While the clerk swore him in, I ran through our several meetings, worrying whether he was adequately prepared. I'd met with Hodges and two other men Janet identified as Fran's most frequent fishing friends, and decided to call him because he was familiar with the court system.

After the oath, he confidently settled himself into the witness box. He would need only a minimum of comfort questions.

"Please give us your name."

"Robert Hodges."

"Where do you live?"

"Los Altos."

"Please tell the jury what your line of work is?"

"I am a consultant to the high tech industry."

"What was your relationship with Francis Dowd?"

"We were friends for many years. We had a few minor business dealings together, but mostly we were close personal friends."

"Had you ever been out fishing on the *Aloha* with Mr. Dowd?"

"Yes."

"Can you tell us approximately how many times?" He gave this some thought.

"I would say thirty times, possibly more."

"Did you always leave from Mr. Dowd's home to drive up to the Sausalito marina?"

"We did, and as far as I recall Fran always drove."

"How long did it take?"

"A little less than an hour."

"Mr. Hodges, after arriving at the marina was there a regular routine you followed to get the boat ready?"

"There were certain things we always did. The tarps covering the back deck were removed and put away, and then stowed the gear we brought with us. The engine spaces were ventilated next. When that was done, Fran warmed up the engines and we were ready to go. The lines were cast off, and Fran backed the *Aloha* out of the slip."

"How long did these preparations take?"

He lapsed into thought. This was an important question we had gone over a number of times and he should have had the answer at the tip of his tongue. He finally said, "Five minutes, ten at the most."

Like Fran's other fishing friends, Hodges had been vague when I interviewed him about Dowd's custom and practice concerning boat handling and navigating. All of them had been out dozens of times on the *Aloha,* but none had any substantive recollections about the courses taken to the various fishing grounds. Dowd was always at the helm doing the navigating, and from what they could see it was a one man job. Once they were underway, other than assembling the rods and preparing the baits, there was nothing for the rest of them to do and they relaxed and enjoyed the ride out to wherever they were going fishing.

The next question was substantive, and I put it to him a little slower.

"Mr. Hodges, on any of the thirty or more trips you were onboard the *Aloha*, did Francis Dowd do anything that you felt put the boat in jeopardy?"

"Not at all, that wasn't Fran's style."

"Was Duxbury Reef a place you frequently went fishing?"

"We went there fairly often."

"Do you recall how you got there, what courses you took?"

"We went under the Bridge, out to the end where the Light House is at Point Bonita. Fran would then make a right turn and go through Bonita Channel up to Duxbury."

I traced the landmarks on the chart as he testified.

"Mr. Hodges, did you ever go through Bonita Channel when the wave conditions made you feel it was unsafe to do so?"

He shook his head and said, "No," without elaboration.

Hodges wasn't keeping eye contact with me anymore. I was starting to get worried and moved to a new area of questioning.

"Did Francis Dowd ever cancel a fishing trip?"

"Yes he did. It happened twice that I can recall."

"What were the circumstances?"

"One time he called the night before. The forecast for the following morning warned of bad weather, and he decided to cancel the trip. On the other occasion, Fran called at four-thirty in the morning. He said he had just listened to the forecast. A small craft warning had been issued, and it would be unsafe to make the trip."

It was a good place to end my direct examination,

"Nothing further, Your Honor. Thank you, Mr. Hodges."

The cross-examination began.

"You were a close personal friend of Francis Dowd, for twenty years I believe you said, is that correct?"

"Yes."

"Are you also a close friend of Janet Dowd?"

"Yes, my wife Jackie and I are close friends with Janet as well."

These questions were a reminder to the jury that Hodges was a family friend, and might not have the same disinterest of a witness who knew none of the parties. My worry was that as a close friend there might be something Hodges had not told me about Fran, out of a desire not to hurt Janet ... negative information that might now be exposed in cross-examination.

"Do you consider yourself an experienced boat operator?"

"No."

"So you wouldn't be a judge of the level of skill or the experience required to be the skipper of a boat the size of the *Aloha*?"

"No."

"Francis Dowd was always at the wheel, is that correct?"

"Yes."

"And you did not pay close attention to the various course changes Mr. Dowd performed as he navigated the *Aloha*?"

"No, I didn't."

"You don't feel that you have the level of experience to know under what conditions it would be safe to take a boat the size of the *Aloha* through Bonita Channel, do you?"

"Not really."

Having established his minimal knowledge of boat handling, Baum was ready to cross-examine him in areas where he might retract some of his direct testimony. He got to the point quickly, and it was a sharp one.

"Mr. Hodges, are you aware that certain required safety items and navigational equipment had been stolen from the *Aloha*?"

"Yes, I'd heard that."

"Do you know if that gear had been replaced?"

"I don't know for sure."

As the questions became more and more detailed, Hodges was becoming increasingly hesitant and overly cautious in his responses. We had gone over what items had been stolen when I prepared him for his testimony, and I informed him what equipment had been replaced and which items there were uncertainties about. I scribbled a quick note to go through the list of stolen items with him one by one on redirect. Cracks seemed to be coming in his composure and I wasn't sure why.

"Mr. Hodges, during the many times you drove up to the marina, were stops ever made for supplies, to fill the car up with gas, or any other reason?"

He gave the question considerable thought before answering, "I don't think so," and then temporized, "we might have occasionally." He finished his answer with more doubt: ". . . I'm not sure."

"Did you always leave for the marina from his house?"

"Yes, we did." And then adding, "as far as I can recall."

The next question was put to him casually, almost conversationally.

"There wasn't a fixed time to leave for the marina, was there?"

Baum was not putting words in his mouth; he was cleverly taking Hodge's guarded responses and turning them into questions that were hurting us. I silently willed him not to retreat from his direct testimony on anything regarding the time issue. I had repeatedly gone over with him what time they left the house for the marina, how long it took to drive up, and the amount of time it took to get the *Aloha* ready to leave the dock.

Hodges lowered his head, apparently in deep thought about the pending question: 'There wasn't a fixed time to leave for the marina, was there?'

The answer should have been right at the tip of his tongue . . . the jury was starting to look at him questioningly.

Hodges finally lifted up his head. "You know . . ." his voice dropped so low the jury leaned forward, straining to hear him, "Fran invited me to go on that trip. But it was a Friday and I had appointments I couldn't break . . . and I had to decline." His head began shaking. "If I hadn't been so busy, I would have been out there with them." He barely got out the last few words before his head dropped to his chest.

Hodges had not mentioned this to me. The question of when they left the house must have triggered this memory, shaking him to the core.

Baum had been hit with an answer he wasn't expecting and concluded his cross-examination. I quickly stood, said I had no redirect, and he was excused.

There were a few questions I could have asked on redirect, but his response had so powerfully moved the jury, I wanted that to be their last impression of Hodges.

Janet was next, and unfortunately, the judge declared a short break. I dearly wanted to get her on the stand right after Hodges, before she had time to agonize, and now she had ten minutes to do so. She put her hands to her face briefly. I expected tears, but whatever was working her lasted only a moment. Excusing herself, Janet stepped out into the hallway to walk a bit and release some of the pressure.

Back on the bench after the break, the judge turned to me. "Call your next witness."

"The defense calls Janet Dowd, Your Honor."

The jury had observed Janet for days, but this would be their first opportunity to make substantive impressions. I had urged Janet to retain her composure no matter what happened while she was on the stand. The jury's reaction to her would in large measure influence their perceptions of Fran. She was absolutely convinced he was not responsible, but those thoughts were dictated by her heart, not logic and facts. The jury would be reaching their verdict on the evidence, not the intangibles Janet so desperately clung to.

Twelve pairs of eyes watched as she took the oath and stepped up to the witness stand, assessing her, taking her in. After settling in, she looked at me, waiting for the first question.

I asked her to give her full name, and also Fran's. Turning slightly toward the jury, she added they were both from Springfield, Massachusetts.

"Your husband was the owner of the *Aloha*?"

"Yes."

Janet's voice was up, her tone steady, seemingly ready for me to begin with substance. I had the same anxiety of a teacher who had been assigned the class play. Everyone knows their part, but when the curtain goes up anything can happen.

I looked up. "Mrs. Dowd, as painful as it must be, I have to ask you about your husband's knowledge of the sea and his use and operation of the boat on his fishing trips." She nodded.

"Your husband was in the Navy, is that correct?"

"Yes, he joined right after high school."

"What were his duties?"

"After basic training he was selected for submarine service, and attended the Navy Submarine School in New London, Connecticut. He sailed on submarines for four years as a sonar operator."

"What was his rating at the time of his discharge?"

"He was a Sonarman First Class."

"Mrs. Dowd, did your husband mention the training he received in small boat handling?"

"Yes, he received small boat instruction during basic training, and further drills while he was in New London."

I strained to phrase a few more boat training questions in a way that would not draw objections. They were not artful, but as good as I could make them. So far Baum had not interfered, but we were not in critical areas of her testimony either.

"Mrs. Dowd, did Fran's family have a boat when he was a boy?"

"Springfield is very far inland. Besides that, he came from a large family. Both of our fathers worked in local mills. There was no money for boats."

This ad lib drew nods from a few of the jurors.

"Was the *Aloha* his first boat?"

"It wasn't. He had what he called a 'ski boat' with an outboard motor that was used for fishing and family waterskiing."

"Was that boat taken out on the ocean?"

"Oh no, it was much too small for that. It was used strictly on the local lakes and reservoirs."

"What prompted him to buy the *Aloha*?"

"He had been out on friends' boats, became interested in salmon fishing, and knew he needed a boat big enough to go safely out on the ocean. Like he did on any new project, Fran read everything he could on the subject, spoke with knowledgeable people, and then started looking for a suitable boat, eventually finding the *Aloha*."

"Before he purchased the *Aloha*, did he have it surveyed?"

Tilting her head slightly, she repeated back to me, "Surveyed?"

Wrong word choice on my part. I rephrased. "Did Fran have it inspected by a professional to make sure it was in good condition?"

"He hired someone to look it over carefully and operate all the equipment to make sure everything was in proper order. The inspector made out a three or four page report, and the few things needing repair were done prior to purchase."

"The *Aloha* was his first big boat?"

"Yes."

"Bearing in mind this was his first big boat, did he obtain any special instruction on its use and operation before taking the *Aloha* out on his own?"

"He did. Fran took a number of lessons from a qualified instructor to make sure he knew how to operate it safely."

I inquired about the number of times he had taken the *Aloha* out on the ocean fishing. She gave this some thought, commenting that the fishing season ran from March through some time in the fall … and estimated fifteen to twenty times a year.

"Mrs. Dowd, how long were you and your husband married?" The sound of a chair scraping backwards intervened.

In a tone indicating his patience with these tangentially relevant questions was at an end, Baum said, "Your Honor, if the court pleases, we object. This is irrelevant to any issue in the case."

The judge turned to me, a questioning look in his eyes, "Counsel?"

I needed this question. Her answer would open a few important portholes into Fran's life that I needed the jury to hear. Vigorously shaking my head in disagreement I responded, "Unhappily, in these times, Your Honor, with divorce so common, I believe it is relevant that Mrs. Dowd be permitted to answer this question so the jury will know that her testimony about Mr. Dowd's experience and actions is based on personal knowledge."

I had never made this argument before, and the expression on Judge Leahy's face made it very clear this was the first time he'd heard it either. He did not appear at all convinced, and was about to say so.

I quickly added a phrase that every judge finds appealing, "I have only a few brief questions in this area, if I may, Your Honor." This had the desired effect, and without much enthusiasm he told me to proceed.

"Mrs. Dowd, how long were you married?"

"Almost thirty years."

"In all this time did your husband engage in anything that might be regarded as high risk activities, such as skydiving, hang gliding, mountain climbing, anything of that nature?"

"No," shaking her head with emphasis.

"Did he ever own a motorcycle?"

"No."

I looked at her expectantly, and after a moment she continued.

"He was sensible and careful about everything he did." Her eyes turned downwards for a moment, connecting with something, before continuing, "If we had been to a party and Fran had more than one drink, when it was time to drive home he would hand me the keys. He was always careful . . . that's the way he was."

"Mrs. Dowd, do you know what time the men left your home that morning to drive up to the marina?"

"I don't know for sure, but I think it was five o'clock."

I knew she was going to be hammered in cross-examination about the time issue and moved the questions to an area where she would be more confident with her responses.

"Do you know if he listened to the marine forecast before he went to bed?"

"Yes. He listened to the forecast on some sort of special radio he had that only received the marine weather forecasts."

"Are you certain about that?"

She sighed heavily before answering, "Yes, I am." I looked at her pointedly. A long moment passed before she looked up again. "I came into the bedroom while he was hunched over listening to that little radio, the one with the marine weather forecasts. I spoke to him, and he shushed me rather abruptly." She stopped speaking for a moment, her lower lip quivering, "I didn't like being spoken to that way, and when he finished listening to the broadcast, we . . . we, had words about it."

It was clear to every married person in the courtroom what happened . . . they'd had a row. Never having listened to one of the broadcasts, Janet was unaware that separate forecasts are given for five different areas along the California coast, stretching from the Oregon border to Mexico. It takes approximately five minutes to go through the whole cycle, and she must have walked in just as the forecast for the San Francisco area was about to begin, prompting his abruptness.

There was one more thing that had to be asked.

"Mrs. Dowd, did your husband speak to you that morning?"

Unless what he said related to the fishing trip the question was irrelevant, but worth the risk of an objection. "Yes, he did."

"What did he say?"

For the first time her grip failed. A noticeable tremor colored her voice as she responded: "He leaned over, said 'I love you,' and kissed me goodbye."

Emotion spilled from her face like a glass overturning. Seeing her reaction, the jury assumed she was on the brink of tears. But she was not. Janet was upset—with me. My question forced her to repeat something of a very personal nature she had told me, probably expecting it would remain private. But I wanted the jury to see Janet's human side, the part she'd so relentlessly hidden from view since the first day of trial.

She quickly regained her composure, waiting for the next question. I broke our eye contact and turned to the judge, "Nothing further, Your Honor."

Except for the intensity of her gaze, Janet remained outwardly calm as she braced herself for the cross-examination that would soon begin. I couldn't say the same for myself.

We had gone over the details time and again, and I knew Janet was ready as far as the facts and figures were concerned, but there was no way to know for sure if she was emotionally prepared to withstand the rigors of cross-examination. A client on the witness stand undergoing cross-examination is the second worst moment in a trial lawyer's life. Only the agony of waiting for a jury to come back with their verdict is worse.

Janet was about to undergo cross-examination, a new and terrifying situation she had no control over. On top of this, she was weighed down by her overwhelming emotional stake in the outcome of the case. Under circumstances like these, it is hard for clients to resist coloring their testimony to fit their own perceptions of reality. I prayed that Janet had kept nothing from me, or for some deeply suppressed psychological reasons maybe even from herself, that Baum would now expose.

The judge nodded toward Baum to begin his cross-examination. He started with the equipment issue.

"Do you know if any of the replacements for the items taken in the burglary were actually installed on the *Aloha*?"

Janet replied: "I don't know for sure, but between the credit card slips, our checkbook, and the conversations I had with Fran, I was able to determine that replacements for all of the stolen items had been purchased. From time to time, he went up to Sausalito to work on the boat, getting it ready for the fishing season. After the accident, the only replacement item still in the garage was the radar set. I concluded everything else had been taken up to the boat."

The cross-examination turned to the conflicting statements she had made about the time the *Aloha* sailed.

"Did you speak to the Coast Guard about the incident?"

"Yes."

"And that was on the evening of the incident, is that correct?"

"Yes."

"How many times did you speak with a Coast Guard representative that evening?"

"Twice I believe."

"Were you the only person in your family who spoke with them?"

"Yes."

"So any statement attributed to 'family members' would have come from you, is that correct?"

"Yes."

"The Coast Guard report indicates on the evening of the incident you told them the *Aloha* sailed from Sausalito at six-thirty that morning?"

"Yes," she responded in a lowered tone.

"Do you recall being sent interrogatories in this case?"

"Yes."

"And you were aware they were to be answered under oath?"

"Yes."

"And you also knew that you had thirty days to think about the questions, and do any research you felt was necessary before answering them?"

"Yes."

Baum then read the interrogatory in question. It asked what time the men left the Dowd home in Los Altos to drive up to the marina. Baum paused, and looked toward the jury significantly. He then slowly read her answer . . . the men had left the house at six-thirty.

Then he asked, "You do recall receiving that set of interrogatories and giving that answer?"

"Yes."

Picking up her deposition, Baum read the part where she stated the men left the house around six o'clock. She acknowledged this was the answer she had given when her deposition was taken.

Baum then summarized the three different times she had stated, and then, with the smoothness of a diplomat, gently suggested perhaps her answer to the interrogatory 'the men left the house at six-thirty' was the correct response. His tone was getting pretty unctuous, and I prayed she would not be tempted to submissively agree with the 'left the house at six-thirty' response Baum wanted her to say.

Janet was now acutely embarrassed about the three different responses she had given about the time issue and did not immediately react. The ensuing silence heightened the intense scrutiny the jury was giving her. Inconsistencies do not sit well with a jury, and they like deliberate omissions even less. But what jurors absolutely won't abide are witnesses with convenient memory lapses about the facts. There are a limited number of times a jury will tolerate lapses, inconsistencies, and omissions before serious doubts about a witnesses credibility begins creeping into their thinking. When that happens, they basically stop listening.

She looked up, the confidence in her voice unraveling as she finally responded. "I'm not certain about the time, because that was one morning I didn't get up with Fran. Ordinarily, when he went fishing I got up and fixed coffee. If it had just been him, our son Jerry and my brother-in-law, John Kennedy, I would have. But that morning I did not, because I didn't want to be in the kitchen in my bathrobe with the other men there."

My head turned reflexively toward the jury box to gauge their reactions. They were staring at Janet with the same intensity of a parent questioning a teenager. I noticed several of the women pursing their lips, weighing what they might have done under the circumstances, searching for the ring of truthfulness in her answer.

Haltingly, she finished. "There's something else. Fran liked to be at work early, before his phone started ringing and things became hectic, so we got up every day at six-thirty. I remember him speaking to me that morning, but because it was before five o'clock I went right back to sleep. If it had been anywhere close to our usual wake up time of six-thirty, I wouldn't have gone back to sleep. I would have got up for the day."

After whispering with Blake, Baum stated he had no further questions and she was excused.

As Janet left the stand I searched the jurors' faces trying to get a sense whether the totality of her testimony provided some insights into the time and equipment issues, but mostly if they'd gained some perceptions about Fran's boating abilities, and Fran himself.

I held her chair out as she sat down, whispering she had done well. She gave no reply. Janet was so tense I wasn't sure she even heard me. Her hand went to her chest in an instinctive movement to assure herself she was still breathing.

The judge looked at the clock; it was just past four. Turning toward the jury, he once again admonished them not to discuss the case and sent them home for the day.

While the jury members filed out, their collective glances were on Janet, taking her in, appraising her intently. When the door leading to the jury room closed behind them, the judge asked if we had anything to bring to his attention. We did not, and he left the bench.

Janet began to express reservations about her testimony. Her face raced with anguish, reflecting . . . none of this was supposed to be. What had happened to our dreams? Gone.

The next day would be entirely for our two experts. I had worked with Captain Seymour over the weekend, and Rae Strange would be in my office at six. Depending on how long they were cross-examined, there was a chance their testimony would be completed tomorrow.

I saw Baum leaving with the Angs and reminded myself of the judge's order to let them know who I would be calling the next day. I finished putting my things away and noticed Blake about to pull his cart through the door. I caught up with him, and said, "Don't you want to know who we are calling tomorrow?"

He whirled around facing me, and began speaking so fast it was difficult to follow his words. "You should have told us about this man, this witness you claim you just found."

He put his cart down. "You should be ashamed of yourself for pulling something like this. You should have immediately informed us."

He was speaking increasingly louder, his anger escalating fast. I knew they had been caught off guard by Captain Phelan's appearance, but so had I by their surprises . . . I couldn't get a reply to form, and there was no chance to speak anyway. Blake was worked up to the point that his voice was fully elevated, giving every appearance of a man ready to start swinging. We were standing only a few feet apart. I stepped back.

Before he could go on, I found my voice. "You have no cause to complain. I've been asking for documents for months, and the first time I saw the China contract was when Mrs. Ang was on the stand." My voice had risen too.

Blake turned his body sideways. I sensed he was ready to start up, and stepped back another pace. I was not going to get hit with a sucker punch. Instead of swinging, he continued in the same angry tone, even louder. "You had an obligation to tell us about this witness."

I cut in, "I had no such obligation, and the judge agreed."

This was not going anywhere, and I had heard enough. "I'm leaving now; either go through the door or I will."

We stood staring at each other. "By the way, I'm calling Strange and Seymour tomorrow." I grabbed the handle on my cart and began moving forward. He did the same and went through the door. I pushed the elevator button. We waited in silence. The elevator in front of me opened. I got in. Blake waited for the next one.

On the drive back to San Francisco the freeway was choked with rush hour traffic and I had to concentrate on driving. After a half hour, traffic thinned out and I'd cooled off enough to think. A long ago conversation I had with my father came to mind. Quite solemnly, he'd said, "Your job is to do everything you can to win your client's case, with one important caveat . . . always within the rules." He thought for a moment. "You probably had a few lectures about 'full and fair discovery' in law school." I nodded. "That's a nice topic for professors and legal theorists in the faculty lounge, but not for a lawyer in trial. You keep in mind that when it comes to a trial you are a gladiator, and your client's interests come first, last, and always. It's a sacred trust. You and your client's case converge, becoming inseparable."

Marsha heard the garage door lift and hurried down the stairs to greet me.

"How did it go today?" and without waiting for an answer continued, "What about Thiessen and Burns?" an apprehensive tremolo in her voice.

"Bearing in mind their feelings about being subpoenaed, they did better than I'd hoped for; I won't need to call you."

Looking immensely relieved, she said, "I'm so glad!"

I told her about the uproar surrounding Phelan, the judge's ruling letting him testify, and how close I felt Blake and I had come to blows as we were leaving the courtroom. Marsha listened without interruption.

When I finished, she said, "It sounds like he was livid."

"He was. But they're going to be a whole lot angrier when it dawns on them that they could have asked the judge to put Phelan's testimony over till tomorrow morning, and request an order that they be allowed to take Phelan's deposition tonight, to find out what he was going to say."

She asked, "Would the judge have granted that request?"

"There's precedent for such an order in circumstances like this, where an attorney is caught by surprise through no fault of his own, such as my finding out about Phelan after the close of discovery. I think Judge Leahy would have granted such a request."

# 24

Marsha and I finished our dinner quickly, and I drove to the office to meet Rae Strange. He arrived promptly at 6:00. I showed him the exhibit Marsha had made of his data, and began preparing him for the next day. After giving him the highlights of Scott Noble's testimony, I told Strange that Blake would probably focus on two issues: the height and location of the waves. After two hours, we both felt ready. Strange said he would review everything again at his hotel that night, and be at the courthouse at one-fifteen the next day.

Returning back home, I went right to work refining the outline for my direct examination of Captain Seymour.

I had devoted a good deal of time over the weekend debating who to put on the stand first. In the end, I decided to start with Captain Seymour, mostly because he would provide some of the foundation Strange would use during his testimony.

In the morning, I had my run and a hurried breakfast. After a kiss from Marsha, I headed for San Jose.

I arrived in court twenty minutes early and unloaded my bags, placing the blue binder for Captain Seymour on the table along with the outline for his direct examination. He arrived just as I finished setting up, and we reviewed the outline for his testimony. He seemed confident and composed.

When Baum and Blake arrived, they maintained a studied refusal to acknowledge my presence. The clerk asked if we had anything to discuss with the judge before we started. We shook our heads, and the bailiff brought in the jury.

191

The door to chambers opened, and the judge emerged as the clerk called the courtroom to order.

I had remained standing. The judge nodded to me. "Call your next witness."

He would have preferred if Captain Seymour had been waiting in the rear of the courtroom, but like most judges he was resigned to the fact that every lawyer wants the day's first witness to make a more dramatic entrance through the courtroom door.

In the hallway, Captain Seymour was already standing, a chart tucked under his arm. I asked if he had any last minute thoughts. He shook his head. I opened the courtroom door, and without a pause he headed for the waiting clerk.

For his court appearance, Seymour had chosen a conservative deep blue pin stripe suit, and a quiet tie. The blue in the suit set off his full head of carefully brushed silvery hair. He had one feature that gave him a very captainly appearance: a large, firmly set jaw with a pronounced dimple.

Seymour had not been to sea for years, but he had a unique personal and educational background that I hoped would capture the jury's interest. The biggest contrast between him and Captain Sheppard, the plaintiffs' expert, was their appearance. Sheppard looked and spoke like an old salt with his rolling gait and neatly trimmed beard. In contrast, Captain Seymour looked more like a captain of industry than the captain of a ship.

He stood at attention in the well for the oath, standing so his face was visible to the jury.

After unpacking his briefcase and settling himself in the witness box, I had him state his name, and then asked, "Would you please tell the jury about your training, education and experience in the shipping industry?"

Directing his comments to the jury, he said, "I had an early interest in a career at sea, and after completing my secondary education I received an appointment to the United States Maritime Academy at Kings Point, New York. Upon graduation, I was licensed as a third mate, which is a junior deck officer." He paused a moment to reflect before continuing,

"As I gained more experience at sea, I took the examinations to advance from third mate to second mate, and then to chief mate, and sailed in those positions on various ships."

"Captain Seymour, at some point did you take, and pass, the Coast Guard examination for a Master Mariner's license, and would you explain to the jury what that license is?"

"A Master Mariner's license is commonly referred to as a captain's license. I took that examination and passed."

I interrupted his narrative. "How old were you when you received your captain's license?"

"I was twenty-three."

"Did you then sail in that capacity as the captain of a ship?"

"Yes, I joined American President Lines in San Francisco, as staff captain for five years, sailing around the world eleven times."

"What was the complement of officers and crewmen on the ships you captained?"

"There were thirty-eight officers and men."

"Captain Seymour, to your knowledge, are you the youngest man ever to have been issued a captain's license by the Coast Guard?"

I had not told him this question was coming, and he hesitated before modestly agreeing this was correct. It was a remarkable achievement to be the captain of a ship at age twenty-three, when many men his age were still students. The jury was clearly impressed.

"Would you please explain what your duties were as captain?"

"As the master, it was my responsibility to see after the operation of the ship, the welfare of the crew, and get the cargoes safely to their destinations."

"During your career at sea, what weather and storm conditions did you encounter?"

He took a moment to reflect. "At one point or another, I probably came across every condition the ocean can throw at a mariner: hurricanes, typhoons, icebergs, and the other hazards that come with a life at sea."

"Captain, do you have any educational experiences in addition to the United States Maritime Academy?"

"I attended the Massachusetts Institute of Technology, graduating with a degree in Marine Architecture and Engineering. After graduation from M.I.T., I worked for several marine architectural firms and ship builders before opening my own marine architectural and consulting firm in San Francisco."

It was an impressive résumé of his educational attainments and practical experience in the maritime industry, which he related without a hint of hubris. He had been testifying in greater detail than I usually want an expert to do in outlining their educational and practical experience, but I felt it was necessary. Captain Sheppard had made a strong impression, and I wanted the jury to take note of the differences in their backgrounds. A few questions earlier I noticed the jurors were beginning to move about in their seats, telling me it was time for substance to begin.

"Captain Seymour, turning your attention to the events of March 9th, two years ago, have you—" From behind I could hear the sound of a chair being pushed back.

Blake interrupted. "We would like to conduct an examination of this witness as to his qualifications to render an opinion in this case."

Blake's request caught me completely by surprise; I was momentarily speechless. A lawyer has the right to ask questions to determine whether the other side's expert has the qualifications to render expert opinions, but with Seymour's education, training and experience in practically every aspect of the maritime industry, how could he not be qualified?

Blake continued. "We do not believe Captain Seymour has the proper qualifications concerning the safe operation, maintenance, and navigation of small craft, and we request the opportunity to voir dire him on his qualifications, if any, on those subjects, before he is allowed to state an opinion on the loss of the *Aloha*."

My mind was racing, but nothing was coming to effectively oppose the motion. Blake could not seriously be thinking that Captain Seymour was unqualified. Other than being born at sea or having salt water in his veins, every other aspect of his life revolved around some aspect of the maritime industry, both at sea and ashore.

I was sure Judge Leahy thought Seymour was qualified, but the safest path for the judge might be to allow Blake to examine the captain on his credentials and then rule he could testify. That way there would be no error to cite if an appeal was made. Denying Blake's request might leave that possibility open. The judge opted for the safer course, and stated, "You may voir dire as to qualifications."

Too late it came to me: I should have immediately asked for a side bar conference, and if the judge agreed to Blake's request, have the examination done outside the presence of the jury as he had done with Phelan.

Blake walked briskly to the lectern. "You have not been to sea in any capacity for years, isn't that correct?"

"Yes."

"In fact, your captain's license is no longer even active, is it?"

"No."

"You do not own a boat of any kind, do you?"

"No."

This was a new Blake. Gone was the flowery British accent, replaced by a strident voice the jury had not heard before. The questions came in rapid bursts, steeped in a tone of disdain bordering on sarcasm, as if Captain Seymour were some sort of impostor.

"You have never been a commercial fisherman or a party boat operator?"

"No."

"You have only limited experience with sport fishing in the ocean, isn't that correct?"

"Yes."

Continuing in the same contemptuous tone Blake asked, "The last time you went through Bonita Channel on a small boat was a few weeks ago, at counsel's request, isn't that correct?"

"Yes."

"And that trip was on a calm day with virtually no waves of any kind, isn't that true?"

"Yes."

The questioning was particularly detailed about his limited experience with small craft, and virtually none concerning navigating through Bonita Channel. Seymour had been in and out of the Golden Gate hundreds of times, but on large cargo ships. Every attempt Seymour made to expand on his answers was cut off by Blake with a demand that he confine himself to 'yes' or 'no' responses.

When Blake exhausted his questions, the judge looked at me. "Do you wish to inquire?"

I was already moving toward the lectern, bringing the notes I had feverishly jotted down.

Captain Seymour looked flushed from the ordeal he had just been put through, that made it appear his expertise restricted him to testify about large ships only, and his education, training, and experience, while broad and unusual, had no relevance to the case at hand.

The main reason for calling Captain Seymour, his vast experience in the maritime industry, had just run aground. I had to bolster the weakest link in his credentials: his limited experience in small boat handling or the judge wasn't going to let him testify.

Using a tone I hoped the jury would find to be in sharp contrast to Blake's hectoring manner, I began, "Captain, when did you first learn how to handle a small boat?" I did not know how he would answer that question, but the probabilities were it would be favorable.

"My father taught me how to sail as a boy. I progressed through a series of larger boats, and as I became more proficient he allowed me to go out alone and for further distances."

"Did you have any instruction in small craft seamanship as a cadet at the Maritime Academy?"

"Yes. We were trained in every aspect of small craft handling, including seamanship, navigation, and safety."

"Was there additional training in small craft handling during your years at sea in the merchant marine service?"

"There was intensive training. The safety of everyone onboard depends on each man knowing his duties and performing them quickly in the event the lifeboats had to be launched hurriedly under hazardous conditions."

A few years earlier, Captain Seymour mentioned a consulting assignment he was working on. It was only of passing interest at the time; now it seemed a heaven sent opportunity to explore in front of the jury.

"Captain, have you done work for clients who build small craft similar in size and type to the *Aloha*?"

"Yes, I have."

"Please explain what you were asked to do."

This was an assignment he particularly enjoyed, and he began an extensive answer. "I was engaged by a well-known boat building firm to determine whether the materials they were considering for their new models were appropriate, and if the boats were capable of safely withstanding the rough conditions out on the ocean. I worked extensively with the company's engineers and designers, frequently operating their prototype boats in all types of conditions out on the ocean with the objective of improving the boats' designs and enhancing their seaworthiness."

It was a good strong note to end on.

Turning to the judge, I said, "Nothing further, Your Honor."

There was an extended whispered conference between Blake and Baum. Finally, Blake rose and said he had nothing else.

Judge Leahy turned toward Captain Seymour, scrutinizing him for a long time. Acutely anxious, I remained standing, waiting on his ruling.

The judge leaned back in his chair, thinking. Almost unnoticeably he raised his hands palms upwards, subconsciously balancing our arguments in the scales, weighing whether an adequate record had been made to support whatever ruling he was about to make. The fate of our case hung in the balance. Without Captain Seymour's testimony on what constituted safe navigation practices on the morning of March 9, we had no chance to win.

He finally spoke. "I will allow this witness to testify in the areas designated," adding, "it will be for the jury to decide what weight to give his testimony," hardly a ringing endorsement of his decision allowing Captain Seymour to testify.

Even though the judge ruled in our favor, I felt little sense of relief. The ordeal he had just been subjected to was bound to have affected Captain Seymour's confidence, and his composure as well. I was equally concerned that he would become overly cautious in answering my questions to avoid putting himself in a position for further derision by Blake on cross-examination. It had been a draining fifteen minutes.

The judge asked me to resume, and I raced to the lectern.

"Captain, please outline the investigations and other work you performed concerning the loss of the *Aloha*."

He responded slowly. "I made inquiries, gathered information, and reviewed the regulations concerning the safety equipment required to be onboard the *Aloha*. I also referred to various charts, tide and current tables, and standard reference works on boat handling and navigation."

"Have you formed opinions and conclusions concerning the *Aloha*'s disappearance?"

"I have. In my opinion, there are three explanations that best account for the loss of the vessel, one of them being more likely than the other two."

Turning so he was facing the jury, he continued. "The most likely explanation, in my opinion, is that the *Aloha* was struck by a large, unexpected, rogue wave which capsized and immediately sank the vessel."

I let his answer hang in the air a moment.

"Captain, please give the jury your full reasoning in reaching this conclusion."

"My information is that the *Aloha* left the Sausalito marina at six o'clock that morning. Based on the boat's length and the size of her engines, I've concluded Mr. Dowd arrived at Point Bonita in about thirty minutes, perhaps a little more. Data obtained from the wave recording buoys leads me to believe the sea conditions were such that a large wave may have arisen which sank the boat."

I had him step down from the stand and trace the course he felt Dowd would have taken from the time he left the marina heading to Duxbury. The jury already knew these details; my purpose was to give him further time to recompose himself. The self-confident Captain Seymour I had known for many years was not the same man on the witness stand now.

When he returned to the witness box, I continued. "You mentioned there were two other explanations. What are they?"

"The *Aloha* may have struck a dead head. This is a piece of floating debris, most commonly a large log or a stump. Such objects are often difficult to see even in daylight. If a boat struck one of them at the right angle, the hull could be pierced causing it to sink."

In a slightly doubting manner, I asked, "Captain Seymour, these dead heads—is this some sort of theory or does it actually happen?"

"They do indeed occur, even causing damage to the propellers of large cargo ships."

"What is the other possibility?"

"The *Aloha* may have been run down by a big ship. A large container ship was in the area that morning which may have run down the *Aloha*."

I paused to look at my notes. I had worked on the next question a half dozen times, and never found a way to phrase it that I liked.

"Based on your many years at sea on large ships, do you have an opinion about whether the personnel, on a containership that is seven hundred feet long built of steel hull plates an inch and a half thick, would always know if the bow of their ship struck a fishing boat?"

"I do not think they would always be aware if they struck a boat the size of the *Aloha*."

As I was looking at the outline for my next area of questioning, the judge's voice intervened. "Would this be a convenient time to take our mid-morning break?" I wanted to finish my direct examination before the break, but answered in the only way the judge wanted to hear.

"That will be fine, Your Honor," and remained standing as the jury moved out of the box. I noticed their entire focus was on Captain Seymour, staring at him uncertainly.

I looked at the captain as well. It didn't take a mind reader to know how upset he was, and I knew full well his anger was not just with Blake for the humiliating experience he had just been put through. He was my witness and, at the very least, I should have shielded him from having the questioning about his credentials done in front of the jury.

When the jurors were gone, he left the stand, walking stiffly over to the table, his face devoid of expression. Speaking brusquely, he said he was going to the men's room and headed for the door.

In his absence, I looked at the notes I'd made on my yellow pad. There was a notation to check something in the Coast Guard report. Rather than hunt for my copy, I walked to the clerk's desk and found the report Captain Sheppard had used. As I glanced through it, an idea sprang to mind. Captain Seymour returned shortly, and I asked him to sit down. There were only a few minutes left before the judge would be back on the bench; not enough time to be anything other than direct.

Not welcoming what I had to do, I spoke hurriedly. "Captain, your credentials have been challenged, and from the tone used in doing so, your integrity has been called into question as well." He eyed me in smoldering silence, waiting for me to continue.

"There's something you can do about that, and under the circumstances I think you should. But you will have to wait until you are being cross-examined to do it." An angry tick jumped on his cheek as I quickly outlined my plan. When I finished, he stared at me in silence. Practically through clenched teeth, he said, "All right, I'll do it." It was the first time he had spoken since returning to the courtroom.

He didn't like my plan, and I didn't either. What I had in mind was going to be based largely on hope, hardly the best light source to travel down unlit paths. The way things were going, the light at the end of this tunnel could easily end up being a bolt of lightning.

The clerk walked over and asked if I was ready.

With more confidence than I was feeling at the moment, I said, "We're ready."

I leaned toward Captain Seymour, repeating what I'd just said about what to do, and to wait until he was being cross-examined. He nodded, walking tautly to the witness box.

After the jury was seated, the judge took the bench, and said, "Mr. Jacobs."

"Thank you, Your Honor," and I turned to Captain Seymour.

"In an incident such as this, involving the death of so many men, how important is the Coast Guard report in determining what caused the loss of the vessel?"

"The Coast Guard's report is of the utmost importance."

Each of my succeeding questions had to be phrased so they hinted broadly towards, but did not actually supply, the answers I wanted him to give. To do it I would have to tread carefully to avoid giving Baum any excuse to start making objections, which would cut off the flow of my questions.

"Did you obtain a copy of the Coast Guard report?"

"It was one of the first things I did. After reviewing it several times, I called the Coast Guard Marine Safety Office and spoke with Dennis George, the officer in charge of the investigation, about his findings."

"How many Coast Guard Accident Reports have you reviewed in connection with your work over the years?"

He gave this some thought. "Well over a hundred. My practice is to obtain a copy of the official report, review it carefully, and then contact the investigating officer with my questions. I followed that procedure in this case."

The next question was at the borderline of being relevant, and I spoke quickly.

"In your many years of working with the Coast Guard's investigating officers, are you familiar with the methods used in training them?"

Thankfully, he began his answer before an objection was made: "They are all career officers, and before being assigned to a Marine Accident Investigation Unit, they receive intensive training on the laws regulating navigation and the safety equipment required to be on a vessel, as well as the rules of the road. They are also taught how to conduct an investigation, and make out an official report. When they are initially assigned to the Coast Guard's Marine Safety Office, they receive additional on the job training, working under the supervision of an experienced senior officer until they are capable of making a proper investigation and report on their own."

"Was the officer in charge of this investigation working on his own?"

"He was. Officer George was well trained and fully capable of acting on his own."

Knowing I was way out on the ice, I asked a follow up question, hoping it wouldn't be objected to, "How do you know that?"

"Because I know who George's superior officer is. That would be Commander James McCartin. The loss of five men was a very serious matter, and Commander McCartin would never give an assignment of this magnitude to an inexperienced man."

I let this nice accolade of Officer George's experience and abilities soak in with the jury for a moment before easing into the next question, hoping I had made it objection-proof.

"Was the Coast Guard report one of the things you relied on in reaching your opinion that Francis Dowd was not careless in his operation of the *Aloha*?"

"Yes, it was."

Hurriedly, I asked, "Did the report corroborate the opinion you reached?"

"It did."

"Captain would you please read the portion of the report which substantiates your opinion that Mr. Dowd was not negligent in—" Before I could complete the question, the sound of chairs scraping backwards once again intruded.

I turned to see Baum and Blake catapulting out of their chairs in an outburst of objections. Judge Leahy's head whipped back and forth between them as the fusillade of objections continued. In the midst of the din, I tried to fathom what possibly could be so objectionable about my question. It might have been more artfully stated, but all I had asked Captain Seymour to do was read from the report. I was mystified by the vehemence of their response, but since both of them were speaking simultaneously, it was impossible to grasp anything more than bits and pieces of their arguments.

Overwhelmed, the judge shot his hand up, demanding one at a time. Blake, continuing in the same loud voice, complained that the document was filled with inadmissible hearsay, further objecting that there was no foundation for the opinions stated in the report, and an array of other objections.

Becoming more agitated, Blake continued: "Counsel knows the question is improper, and it is misconduct to ask Captain Seymour to read from the report in front of the jury."

Sensing another dog fight was in the offing, the judge cut in sharply, "Just one moment."

His fiery face clearly communicating he was at the end of his rope with our brawling in front of the jury.

Making eye contact with me, he said, "Do you wish to be heard?"

In a voice more confident than my stomach was registering, I responded. "Your Honor, their objections of hearsay, lack of foundation, and their other objections concerning this document are not well taken. The Coast Guard report was put into evidence by them, while their witness Captain Sheppard was on the stand; and they cannot now object to Captain Seymour testifying about it—"

The judge jerked his hand up. I stopped instantly. Surely he was not going to make his ruling without letting me complete my argument. Keeping his eyes fixed on me to ensure I said nothing further, he leaned down to the clerk. With an impatient, beckoning gesture, he ordered her to hand him the exhibit. I frantically scrolled through my mind trying to remember what I'd done during the break. All I could recall was there had been very little time, and I was rushing when I pulled the Coast Guard report from the clerk's evidence box, and skimmed through it. The thought hadn't entered my mind to look at the exhibit sticker to see if it had been admitted into evidence or just marked for identification. If the report was marked for identification only, and not admitted, I was going to be in for the very humiliating experience of the judge unloading on me in front of the jurors. They would conclude I was trying to pull a fast one by improperly attempting to have Seymour read from a document which had not been admitted.

My credibility hung in the balance as the judge examined the exhibit. When he finished, he asked the clerk for her exhibit log, carefully comparing the exhibit stickers on the report with her log entries. Putting the documents aside he looked down, contemplatively.

Finally looking up, he turned to Blake. "It appears the documents were admitted into evidence, apparently at your request."

The breath I had been holding shot from my chest in relief.

The judge continued: "You are objecting on the grounds of hearsay?"

Blake immediately said "Yes," and began arguing, but the judge wanted a 'yes' or 'no' answer, and held his hand up cutting off further comment.

The nature of their hearsay objection was plain enough: hearsay is a statement made by someone who is not present in court. Officer George was obviously not in court to testify about the opinions he had stated in the report, clearly making the document hearsay. There were even a few instances in the report of hearsay on top of hearsay . . . where George had inserted information that other people had told him.

Looking at Baum and Blake, the judge asked, "In addition to hearsay, and your other objections, you are also requesting that the Coast Guard report be withdrawn on the grounds that it was mistakenly offered into evidence?" They were.

A long period of silence followed as the judge considered his alternatives before making his ruling. The parts of the report that were hearsay could possibly be redacted, but there was no practical way to do that. The report was five or six pages and the jury would have to leave the courtroom, or more likely be sent home for the day, while the court reporter read Captain Sheppard's entire testimony to Judge Leahy, so he could determine what parts of the Coast Guard report Sheppard referred to during his testimony. As the judge considered what to do, it must have become increasingly apparent to him that it had been a major mistake to admit the report in the first place.

He leaned forward. "Submitted, gentlemen?"

Without much enthusiasm, we said, "Yes."

Tilting his chair back, he pursed his lips, immersed in thought, thinking through his options.

The thought kept drumming in my head . . . this was not the time for Judge Leahy to come up with a 'split the baby, King Solomon ruling.' As the seconds ticked off, my fear escalated he was considering doing just that.

He finally looked up, clearing his throat. "Plaintiffs' objections of hearsay, and their other objections, are overruled."

As he began considering his next ruling, the perturbed look on his face indicated his mind was not made up. It was going to be a close call.

The judge brought his chair up slowly. "Plaintiffs' motion to withdraw the Coast Guard report, Exhibit 11 A, and Exhibit 11 B, is denied."

I was hugely relieved; the jurors would not only hear Seymour read from the report, they would also get to read the document during their deliberations in the jury room. The thought came to me: if there was a patron saint for jurors, it would probably be Thomas . . . who only believed what he saw.

His words, and even more so his facial expressions, made it abundantly plain Judge Leahy was far from pleased with either of his rulings, but there was no indication what displeased him, or toward whom his displeasure was directed. I sensed the judge decided he had made a major mistake in letting the Coast Guard report come into evidence in the first place, but he had also concluded that any error on his part in doing so was expunged by the doctrine of Invited Error. Under this legal doctrine, if a judge erroneously admits a document into evidence at the request of one of the lawyers, the judge's mistake cannot later be claimed by that lawyer as erroneous since he was the one who 'invited' the judge to make the error.

The judge looked at me. "You may continue your examination."

Buoyed with relief, I quickly returned to the lectern.

"Captain Seymour, before your testimony was interrupted by counsel, I believe you were going to state whether your opinion, that Mr. Dowd was neither careless nor negligent in his operation of the *Aloha,* was corroborated by the Coast Guard. Please do so now."

He cleared his throat and turned toward the jury box, "The Coast Guard, in their official report, stated there was no evidence of operator negligence."

"At this time, would you read to the jury the part of the report you are referring to."

Turning to fully face the jurors, the Captain began: "On page one, section 1 (c), the report states—" I cut him off. He was reading way too fast. I wanted the jurors to not only hear the words, but have time to fully absorb their meaning.

"Captain, would you please read a little slower, so the jury may better understand you."

Elevating his voice, he began again, slowly pronouncing each word as if it were ten syllables, and he was speaking to a group of people for whom English was their second language.

"The Coast Guard report states: 'there is no actionable evidence of . . . misconduct, incompetence, or negligence.'"

When he finished, I let those redolent words hang in the air for as long as I thought the judge, bearing in mind his present mood, would tolerate before continuing.

"Captain, what you just read is the exact language, word for word, from the official Coast Guard report concerning the loss of the *Aloha*?"

"It is."

"And the report states: 'No misconduct,' is that correct?"

"That is correct."

"And, 'No incompetence?'"

"Correct."

"And, 'No negligence.' Is that correct?"

"That is also correct."

Turning to the judge, "I have nothing further for Captain Seymour," adding an escape hatch for myself, "—at this time, Your Honor."

Captain Seymour's attention instantly switched from me to Blake who was charging the lectern as if he had just been unleashed.

Using the same derisive tone he used in examining Captain Seymour about his qualifications, Blake immediately drew the jury's attention to the captain's weakest link, his limited experience with small craft.

He had Seymour repeat that he no longer owned a boat, seldom been through Bonita Channel, and had no real interest in or knowledge about fishing. Seymour did the best he could to put his limited small craft experience in a favorable light, but the substantial difference between his expertise and Captain Sheppard's concerning small boat handling was being minutely underlined in front of the jury. Each question painted Seymour further and further into a corner, and Blake had a lot more paint to use.

"In fact, most of your work involves the design of large ships?"

"Yes."

The cross-examination turned to when the *Aloha* sailed. Broaching the issue cleverly, Blake asked, "The open ocean begins at the entrance to the Golden Gate out by Point Bonita, correct?"

"Yes."

"It would have been negligent to take the *Aloha* past the protected waters of the Golden Gate after the small craft warning had been broadcast at eight o'clock, isn't that correct?"

"It would have been."

"You are aware of the considerable discrepancies given by the defense about when the *Aloha* sailed . . . first to the Coast Guard on the night of the incident; then a different time was stated in the answers to interrogatories; and still another time was stated by Mrs. Dowd in her deposition; and a still different time here in court?"

The captain took a moment to consider his response.

"It is my understanding from those who most frequently went fishing with Mr. Dowd that they left his house at five o'clock, and it took about an hour to drive to the Sausalito boat harbor. If that is correct, the *Aloha* would have been well past Point Bonita and through the Channel by eight o'clock. Since Mrs. Dowd apparently did not get up with her husband that morning, I don't think she really knows when they left the house that day."

After studying his notes, Blake went to a new topic. "Your principal opinion is that the *Aloha* was capsized by a large wave?"

"That is the most likely cause."

"Your two other theories are not real explanations at all, are they. They're mere possibilities, isn't that correct?"

Without waiting for an answer, Blake pulled out Captain Seymour's deposition.

"In fact, you stated in your deposition that besides being run down by a large ship or sunk by a log, the *Aloha* might have been captured by pirates?"

The jurors looked at Captain Seymour incredulously. Some were sniggering, unable to stifle their laughter.

I shot out of my chair. "Just a minute here, Your Honor. When counsel took Captain Seymour's deposition, he asked him to state every explanation he could think of to account for the loss of the *Aloha*. Counsel has no right to come in here now, when he was the one who asked the captain to speculate on every possible cause, and turn it against him. I will stipulate the *Aloha* was not pirated, and a meteor didn't fall on it either." I was practically shouting with anger.

Before I could blow off more steam, the judge fortuitously intervened.

"Counsel, please state your objection in the proper form."

There was no real objection to a question of this nature, but I sensed if I could come up with anything, the judge would sustain it.

"Your Honor, I request that this misleading and insulting question be withdrawn. Or that the entire series of questions he asked the captain in his deposition be read to the jury so they can see that Captain Seymour was responding to counsel's question, asking him to speculate on every possible explanation, no matter how remote."

This long-winded speech was more ventilation on my part than an objection with any real chance of being sustained.

Before the judge could rule, a calm voice, seemingly from somewhere else, intruded. It took a moment to realize it was Captain Seymour who had spoken.

"If I may, Your Honor, I would like to answer that question."

Without bothering to ask either of us for comment, the judge immediately consented.

Seymour turned to Blake. "I did say that about pirates when you asked me to state every possible cause that might account for the loss of the vessel. Modern day pirates do stop ships in Southeast Asia and the Arabian Sea, but it has never happened here." In a tone that sounded like glass being ground up, he continued, "I thought I made that clear in my deposition."

I knew Captain Seymour well enough to recognize he was at the red line. I didn't know how much more sarcasm he was going to take without erupting. Looking coldly at Blake, he indicated he had not finished his answer.

"As I have previously stated, my belief is there are three possible explanations to account for the loss of the *Aloha*. The most likely cause was that a large wave capsized the boat. The run down and dead head explanations are less likely, but both do occur. I have personal knowledge of a dead head sinking a fishing boat off Half Moon Bay. And the most recent incident involving a large ship running down and sinking a fishing boat occurred just a few months ago when an oil tanker named the *Golden Gate* ran down a fishing boat called the *Jack Jr.*"

Changing topics quickly, Blake asked, "Do you agree it would have been improper to take the *Aloha* through Bonita Channel if large breaking waves were present?"

"If Mr. Dowd had seen a significant number of large breaking waves, it would have been improper to enter the Channel." Before Blake could cut him off, Seymour added, "But based on what I know about the level of Mr. Dowd's skills and his experience, I do not believe he would do that. I might add this is also the opinion of the Coast Guard." He calmly picked up the report, and for the second time read to the jury. "There is no evidence of . . . incompetence or negligence."

In the few moments we had at the end of the break, I told Captain Seymour when he was undergoing cross-examination to use the Coast Guard report to reinforce his opinions every chance he got. He was doing so now, not as a club as I had suggested, but more like a scalpel, cutting Blake's cross-examination to bits.

Blake continued, probing for holes in Captain Seymour's direct testimony to exploit.

"If the *Aloha* left Sausalito as you suggest at six o'clock, and arrived at Point Bonita thirty to forty-five minutes later, then the fifteen other boats that left at the same approximate time would have been at Point Bonita at the same time as the *Aloha*, isn't that true?"

It was a highly probative question, and the jury leaned forward to take in his response.

"If the other boats maintained the same course and speed, they would arrive within that same broad time frame."

"Captain Seymour, despite all the publicity and the considerable efforts made by the Coast Guard and others to locate witnesses, are you aware of the fact that not one person has come forward stating they saw the *Aloha* that day?"

He replied: "Several points come to mind. It was still dark out, and the fishing boats do not go out as a flotilla. Each boat has different design characteristics and engine capacities which affects their speed through the water. It is also prudent for a mariner to keep a safe distance from other craft in the event another boat makes a sudden change in speed or course." Blake was not easily put off his point, and immediately followed up. "From Sausalito to the Golden Gate Bridge is a distance of three miles, and takes fifteen minutes, yet no one saw the *Aloha*. From Golden Gate Bridge all the way to Point Bonita is an additional three miles in tightly confined waters, and again no one observed the *Aloha*. Doesn't it seem odd to you, in all that time and all that distance, no one on any of the other boats saw the *Aloha*?"

It was a tightly framed question giving him little running room with his response. But Captain Seymour was getting his second wind, his confidence returning. He began responding almost as soon as Blake stopped speaking.

"A boat operator must of course stay aware of the other vessels in his general area, but he cannot focus on them exclusively. He has a number of additional operational things to do as well: besides the other boats, he must observe the sea conditions around him, maintain a safe distance from the headlands, and keep track of the buoys, lights, and other navigation aids. It is very much like driving a car. A driver has to know where he is going, and stay alert to the traffic conditions around his vehicle, but he must keep his primary attention focused on the conditions ahead of him that may become hazards if he is not paying attention." He picked up the Coast Guard report. Taking his glance from Blake, he turned to the jury. For the third time he read that no finding had been made of inattention or negligence on Dowd's part.

There was a brief whispered conversation between Blake and Baum, before Blake said his examination was concluded.

The judge looked inquiringly at me. I stood. "Nothing further, Your

Honor." Turning toward the witness stand, the judge said, "You are excused."

After placing the files back in his briefcase, Captain Seymour made for the door. His head up, shoulders squared back, no longer the look of a humiliated, defeated man.

The thought of working in the claustrophobic room down the hallway prompted me to ask the clerk whether I could stay in the courtroom over the noon break to work. She agreed. Before starting, I took a moment to reflect on the morning session. The tumult surrounding Captain Seymour had been so hostile it was hard to know what interpretation the jurors made of his testimony. There was no time for parsing his testimony now. I had work to do, and began sorting through my notes about our final witness, Rae Strange.

The first document in my binder was the "Graveyard of Ships" news story. Scanning it quickly, I noted the considerable attention given to the event that occurred one year before the *Aloha* incident, when a big wave swept three men off the stern of a fishing boat that had been steered too close to the edge of the Channel. The article speculated that the *Aloha* might have done the same thing. I was concerned that plaintiffs' team had seen this article too. If so, they could not have missed the similarities between the two incidents. The potential negligence of taking a boat too close to the edge of Bonita Channel had not been raised during Blake's cross-examination of Captain Seymour, but that did not mean the issue was dead.

Strange's greater knowledge of wave formation made it possible to raise the issue through him when he was cross-examined; and it was far from a trivial liability question. The applicable law was quite clear: a person engaging in any activity has a duty to act with care, and that duty includes making reasonable efforts to learn of the dangers involved and take steps to avoid them. Lack of awareness of a specific danger is not a defense. Sailing close to the edge of Bonita Channel looks safe, and no warning is stated on the charts not to do it, but the danger of doing so was a risk well known to the party boat captains. The judge would instruct the jury that the question of Dowd's negligence was not limited just to the dangers he was aware of, but the dangers he should have known about as well. 'Ignorance of the law is no excuse.'

The sound of voices intruded into the courtroom. I turned around to look at the spectator area, it was empty. I then noticed the door leading to the jury room was slightly ajar; the voices were coming from there. Some of the jurors must have remained over the noon recess. A few moments later, the voices became loud enough to recognize: it was Baum and Blake. They were speaking about the Coast Guard report. Blake was adamant about the point he argued to the judge that the report had been mistakenly admitted into evidence.

Their conversation seemed as if it would continue, and I felt I should announce my presence. They had probably gone into the back hallway leading to the jury room to speak privately, unaware I had stayed in the courtroom.

As I was getting up, Baum spoke, "Forget about the ruling. If it was a mistake, we made a record and can deal with it later."

I was about to head for the door when Baum spoke again, "Don't focus on anything else except this next witness," he continued, his voice filled with confidence, ". . . don't worry about it, we're way ahead."

Just then the door opened and they entered the courtroom. I sat down, and bent my head over the file. They put their trial books away and walked out together without speaking. In the silence, Baum's confident words drummed in my ears. It took a few minutes of determined effort, forcing myself to concentrate on the outline.

# 25

I asked Strange to be at the courthouse at one-fifteen. When the time came, I went to the hallway to see whether he had arrived. He was seated on one of the benches reading his file. I beckoned him to come in. He stood and began walking toward me. At first I was uncertain what I was seeing. By the time he got to the door, I was so distracted I did not at first notice his outstretched hand. To my astonishment, he was wearing a green polyester suit with thin white stripes. The suit, and his tie as well, had gone out of style generations earlier. The night before when we met in my office, he was dressed in slacks and a handsome tweed jacket. On every other occasion he had been similarly well attired. His hotel was out by the airport, and there was no time to send him back for the tweed outfit. With considerable effort, I forced myself to stop gaping.

As he passed in front of me, I gave his suit one more look. In the harsh glare of the courtroom's fluorescent lighting, the polyester was shining. To put a positive spin on the situation, I told myself: showing up for court looking like this, the jury will have to think: 'this guy has to be for real.'

We sat at my table and reviewed what I would be asking him on direct, and areas where he should be on alert during cross-examination. I told him Blake was going to be concentrating on two things: the size of the breaking waves and their location.

The judge resumed the bench, directing me to call my next witness. Strange came forward for the oath and took the stand.

When he was settled, I asked, "Please give your name for the record."

"Ralph Rae Strange," and added that he went by his middle name, Rae, which he pronounced Ray. His credentials were next.

In our final preparation session the night before, I said I would ask him to give the jury a thorough exposition of his education, training and experience to help them evaluate his testimony. He initially balked when I told him I would in essence be asking him to catalog his résumé. It took some doing to convince him that this part of his testimony was not a time for modesty.

"Mr. Strange, would you please give the jury your educational background?"

"I graduated from the University of California at Berkeley, in geology."

"Do you have any postgraduate education?"

"After graduating from Cal, I joined the Navy for three years, and was sent to the Naval Post Graduate School in Monterey."

"Please elaborate on the focus of your studies at the Navy postgraduate school."

"A number of years ago, the Navy set a high priority on accurate weather forecasting and knowledge about the tides. They established a special degree program to train officers in meteorology and oceanographics."

"Your selection by the Navy to receive this highly specialized training must have been quite an honor?"

We had not gone over this question, and he began a fumbled attempt to answer, finally saying he didn't know how to respond.

"Mr. Strange, I know you are trying to be modest, but to do their jobs properly, the jury has to compare your training and experience with the other experts who have testified."

He finally managed to get out, "I did feel quite honored to be asked to attend the school."

I turned the questioning to his work experience after his discharge from the Navy. More at ease with this line of questions, he turned toward the jury, mentioning he had been an operations analyst at the Stanford Research Institute for three years. The excellent reputation of Stanford's research institute was well known to many of the jurors who nodded their recognition.

After that, he had worked as the chief meteorologist and director of forecasting for several firms which provided specialized forecasting services to businesses with a need for long term weather forecasting, such as large construction companies, utilities, and industries that relied on agricultural commodities.

"What is your present position?"

"Ten years ago, I founded my own firm, Pacific Weather Analysis, Inc."

"Please explain to the jurors what your field of expertise is."

"I am a marine meteorologist and oceanographer."

"What services does your firm provide, and tell us a little bit about your clientele and the type of work you do for them?"

"We provide short and long term weather forecasting as well as coastal engineering services. One of our specialties is to determine the effect of waves on various structures built in the water. A client might be planning to dredge a harbor and need data on wave patterns, currents, and tides. Other clients are large contractors building breakwaters and piers who need similar information. One job I did involved preparing an in-depth analysis of what effect the waves and currents would have on the cooling outfalls of a proposed power plant."

Every time I met with Strange in my office, he seemed relaxed and composed. Now, he was continuously pulling on his tie and shifting around in his chair. He was plainly nervous, and becoming more so. I had no idea what was making him so ill at ease, and I was fast running out of 'comfort questions' about his background that ordinarily puts a witness at ease. I hoped the substantive questions about his opinions would distract him from whatever was putting him on edge.

"Mr. Strange, have you formed an opinion on whether the waves existing on the morning of March 9th were capable of capsizing and sinking Mr. Dowd's boat?" I flinched as soon as I finished stating the question, half expecting Baum and Blake to once again jump out of their seats, challenging his credentials the way they had with Captain Seymour. Thankfully, there was silence from behind me.

Strange turned slightly toward the jury. "I have reached certain opinions and conclusions about the loss of the *Aloha*."

"Please outline for the jury what investigations you've made, and describe the documents and other data you analyzed?"

"I referred to the Coast Pilot and other reference works, examined various nautical charts and tide tables, and analyzed the data from all the available wave recording buoys."

"Before getting to your opinions, would you please give us some background information on how waves are created?"

"Waves are formed in only one way—by the wind."

Fully turning toward the jury box, he continued. "There are three important things to know about wave formation: first, the speed of the wind; second, the amount of time the wind blows; and, third is the fetch. The term fetch means the size of the area over which a particular wind system is blowing."

At this point he got up unexpectedly, heading for the blackboard. Picking up the chalk, he wrote: Speed, Time, and Area. He then drew a schematic map of the north Pacific on the blackboard showing the West Coast, the Aleutians, and Hawaii. He stepped back momentarily to critique his art work before returning his attention to the jury.

"This incident occurred on Friday, March 9th, two and a half years ago. Earlier that week, a major weather system had been building 1,500 miles northeast of Hawaii. The peak intensity of the storm system occurred on Wednesday, March 7th, attaining gale force winds. The winds drove the waves created by the storm in an easterly direction toward the California coast. Those waves struck the coastline around San Francisco on March 9th."

This tutorial on wave formation, and the connection between the storm in the Pacific and the waves arriving along the coast on March 9, had been done without a single question from me. Strange, who had no training in teaching techniques, was very effectively utilizing the methodologies of an experienced professor: maintaining eye contact, searching the jurors' faces to make sure his explanations were understandable, and frequent use of the blackboard and charts to illustrate his points. The jury was absorbed.

I put a chart on the easel, and asked him to resume his seat.

"Mr. Strange, what effect did the shallow water around the San Francisco Bar have on the waves coming in that morning?"

"In the deep ocean, the gently rolling shape of a swell is not affected by the bottom hundreds of feet below, but when the depth of the water is less than half the length of a wave, there is an effect."

Once again he was spontaneously out of his seat. At the blackboard he wrote: 2:1, and the words 'length to depth' underneath.

Turning to the jury, he pointed to what he'd written on the board.

"2 to 1 is a formula. For example, let's say a wave one hundred feet in length passes over an area where the water is sixty feet deep; there would be no change in the shape of the swell. But, if that same one hundred foot long wave went over an area where the depth is fifty feet or less, the shape of the wave would begin to change."

Looking directly at the jury he asked rhetorically, "Why would that be so?"

Using the pointer, he tapped the 2 to 1 figures he had written on the blackboard, and said, "When this hypothetical one hundred foot long wave rolls over an area deeper than fifty feet, there will be no change in its shape. But, when it passes over a location fifty feet or less in depth, there would be a change in its shape ... because that wave is then in a 2 to 1 ratio with the bottom." There were nods of understanding from the jury box.

He then pointed to the nautical chart on the easel, and asked the jury to note how quickly the water depth changed from hundreds of feet deep outside the San Francisco Bar, to only twenty-three feet on the Bar itself.

He continued: "A number of things were happening to the waves coming in on the morning of March 9th. As those swells passed over the increasingly shallow area around the Bar, they gradually changed from smooth rollers into waves with more sharply pointed crests, and their speed decreased as well because of friction with the bottom."

He turned to the jury, summarizing, "The following things happened: the waves became more compact, their height increased, and their speed decreased." He paused a moment. "Oh, and one more thing took place that is important to understand . . . the shallow depth of the Bar caused those incoming waves to refract."

Seeing twelve blank faces staring at him from the jury box, a self-effacing smile crossed Strange's face as he quickly added, "Sorry, let me state this a little more simply. The oceanographic term 'wave refraction' simply means that . . . a wave bends."

Other than the engineers on the panel, the rest of the jurors' knowledge of physics was probably limited to a course in high school. Observing that most of the jurors were still not comprehending, he elaborated. "When the swells coming in that morning came in contact with the shallow depths of the Bar, they refracted, or bent, around the Bar like this." He stood quickly, making a 'bear hug' gesture with both arms.

Noticing a look of confusion, he said, "Let me see if this will help."

He stepped down, walking swiftly to the stack of exhibits leaning against the clerk's desk. Leafing through them, he picked out one of Baum's exhibits, a two by three foot blow-up photo of the Marin Headlands. After studying it a moment, he stepped closer to the jury box, pointing to several locations on the photograph where he said wave refraction was taking place. He had me hold the photo up, and together we walked it down the jury box while he pointed and explained to two or three of the jurors at a time.

"Look here and here, do you see where the waves are bending and wrapping around these big exposed rocks?" His arms were flying as he repeated the bear hug gesture.

"The bending of these waves around the obstacles you see in this blow-up is what wave refraction is all about."

During the several minutes it took to do this 'show and tell' for the jury, a connection between what Strange was explaining about wave refraction and a different type of wave that oceanographers refer to as 'waves of coincidence' came together in my head.

There are two times when a lawyer is rendered speechless. One is when he is caught completely by surprise, and the other is when an epiphany of good luck appears out of nowhere. One of them had just occurred, and I wasn't sure which.

In one of our meetings months earlier, Strange briefly mentioned 'wave coincidence.' What he said at the time seemed to have no connection to the case, and I'd forgotten about it until hearing his testimony about waves refracting around the rocks and then coming together behind them. Now, it seemed very relevant to what happened to the *Aloha*.

A wave of excitement swept over me, and just as quickly subsided on the reef of reality. Any questions I asked Strange now about coinciding waves would be in entirely unrehearsed territory. All the work we had done preparing his direct testimony would have to be put aside, and every question I put to him on this unrehearsed topic of 'waves of coincidence' would depend on what his last answer had been. It would be the same as performing a new composition in front of a critical audience without a musical score.

I tried to convince myself if his testimony got too close to the rocks, I could steer him away. Not much of a risk management plan, but something in my head was prodding me . . . 'you can't eliminate all risk in a trial.' If that thought wasn't foolish enough, the inner voice was adding, 'by risking nothing—you risk losing everything.' I told myself this is the sort of logic that appeals to teenagers and others flirting with thoughts of invincibility.

By the time Strange was back in the witness box, I'd decided.

"Mr. Strange, do you have an opinion whether these 'waves of coincidence' you've been telling us about could have formed in Bonita Channel that morning?"

"Yes, they could."

I needed a little foundational testimony before I could go further with this new line of questioning.

"What was the height range of the waves coming in that morning?"

He referred to his summary. "According to the buoy measurements, the height of the top one-third of the incoming waves averaged 11 feet. The top ten percent were 13 feet high. The top one percent averaged 18 feet in height."

I asked him to tell the jury what would happen if two of those waves refracted around the Bar and then met in Bonita Channel while they were in phase. Putting his summary aside, he turned to the jury.

"Let's say two of the eleven foot waves in the top one-third coincided while they were 'in phase,' the combined wave would be approximately 22 feet in height. For scientific accuracy, ten percent is subtracted from that combined figure which would be around two feet, making the newly formed wave approximately 20 feet high."

I asked him to do the calculations for the top ten percent and the top one percent of the waves that morning.

He took a moment and began doing the math out loud.

"The waves in the top ten percent averaged 13 feet. Two times 13 is 26. You then subtract three feet for the ten percent reduction, making the combined wave around 23 feet. The top one percent was 18 feet. Two times 18 is 36. Subtracting four feet for the ten percent reduction would make a 32 foot wave."

I wanted to take a moment to let those figures, which had plainly impacted the jury, sink in, but my fear of objections forced me to move on quickly. I asked, "Since one of these newly created coincident waves is nearly doubled in size, would the power of this new wave be doubled?"

He shook his head emphatically, "No. The energy carried by the new wave is not doubled. It would be nearly quadrupled in its power and destructive force."

This answer was a complete surprise. I had expected him to say there would be a slight increase.

"Mr. Strange, would a breaking wave, 32 feet, 23 feet, or even 20 feet high, have been big enough to capsize and sink a boat the size of the *Aloha?*"

"Any of them could have. Bearing in mind the weight of the water, plus the force generated by breaking waves that size, the capsizing would have been immediate."

The past fifteen minutes of questioning had been entirely in uncharted waters. As tempting as it was to go on, the risk of asking a land mine question was too great. I decided to quit on the power of his last answer.

"Nothing further, Your Honor."

Baum and Blake were whispering intensely, and asked for a moment which the judge granted. Strange shifted nervously in the witness box, waiting for cross-examination to begin. When Blake was ready, he moved to the lectern.

"Did you consider the tidal conditions for March 9th?"

"Yes, I did."

"What was the state of the tide at six o'clock, March 9th?"

Strange said he didn't know without looking, and began rummaging through his files strewn on the desk top. After a good deal of searching, he said, "I don't seem to have the tidal data with me, but I did look it up and considered it . . ." he paused, "and think it was an outgoing tide."

"Do you know what time high tide occurred that morning?"

"No."

"Do you know when low tide was?"

"No."

Blake appeared puzzled—almost certainly an affectation for the jury's benefit.

We were less than two minutes into Strange's cross-examination and Blake was making him look disorganized and flustered. I should have gone through his files with him in the office and made sure everything he based his opinions on was in the files, and in some sort of order. The tenor Blake used in his questions implied this was important data that Strange should have at the tip of his tongue or, at the very least, readily available in his file. Jurors can accept nervous witnesses, but they don't bond well with experts who look unprepared.

Blake moved to a topic that had been a battleground with every other expert: the height and size of breaking waves in Bonita Channel. He began tangentially. "Mr. Strange, can you define the term 'long period waves'?"

"It is a measurement of time, expressed in seconds, for a wave to pass a fixed point."

"A twenty second time period for waves in the San Francisco area is a rare occurrence, is that correct?"

"Yes, it only happens two or three times a year. I examined data from the National Weather Service, and the wind speeds could not have created the long period swells occurring in the San Francisco area that morning. The swells that existed in the early morning hours of March 9th were created by the storm I mentioned earlier, centered northeast of the Hawaiian Islands, not local wind conditions."

Blake then asked, "Would the existence of large swells be an indication of danger to a careful mariner?"

Strange responded from a scientist's viewpoint, rather than a boat operator's perspective.

"With their smooth rolling contour, swells are not a hazard; only breaking waves pose a threat."

"Mr. Strange, wouldn't the presence of large swells be a warning sign to a careful boat operator of potential danger in areas of shallow water?"

Too late, Strange saw the trap that had been laid for him.

"They would be," he replied.

Blake went on quickly. "So, in areas of shallow water, such as around the Bar, the presence of large swells would be an indicator that breaking waves might form, and under those circumstances, a boat operator should avoid those areas, isn't that correct?"

Strange hesitated uncomfortably before answering, "Yes."

Blake paused, letting the jury scrutinize Strange twisting in his chair, before turning his questioning from the general to the specific.

"If there were large swells in Bonita Channel, that would be an indication of danger, wouldn't it?"

"That would depend on the size of the swells."

Blake took my four foot by six foot exhibit which depicted the height of each wave that had been recorded on March 9, and put it just below the witness stand, facing the jury. When it was in place, Blake asked, "Wouldn't the highest of the hundred or so waves listed here have turned into breaking waves?"

Strange was having trouble with the question. As he hesitated, Blake took a black marking pen and in rapid fire order began circling the highest waves, asking Strange, "Couldn't this one have been a breaking wave?" Without waiting for an answer, he added, "Couldn't this one?"

I was on my feet, but not before Blake circled two waves and was starting on the third. Moving fast, I pushed myself between Blake and the board.

Turning to the judge, I began speaking, my anger rising, "Your Honor, this exhibit has been admitted into evidence, and it is improper for counsel to mark it up."

My finger was pointing at Blake who stepped back. I sucked in a breath to get my voice under control before continuing. "I ask that you order counsel not to mar this exhibit. He can either provide a piece of plastic sheeting to cover the exhibit, and mark up the plastic, or get his own exhibit." Blake cut in, to argue his reasons for marking the exhibit. The judge held his hand up, and in a sharp tone said, "All right."

Moving his look to Blake, who was still arguing, the judge said, "Do not mark it." He shifted his weight several times in his chair before ordering Blake to proceed.

The large black circles drawn around the first few high numbers made the handsome exhibit Marsha had spent hours preparing over the weekend look like the victim of a graffiti attack.

The encounter had an effect on Strange who was now sitting stiffly erect in the witness box, waiting for Blake to continue.

"The swells in Bonita Channel that morning were of sufficient size to turn into breaking waves, weren't they?"

There had been extensive testimony on that subject, much of it in conflict. The jury waited attentively, but Strange made no attempt to begin answering. It was as if his mind were elsewhere.

After a prolonged silence, Blake asked in a lowered voice, "Do you not understand the question?" His tone plainly implied that this was not a possibility. Strange remained silent.

As the time continued to drag out, I willed him to respond, to say something—anything—to break the lengthening silence. Doubts about Strange's credibility were going to start imbedding in the jurors' minds if he didn't start speaking immediately, if they hadn't already come to that conclusion.

Looking directly at Blake, he finally said, "I understand your question."

The manner in which Strange spoke did not convey that he really had. Another painful pause ensued before he continued in an apologetic tone. "This is probably my fault for not making my earlier testimony clear, but the trouble I'm having with the question is that your premise is incorrect."

Strange then began explaining to Blake the mistake he was making. "There are only two ways a swell can turn into a breaking wave: either by coming into shallow water, or because of high wind conditions. The wind speed that morning, as recorded by the National Weather Service, was not anywhere near high enough to create large numbers of breaking waves in the Channel. There may have been occasional wind gusts sufficient to create intermittent whitecaps, but not on a massive scale, and not for sustained periods. The only other way a swell can turn into a breaking wave is if the height of a wave is in a 1 to 1.3 ratio to the bottom."

Strange reflected for a moment before continuing. "My statement that breakers were not consistently occurring in Bonita Channel is not a supposition or guesswork on my part. The 1 to 1.3 ratio I mentioned is a law of physics, and the waves that morning, as measured by the recording buoys, simply weren't high enough to turn into breaking waves all across the Channel."

This was an answer Blake had not expected, and he hurriedly moved to another area. In the momentary silence, my relief ballooned.

"Are you aware of the fact that no other boat reported seeing any large solitary waves that morning?"

Strange replied, "I am not aware of that," adding that he was not surprised, and then repeated his previous testimony, "One of the characteristics of coinciding waves is their brief existence. If two waves refracting around the Bar from opposite directions met in the Channel, as I showed happening on the blow up photograph, they would form into one large wave, break over, and then disappear all in a time frame measured in seconds, not minutes."

This was an excellent answer, but every time Strange gave an extended response, my heart dove into my stomach. He seemed to have completely forgotten my admonition that long answers provided fodder for more, not less, cross-examination. Even though I was sitting at the edge of my chair with a look that must have communicated my anxiety, Strange was either ignoring, or not picking up on my concern. My only relief was that his last few answers were not what Blake had been expecting. If Strange kept reinforcing his answers with the best parts of his direct examination, he would not be in the witness box much longer.

Blake then asked, "The unusually long period waves existing that morning would have allowed breaking waves to occur in the Channel?"

Strange shook his head. "The length of a wave has nothing to do with its height. In order for breakers to be present all across the Channel that morning, the waves would have had to be much higher." He quickly added, "I apologize again for not making my prior testimony clear on two points you are apparently confused about."

Strange began again, speaking slowly and emphatically. "The *profile* of a smooth rolling swell will change when its length comes into a 2 to 1 ratio with the depth to the bottom. However, the factor that causes swells to turn into *breaking waves* is not their length, but their height in relationship to the depth. That is calculated by an entirely different ratio, the 1 to 1.3 formula I mentioned earlier."

He paused. "I might add that when and where swells change from smooth rollers into breaking waves is not based on speculation or assumptions on my part, but the laws of physics."

This was the third time Strange had given a clarifying reminder of his prior testimony and apologized for not making himself clearly understood. This time it evoked a few smiles from the jurors as Blake, once again, had his paper corrected in front of the class by the professor. The only person in the courtroom who seemed to be unaware that Blake might have an agenda in mind with his cross-examination questions, other than discussing the application of the laws of physics, was Strange.

The questioning turned to the size and shape of the waves in the Channel.

"Isn't it true that in order to combine, two coinciding waves have to be the same size, speed and height, and be in phase with each other as well?"

Strange shook his head. "No. If that were the criteria, coinciding waves would never happen. The reason is because no two waves are ever exactly alike. The only place exact duplication takes place is in the controlled conditions of a wave tank in a laboratory. In nature, all that is required is for close approximation of a wave's size, shape and speed, and that their tops be approximately in phase. When that occurs, the two waves can coincide, turning into one wave nearly doubled in size. No boat the size of the *Aloha* could withstand the destructive force of a wave nearly 20 feet high collapsing down on it."

In the silence, you could practically hear the roar of water smashing open the door, instantly flooding the cabin, sending the *Aloha* to the bottom.

There was an extended whispered conference. During Blake's cross-examination, Baum had been taking notes which they were now discussing. Blake finally lifted his head, saying he had nothing further. The judge turned to me.

While they had been conferring, I looked at the notes I'd made of Blake's cross-examination which, for the most part, consisted of a few barely legible scribbles. I never take my eyes off a witness long enough to take elaborate notes, and this applied doubly with Strange. Every time he answered with anything more than 'yes' or 'no,' which was frequent, a visceral reaction of dread clutched me. At one point or another during Blake's cross-examination, Strange had managed to break, disregard, or ignore every bit of advice I'd given him despite hours of drilling in our preparation sessions. Any further questions I put to Strange would only provide additional opportunities for Blake to cross-examine him about, and I wasn't sure my nervous system could take the stress. I stood hastily.

"Nothing further, Your Honor."

The judge turned to Strange and excused him. A visible wave of relief washed over his face as he began stuffing the scattered papers into his briefcase. Looking up, he thanked the judge, and with a deep nod bade farewell to the jury. I was waiting for him in the well. He gave me a damp hand to shake, mumbled something about catching a plane, and without further delay made for the door.

As the door began closing behind him, the release of tension in the courtroom was palpable.

The judge asked whether I had further witnesses.

"The defense rests, Your Honor."

Judge Leahy turned to Baum and Blake. "Do you have any rebuttal witnesses?"

There was no immediate response to the judge's question as they conferred.

There was a click at the back of the courtroom. My head snapped around, half expecting to see Officer Dennis George, resplendent in his dress blue uniform, stepping through the doorway, ready to modify the opinions he'd stated in his report which had caused such an uproar.

No one was there. The door had not fully closed behind Strange, belatedly clicking shut.

Baum finally spoke. "No rebuttal, Your Honor."

The judge turned to the jury, informing them that all the evidence in the case had been presented. The next day would be final arguments from me and Baum, and then he would instruct them on the law they were to apply. They would then begin their deliberations.

Looking at them very somberly, the judge concluded, "Even though the evidence phase of the case is completed, the admonition I have given you remains in effect. Do not discuss the case with anyone, or allow anyone to discuss it with you. Do not conduct independent research on any aspect of the case. Go home, put the trial out of your minds, and assemble in the jury room tomorrow morning at 9:30." He then wished them "good evening," and they filed out of the courtroom.

Our work, however, was not over.

It is the duty of the trial court judge to determine what instructions a jury receives on the law they are to apply. Before deciding, the judges confer with the attorneys from both sides, seeking their input on which instructions are applicable to the case. Judge Leahy had previously ordered us to submit a list of the instructions we wanted him to give the jury. For the most part, our requests were undisputed boiler plate matters the judge would read directly from the Book of Approved Jury Instructions.

Judge Leahy had us come into chambers, and we spent the better part of an hour going through the instructions he would give in the morning. Baum had one additional instruction he wanted read to the jury concerning the doctrine of Res Ipsa Loquitur. It was a critically important one that Baum was determined to have, and I was equally opposed. There was going to be a lot of argument on it from both of us. The judge was tired and deferred argument on this pivotal matter until the morning.

He informed us closing arguments would begin at nine-thirty, and each side would have a maximum of one hour.

# 26

Marsha made an effort to discuss things not related to the case while we ate our salmon supper. Afterwards, she opened the leaves of the dining room table to accommodate all my files.

I made a rule not to work past midnight during a trial, but that did not apply to preparing my final argument. I would not go to sleep until I felt satisfied that I had the outline of what I was going to say to the jury committed to memory; not the exact words, but the essence of what I would say to them. Juries won't stand for canned speeches.

Because of the unexpected twist in Rae Strange's testimony, the outline I gave the jury in my opening statement about what the evidence would be had little application now. They'd had three weeks of food for thought; now I had to chop it into digestible pieces.

It was close to eleven o'clock before I had a gut sense of what I would say to the jury in the morning, trying to convince them that Francis Dowd was not careless or negligent. I wanted to continue refining my outline, but I had to prepare my opposition to the Res Ipsa instruction Baum so badly wanted Judge Leahy to give the jury. Rolls of parchment and reams of paper had been expended writing on the legal issues behind this instruction. It was going to be a long night.

Roughly translated, the Latin phrase Res Ipsa Loquitur means 'the thing speaks for itself.' The instruction was based on an English case, Byrne v. Boadle. Despite being over a century old, the basic holding in Byrne was still followed in California. If the judge gave this instruction, it would be a real problem.

I remembered Byrne v. Boadle from law school. The manner in which the case came up for discussion in our torts class made it quite memorable. Professor Jones called on one of us to give the facts of the case. Before the selected student could begin, someone in the back started murmuring a familiar tune. In a few moments, the entire class was loudly chorusing: 'Roll out the barrel, we'll have a barrel of fun. Roll out the barrel, we'll put the blues on the run.'

The professor grinned, nodding his head to the tune. After the howls of laughter subsided, he turned to the student, and somehow managing to keep a straight face said, "I believe you were giving us the facts in Byrne v. Boadle."

The basic facts were: Mr. Byrne, the plaintiff, was walking down a street in London in 1863 and was injured when a barrel of flour rolled out of the second story of a warehouse owned by a merchant named Boadle. The plaintiff sued the merchant for his injuries and lost. The trial court judge ruled: since the plaintiff had not put on any direct evidence demonstrating that the flour merchant had been negligent, the judge held that the merchant could not be held at fault.

Byrne appealed. The English court of appeals reversed the trial court's ruling, stating that a barrel does not fly out of a window without someone being negligent, noting that the barrel was entirely in the hands of the merchant. In the court's decision, the Latin phrase Res Ipsa Loquitur, 'the thing speaks for itself,' was used for the first time.

The holding became the foundation of a new legal doctrine applicable in situations like our case where a party who has been harmed is unable to offer direct evidence of what happened, but there is evidence that at the time of the accident the object causing the injury was in the hands of the defendant. If those two conditions are shown, the defendant then has to come forward with proof that he was not negligent in handling the object.

If Judge Leahy decided to give the Res Ipsa instruction, the jury would be allowed to infer Dowd had been negligent if they found the sinking of the *Aloha* was the type of incident that does not happen in the absence of someone's negligence.

Awakening at six, I ran around the park before sunrise. Despite the accumulated pressure of three weeks in trial and not putting my work aside until one o'clock, the run refreshed me. After breakfast, Marsha walked with me downstairs to the garage. She was doing some investigation work with a tight deadline for another firm, but promised to be there for my closing argument.

Squeezing my hand, she said, "I know you'll do well," and leaned through the car window kissing me goodbye.

I arrived at nine. The clerk told us the judge would see us shortly, and in a few minutes we were summoned into chambers.

The judge was aware Baum fervently wanted the instruction, and I was just as firmly opposed. He also knew that no matter how he ruled, this was the only instruction with any real risk that his ruling might be reversed on appeal if he did not make a careful record.

Baum spoke first with a well-organized and persuasive argument that Res Ipsa applied to the facts in this case and should be given, repeatedly reminding the judge that none of the other boats out that day had been lost.

Judge Leahy tilted his head back, pondering Baum's argument. He then nodded for me to begin. I put my notes aside. "One of the requirements that must exist before the Res Ipsa instruction can be given is plaintiffs must show that the instrumentality causing the injury is in the 'exclusive control' of the defendant. Our expert, Captain Seymour, testified about three explanations to account for the loss of the *Aloha*: a run down, dead heads, or a big wave. . . ."

With little attempt at masking his impatience, the judge cut in. "You're not really suggesting the *Aloha* was sunk by a dead head are you?" Before I could continue, the judge commenced answering his own question. "Your own expert said this virtually never happens, and there's no evidence of a run down occurring that morning either." His voice, face, and tone left no room for misinterpretation that he found either theory plausible.

"Your Honor, I rank the likelihood of these three possibilities occurring the same way the experts did. The most likely cause being a large breaking wave; second would be a run down; and a dead head third. But no matter how they are ranked, all three of our theories underline plaintiffs' shortfall in meeting the key requirement for giving Res Ipsa, which is that the defendant must have 'exclusive control' of the element causing the harm before the instruction can be given. No one would seriously argue Mr. Dowd had control over a wave or a dead head, but it is the run down theory that most clearly demonstrates plaintiffs' failure to meet the 'exclusive control' requirement."

The judge was already shaking his head, once again interjecting himself. "But Captain Going testified small craft are a constant concern, and he always stays alert for them. He had no personal knowledge of a collision with a small boat, and no such incident was reported to him by the captain or the crew."

"That's true, Your Honor, but Captain Going also testified that he knew about the run down involving the *Jack Jr.*, and that the Coast Guard interviewed everyone on the oil tanker and no one said they saw, heard, or felt the impact when it ran down the *Jack Jr.*, with the loss of three lives."

The judge asked if we had any further argument. We did not.

This was a precarious ruling for Judge Leahy, and he listened to our arguments with the same level of attention a concert master would use when trying to differentiate between sharps and flats.

He knew the likelihood of a run down or a dead head was remote, but Captain Seymour testified they were not hypothetical events either. The recent tragedy involving the sinking of the *Jack Jr.* gave grim witness to the fact that run downs can occur without the knowledge of the officers and crew of a big ship.

We waited in silence. Any attempt to speak would have been an unwise intrusion into his thought process. When he finished, he tipped his chair forward. "Submitted, gentlemen?"

"Yes," we murmured.

He took considerable time before speaking. "I am not going to give this instruction."

A rush of relief swept over me. The instruction would have been a huge obstacle to overcome in closing argument. In the absence of direct evidence about what happened to the *Aloha*, the Res Ipsa instruction would have given the jury carte blanche to infer that Francis Dowd was at fault. Infer is a very malleable word the jury could twist into covering almost anything if they chose to do so.

The judge announced he would take a short break, and then bring the jury in for our closing arguments.

I had been on tenterhooks for three weeks fearing that at some point the *Marine Sulphur Queen* case would be cited to the judge by Baum and Blake. The factual similarity of both vessels disappearing with no survivors or witnesses would have made an argument that the rule in that case applied to the *Aloha* very persuasive. It would also have set a precedent in having the Federal rule apply to California cases.

I was equally relieved when no request was made for a Negligence Per Se instruction which would have allowed the jury to infer that Francis Dowd was negligent if they found one of the statutes regarding safe navigation or safety equipment had been violated.

In a few minutes, the hundreds of hours spent over the past two years on discovery—and three weeks in trial—would all come down to less than an hour of closing arguments.

As I took my seat at the table, I noticed Janet sitting as she had throughout the trial, gripping her emotions with the same rigidity that she now was doing with her hands, clutching the armrests of her chair. With so much at stake for her personally, the passions coursing through her must have had a heartbeat of their own.

As the jury filed in, the clerk rose, addressing the filled courtroom. "All rise, Department Six of the Superior Court of the State of California is now in session, the Honorable David Leahy, judge presiding."

The judge entered quickly. After glancing at the jury box and counsel tables, assuring himself everyone was present, he began. "Ladies and Gentlemen, the lawyers for each side will shortly be giving their final arguments for your consideration. First, I am going to give you some preliminary instructions on the law that you will be applying in this case. After their arguments, I will give you further instructions."

Keeping his voice well elevated so the jury could hear without straining, Judge Leahy began in a richer, fuller tone than he had used previously, lending a compelling sense of importance to the instructions on the law they were to apply.

When he finished, he looked at Baum. "We will hear from plaintiffs first."

Baum walked toward the well of the courtroom in an unhurried manner, standing to the side of the lectern to directly face his audience in the jury box.

"May it please the court, counsel, and Ladies and Gentlemen of the jury. Mrs. Ang has asked me to thank you on behalf of herself and her children for your attentiveness throughout the trial."

Adopting a more somber tone, he continued. "I would like to remind you of the comments I made in my opening remarks concerning what the evidence would show, and that the facts would support a verdict in favor of Mrs. Ang and her children at the end of the trial."

He moved his eyes slowly around the jury box. "I regard those statements as promises made to you." Gravely, he added, "And I believe I have fulfilled those promises.

"The evidence we presented overwhelmingly supports a finding in favor of the Angs, and I would like to review that evidence with you now."

Baum then paused as if he were groping for his next words. It was way past the point where he would have been uncertain about what he was going to say. It was effective theatre, heightening the jury's attention.

Looking up, he continued. "Before I begin, I want to make one point clear: there is no evidence from either side, nor do I personally believe, that Francis Dowd was anything other than a fine man. He was an important executive of a large corporation who accomplished much in his lifetime. But you know from your own experience in life that good people sometimes make mistakes; and even the best intentioned among us can have momentary lapses in judgment." Very adroitly, Baum was providing a non-condemnatory way for the jury to find Francis Dowd had been negligent without putting them in a position where they would have to be reproving about doing so. In the jury box heads were nodding.

Speaking in a firm tone, refocusing their attention, he said, "I would like to review the important facts with you. They are quite simple really, and for the most part uncontested. Of all the evidence presented, the one fact that has been most conclusively proven is this: fifteen or more boats went out that day, and every one of them came back safely, all except one, the *Aloha*. Here is another fact which remains uncontroverted: no other boat reported encountering the huge wave the defense offers as an explanation for the loss of the *Aloha*. Not only did no other boat encounter any such wave, not one single person on those fifteen boats reported even seeing a wave which the defense claims was thirty feet high.

"Ladies and Gentlemen, the only explanation supported by all the evidence to account for the loss of the boat is this: the *Aloha* was capsized while attempting to go through Bonita Channel when it was unsafe to do so."

Baum resumed his normal speaking voice. "Captain McGee, a man of thirty years' experience, looked up Bonita Channel, saw waves breaking all the way across, and recognized it would be unsafe to attempt going through. He immediately turned his boat around and went out safely through the Main Channel."

He looked at each juror carefully. "There is something else about Captain McGee I would ask you to remember: he brought his log book with him when he came to court."

Pausing to add emphasis, he continued. "I'm sure you recall his testimony that the three or four boats ahead of Captain McGee, and the same number coming behind, did the same thing. They all turned around and went safely to Duxbury, going out through the Main Channel.

"It is also uncontroverted that no other boat reported seeing any distress flares shot up, nor were there any calls for help on the two-way radios which all the boats monitor. If the *Aloha* left at six o'clock, the same time as the other fishermen, Mr. Dowd would have seen the danger which was so obvious to Captain McGee and the others, and safely followed them out through the Main Channel, wouldn't he?"

He moved his glance over the jury box. "Since no one on the fifteen or twenty other boats reported seeing the *Aloha* that morning, the only logical conclusion to be drawn from this evidence is this: the *Aloha* left much later than the rest of the boats. That's why no one saw him." Baum gave a lengthy pause, underscoring his point.

"Here is another uncontroverted fact. The *Aloha* was burglarized shortly before the incident. The two-way radio, the radio telephone, the flare gun and flares, and the radar set were all stolen. It was initially thought that the replacement radar set had been installed on the *Aloha*, but it was subsequently discovered that it had not been replaced."

He looked at the jury questioningly. "Isn't it just as likely that the radio had not been installed either, or the flare gun and flares? I remind you, no radio message was received from the *Aloha*, and no other boat saw a distress flare shot up that morning."

He turned to one of the most important jury instructions the judge had read. "One of the things you will be doing in the jury room is to weigh the qualifications and experience of the expert witnesses you have heard testify. Our boat handling expert, Captain Peter Sheppard, does not have a degree in engineering or naval architecture, and he has not been the captain of a big ship, but this case isn't about designing big cargo ships, or sailing them around the world, is it? They are not issues in this case. What this case *is* about is the safe navigation and handling of small craft which Captain Sheppard has done exclusively. For the past ten years, he has operated hundreds of power boats, delivering them up and down the Pacific Coast, even to Hawaii. He is thoroughly familiar with the waters off the Golden Gate from the perspective of a small boat operator, and safely navigated small boats through Bonita Channel many times.

"Captain Sheppard stated unequivocally that taking a boat the size of the *Aloha* through Bonita Channel, when waves were breaking across it, was unsafe and should not have been attempted. He testified the prudent thing to have done was go out Main Channel like Captain McGee and the fifteen other boats. And, under no circumstances, should an attempt have been made to go through Bonita Channel."

In the last few minutes, the cool composure Baum had displayed from the first day of trial metamorphosed into a harder edge.

"Ladies and Gentlemen, all the defense witnesses lied," he said, looking at the panel sharply.

This was too much. I angrily jumped out of my chair demanding that he apologize to Mrs. Dowd. Before the judge could intervene, Baum quickly amended his remark, "Except Mrs. Dowd." He then added, "The defense experts lied when they said they knew what happened to the *Aloha*, when all they were really doing was reciting their so-called theories."

He moved swiftly to a different topic. "I'm sure Rae Strange is an experienced oceanographer, but the focus of his experience is down where he lives in Santa Barbara, not up here in the Bay Area where our wave expert Scott Noble lives and works. Can there be any doubt in your minds as to which of them is more knowledgeable about the winds, waves, currents, and the other conditions unique to the Bay Area?"

He turned to the theories I'd offered about how the *Aloha* went down. I stirred uneasily. "First, the defense claims a big wave came out of nowhere—which I remind you no one else saw. Next was the theory that the *Aloha* had been run down by a large ship, and no one saw that either. Finally, the defense offered the most implausible explanation of all: a piece of wood came floating along and, in some unexplained way, pierced the *Aloha's* hull, causing it to sink so suddenly that no one was able to don a life jacket, send up a flare, or make a radio call for help, assuming that flares, a radio, or life jackets were even onboard."

Shaking his head, "No, Ladies and Gentlemen, you will recognize these so-called theories for what they are, mere possibilities completely unsupported by any credible evidence. Nothing more than red herrings designed to distract you from the only logical explanation which does account for the loss of the *Aloha*: the boat sank because Mr. Dowd tried to go through Bonita Channel when it was unsafe to do so."

Gesturing in my direction, he went on. "If a wave as tall as a three-story building, which defense counsel wants you to believe, actually occurred, surely someone would have seen this huge wave and reported it. Is it credible to believe if such a wave actually existed, and Mr. Dowd left at the same time as the other boats, wouldn't someone on one of the other boats have seen this enormous wave too?"

Baum shook his head. "This big wave theory is just another speculation, and like the run-down, and dead head theories ... completely unsupported by the evidence. None.

"What did happen is what Captain McGee observed with his own eyes, not some theory by a meteorologist from Santa Barbara who wasn't there and knows nothing about the local conditions. Captain McGee saw large waves breaking all the way across Bonita Channel, and he changed course and went out Main Channel to Duxbury. The boats in front of him, and the boats coming behind him, saw those same dangerous conditions and did the same thing."

Baum's voice fell, vividly underlining his point like a brush stroke. "And every one of them ... came back ... alive."

This was Baum's second or third reminder that the *Aloha* was the only boat lost, and from the jurors' faces his argument seemed to be tipping Lady Justice's scales in plaintiffs' direction.

Smoothly switching to a persuasive voice, Baum turned to the subject of damages. He recited the testimony about Andy Ang's humble beginnings in China, his immigration to the Philippines where he arrived with virtually nothing, and by hard work and determination gained an education and developed a successful business. Baum mentioned the amount of lost income that would have been received under the new contract Andy signed with Raytheon. The contemplative look on the jurors' faces indicated that Baum's understated presentation of the Ang family's monetary loss was getting through to them.

Moving to the present tense, he turned to the intangible losses Mrs. Ang and her five children had already suffered, and would bear in the future by the loss of care, comfort and society from Andy Ang's death. He said the judge would instruct them that under the law they should award reasonable compensation to Mrs. Ang and her children for the loss of a loving husband and father; strongly hinting that a sum equal to the amount of lost income would be appropriate. I noted the women on the jury, particularly those Mrs. Ang's age, were listening in rapt attention to every word.

Returning to the jury instructions, he refreshed their memory as to what the judge had instructed them. "Under the law, negligent conduct is defined as the failure to do something that a reasonably prudent person would do. In this case, the overwhelming flow of evidence points to only one conclusion. For whatever reason, Francis Dowd took the *Aloha* into Bonita Channel when it was not safe, with the tragic loss of everyone onboard. No matter how hard the defense tries to do so, one fact cannot be refuted: fifteen boats went out that morning and every one of them came back safely; all except one. Due to some momentary lapse in judgment, Ladies and Gentlemen, the *Aloha* did not return."

He thanked the jury and nodded to the judge.

On the surface, Baum's summation appealed to the jurors' sense of reason and logic; the emotional element of his argument was so subtly interwoven they were probably unaware. It was the work of a master dramatist.

'The facts speak for themselves' may have validity elsewhere, but not in a trial. During closing arguments it is the lawyers who speak for the facts, using all their powers of persuasion to convince the jurors that their interpretation of the evidence is correct. But to be effective, a jury must believe that what they are being told is the truth. The more a jury trusts they are being guided toward the right path, the more likely they are to take it. Watching their faces, it seemed Baum had given them reason to do so. It was one of the best closing arguments I had ever heard, and under the rules he was going to be allowed a rebuttal argument when I finished . . . a second chance to persuade them.

The judge declared a short break and left the bench. My nerves were ratcheted so tautly, it took an effort to concentrate on the notes I'd made of a few points Baum had raised. Failing to respond to them would be interpreted by the jury as an admission they were correct. When I finished, I glanced at the spectator area. I was pleased to see that Marsha had come in, sitting at the back.

The clerk walked over, asking if I was ready. I nodded. As the judge headed for the bench, Janet looked at me. Nothing moved on her face, but her eyes exuded a warmth that heartened me.

When the judge was settled, he looked toward me. "We will now hear from the defense."

Walking toward the lectern, I gave myself a final reminder to stay in check.

Thanking the judge, I nodded to Baum and Blake and turned to face the jury box. "Members of the jury, you have heard testimony from sixteen witnesses these past three weeks. A considerable part of the testimony was technical in nature, and not always easy to follow. Mrs. Dowd has asked me to thank you for your close attention to the evidence.

"I know you do not have an easy task ahead of you, but after weighing all the evidence, I feel you will come to the conclusion that a large wave suddenly struck the *Aloha*, causing it to capsize and immediately sink."

I began my review of the evidence. "You've heard a lot of testimony about the time the *Aloha* sailed. Rodney Thiessen and Karen Burns, two witnesses with no connection to any of the parties, unequivocally established that the *Aloha* left the marina at six o'clock."

There was a lot more to argue on this point, but I wanted to get off the time issue as quickly as possible. Every word I said would only add more bricks to the foundation Baum was building for two of the strongest parts of his argument: if Dowd left at the same time as the fifteen other boats, how can it be true that no one saw the *Aloha* . . . and how is it possible that none of the other boats encountered the big wave we claimed had arisen? The brevity of my argument about when the *Aloha* left the marina wasn't giving the Emperor a lot of clothes, but if Thiessen and Burns hadn't convinced them Dowd left the dock at six o'clock, nothing I could say would. I moved to our three explanations.

From this point forward my arguments would be free-form, carried by their own momentum, letting the jurors' faces tell me if I was getting through to them. I gave a final glance at my outline on the lectern and moved into the well of the court to directly face the jury. For the next thirty minutes I would be swinging from one point to the next with no safety net.

"Ladies and Gentlemen, Captain Seymour discussed three theories with you that might account for the loss of the *Aloha.* The least likely explanation was striking a dead head. He stated they are rare, but it is inaccurate to say incidents involving dead heads never happen. On your visits to the local beaches, you've seen large stumps with sharp points which are very capable of piercing the hull of a fishing boat."

I quickly turned to the run down theory. "You recall the extensive cross-examination of Captain Seymour about the run-down issue, with the implication by plaintiffs' counsel in every question that the run down theory was a red herring that didn't happen . . . despite the fact that the most recent event in the long history of incidents involving big ships running down fishing boats occurred just six months ago, and all three men onboard that fishing boat, the *Jack Jr.*, lost their lives. I wonder if the widows of those three men consider a run down, which cost their husbands their lives, just 'a mere possibility' as counsel so dismissively referred to that incident."

I made my commentary on the run down and dead head theories as brief as possible. What I really wanted to do was apologize to the jury for making them sit through endless testimony on dead heads and run downs when my main purpose was to keep Judge Leahy from giving the Res Ipsa Loquitor jury instruction Baum wanted badly.

"Counsel raised the issue of Captain Seymour's credentials, and I feel it's necessary to respond. I called the captain for one reason: he is the most well rounded person I know concerning maritime matters. You heard his testimony about learning to handle a small boat from his father. Later on, after winning an appointment to the United States Maritime Academy, he received intensive training in small boat handling. Do you recall that I practically had to drag out of him something I learned, not from him, but someone else, that at age twenty-three he was the youngest man ever to receive a captain's license in the U.S. Merchant Marine, I believe it says a great deal about his intelligence and his capabilities to have successfully handled that responsibility when many men his age were still in school."

I moved to within a few feet of plaintiffs' table, pointing to Blake. "If counsel felt Captain Seymour's opinions were incorrect, or his theories were based on inaccurate information, those are legitimate grounds for cross-examination. But is it acceptable to put him through the demeaning experience of trying to make it appear Captain Seymour actually believed a gang of pirates abducted the *Aloha,* when he was the one who asked the captain during his deposition to state every possible explanation to account for the loss of the boat. That's not right."

My voice reflected the anger I was inwardly directing at myself for failing to prevent the humiliating examination of Captain Seymour from taking place in front of the jury.

Trying to rein in my emotions, I zeroed in on wave technology. "Of all the science that has been testified about in this case, a 'wave of coincidence' is the easiest scientific principle to understand. All of us understand the meaning of the word 'coincide.' It means coming together at the same time and place, doesn't it?"

I found myself emulating Strange's 'bear hug' gesture as I continued. "He testified the conditions existing that morning would have allowed waves of coincidence to form when two waves, after refracting around the Bar, met in Bonita Channel. He told us that such a newly formed wave would be much larger than the others around it. The new wave would also be very unstable, causing its top to immediately break over with great destructive force. After breaking over, the sea would revert to the same appearance as before. This entire sequence takes place in a matter of seconds, not minutes. In fact, Mr. Strange said a hallmark of these 'waves of coincidence' is their sudden and unpredictable occurrence. This is why no one else saw the wave that struck the *Aloha* in the pre-dawn darkness that morning."

I had one more point to add before going on. "Mr. Strange testified that waves typically come in sets; something you've observed many times at the beach. A group of large waves will come in, followed by a sequence of smaller waves, varying back and forth, which accounts for the different wave conditions observed by Captain Phelan versus what Captain McGee saw. I would like to remind you that Captain McGee testified he left the Sausalito marina at 6:10, whereas Captain Phelan left at 6:00 from San Francisco."

It was time to address the ultimate question the jury would have to determine: was Francis Dowd negligent?

Departing from orthodoxy, I decided to make the focus of my argument not on the testimony of the witnesses I called, but plaintiffs' witnesses.

"Do you recall their expert, Captain Sheppard, agreed that service on a submarine was difficult and exacting duty . . . a place where sound judgment is a prerequisite, and keeping a cool head under stress a necessity? I'm sure you also remember Captain Sheppard agreed that a man given to acting irrationally would not last very long in the submarine corps?" I let this linger a moment.

"When there is so much scientific and technical testimony in a trial, sometimes small but very important points can be overlooked. With that in mind, I would ask you to consider this: Francis Dowd attained the rating of Sonarman first class. A rating of petty officer first class in the Navy is the equivalent of sergeant first class in the Army and Marine Corps. Attaining this rating in one four year enlistment is a remarkable achievement, as anyone who has served in the military will tell you." I made eye contact with the man who had served in the army. He pursed his lips, considering what I said, and nodded slightly.

It occurred to me with no eyewitnesses, and no physical evidence, the jurors would be asking each other endless questions about what happened. The best, although certainly the most unconventional, way to present the remainder of my argument might be to throw rhetorical questions at the jury, and trust them to come up with the right answers. I decided to begin with a subject that was bound to come up during their deliberations: Dowd's boat handling abilities.

"I ask you to reflect for a moment on Dwight Ang's testimony. He told you his father had been fishing on Mr. Dowd's boat on three or four prior occasions, and never said Mr. Dowd handled the boat in a way that made him feel unsafe. Something else Dwight said was that his father never stated Mr. Dowd did any drinking while he was onboard. On that subject, do you recall Janet Dowd's testimony about how responsible he was about drinking and driving? If he had more than one drink, she drove home, and she never had to get after him about it." When a few of the women nodded knowingly, I added, "Isn't it just as likely a safe driver is going to be a safe boat operator?"

For the first time it felt like I'd found my voice, quilting seemingly insignificant bits of testimony that made sense when pieced together. I picked up the pace, turning to Stan Karp's testimony.

"He told you Francis Dowd was a vice president of Raytheon, in charge of their West Coast operations, including the facility here in Mountain View where 1,500 people work." In the same rhetorical tone, I continued. "You are probably asking yourselves: well, so what? What does that have to do with this case? Where's the relevance?" I stopped to make eye contact with each of them. "Ladies and Gentlemen, it's significant for two important reasons. First, Francis Dowd had been with Raytheon ever since he graduated from college, thirty years ago. Doesn't that say something about stability? Secondly, Raytheon is a big company employing tens of thousands of people worldwide. Is it conceivable to you that Francis Dowd would have been promoted to his position of responsibility as a vice president of this large multinational company if he were rash or impulsive?

"There is something else I would ask you to consider. His father had a large family to support. Francis Dowd was determined to get an education, but realized under his family's circumstances he would have to obtain it on his own, which he did with the G.I. Bill, earning his degree in the difficult field of physics. He had no family connections or social position smoothing his path. His record of accomplishment was based entirely on his own merits, further evidence of clear headed thinking and stability."

Standing alone these were not vital facts, but the inferences that could be drawn from them by the jury about Dowd's temperament were critical. They were listening attentively but, just as they had throughout the trial, their reactions, for the most part, remained frustratingly undecipherable. I decided to press the point to evoke some overt response from them . . . not to just hear my words, but feel them.

"When you consider the character traits of Francis Dowd concerning the operation of the *Aloha*—"

Baum jumped to his feet, speaking heatedly. "Objection, objection, Your Honor. Francis Dowd's character is not on trial."

The look on his face stated he had a lot more to say, and was about to continue. Before he could, the judge sustained the objection, ordering me to move on.

While the judge was ruling, a light went on in my head. The ruling was correct. Evidence of a person's character is not admissible to demonstrate what he may have done on a specific occasion. Baum's objection stimulated me to put the semblance of a plan together. When I finished my outline the night before, it was adequate, but something was missing, and I'd been too tired to recognize how effectively Baum, throughout the trial, had employed the hypothesis used by every good scientist: 'the simplest explanation of a problem is invariably the best one.' Now, in closing argument, Baum focused on one simple theme: McGee and fifteen other boats came around Point Bonita, looked up the Channel, had seen big waves, decided it was dangerous to go through and gone out via the Main Channel . . . and they all came back alive.

What I had to do now was change the question from whether or not Dowd entered the Channel when it was unsafe to do so, to a different focus . . . was Francis Dowd the type of man who would do such a thing? I would use another old adage: 'to know what a man might do, you have to know the man.'

It was a good idea with one major shortcoming: to do it I would be on perilously thin ice with the judge. He had just ruled I could not argue Dowd's character to the jury. To get my argument across without drawing another objection I would have to tread cautiously. The judge had sustained Baum's objection without making a production out of it, but if I disregarded his ruling and it came up again, I would be risking an explosive rebuke from the judge, done in front of the jury, that might prove fatal to our case.

I put the wheel 'hard-over' in my head. Reestablishing eye contact, I continued. "You will, of course, have to consider plaintiffs' explanations. But when the veneer of their carefully chosen words and smooth delivery is stripped away, what you're really being asked to do is ignore the mountain of evidence you've heard about Francis Dowd's care, caution, and experience in boat handling, and in its place they would have you believe Francis Dowd did this."

I went to the clerk's evidence box for the photograph of the waves they put in evidence through Captain McGee, and began slowly walking it down the jury box.

"This is what plaintiffs' counsel would have you believe," I said, pointing to the photograph. "Make no mistake about this, Ladies and Gentlemen, if you're going to accept their position, this is the fantastic story you will have to accept. Plaintiffs would have you believe that Francis Dowd, who learned seamanship and safety in three and a half years at sea, where if you disrespect the power of the ocean lives are lost—instead, they want you to suspend your common sense and believe that Francis Dowd, whose entire life was dedicated to thinking logically, planning carefully, and acting responsibly, would somehow . . . in complete contradiction to the entire flow and direction of his life . . . do this."

I was so livid the photo was shaking in my hand, the words spilling out of me. "They would have you believe he would do something so dangerous, and so patently foolish as taking his boat through water like what's shown in this photograph when every scrap of evidence you've heard in this courtroom states, in fact cries out, that just the opposite is true!"

I needed another drink of water, but when I tried to refill my glass I discovered I'd emptied the jug on my table. The bailiff gave a quick gesture to approach, filling my glass from her flask. I gulped it down, my throat dry and raw. I had to slow down, and critically needed to moderate my tone.

Walking back toward the well, I resumed. "Don't take my word for it that Francis Dowd wasn't negligent."

I paused, pulling each word out, one at a time. "That's right, Ladies and Gentlemen, I do not want you to take my word for it." They stared back, doubt etching their faces.

"The best evidence that he was not negligent doesn't come from me, it comes from their own witness."

I paused again, letting my words settle in their minds before continuing. "Do you recall at the beginning of my cross-examination of their first witness, Captain McGee, I asked if he knew Mr. Dowd, and he responded, 'I've *heard* about him.' He didn't say he knew Mr. Dowd, or that he'd talked with him. When McGee said that, I decided to explore just what it was that he'd *heard* about him. I asked the captain if he'd heard that Mr. Dowd served in the United States Navy for four years? Or been at sea on submarines most of that time? Or that Francis Dowd hired a professional skipper to give him instructions when he first bought the *Aloha*? Or been fishing out on the ocean a hundred or more times and never had any problems?"

I dropped my voice. "Captain McGee testified that he had not been told any of those things."

I had been moving backwards towards plaintiffs' table while speaking, and stopped next to it so the jury would be looking at Baum and Blake as I completed my thought. "It looks like whoever was feeding information to Captain McGee about Francis Dowd wasn't giving him a very complete picture, were they?" I moved my eyes back and forth between the jurors and Baum and Blake for as long as I thought Judge Leahy would permit.

The judge finally shifted in his chair, my cue to return to the well of the court.

"Do you recall I handed him the photograph, requested that he study it carefully, and then asked, 'Captain McGee, taking a boat like the *Aloha* through wave conditions like those shown in this photograph, that wouldn't just be careless or negligent, that would have been the act of a madman, wouldn't it?' I know you remember his response, Ladies and Gentlemen. He said, 'Yes, I suppose it would . . . yes.'"

Shaking my head, I said, "The irony is if you accept this story of theirs, you will be accepting a tale even their own witness rejected." I paused to make eye contact with them again.

"Once Captain McGee got the straight dope about Francis Dowd for the first time right here in court. . . ." I stopped in mid-sentence, walking over to the witness stand, putting my hand on the railing. "He sat here, Ladies and Gentlemen, right in front of you, so you not only heard what he said, you got to study his face as he answered the last question I put to him: 'Captain McGee, based on what you *now* know about Mr. Dowd, this doesn't sound like something he would do, does it?'"

I lowered my voice. "And the captain responded . . . 'No, I don't think he would.' Once Captain McGee had been told the *truth* about Francis Dowd, even their own witness wouldn't believe he would do something so foolish."

My allotted time was coming to an end. It was time for my concluding thoughts.

"Francis Dowd was many things in life: sailor, husband, and father. He was a man whose outstanding achievements, from very humble beginnings, were attained by hard work on his own merits. He was not perfect, but as Captain McGee himself said: Francis Dowd was not a madman."

Ordering myself to cool off didn't seem to be having much effect. I felt I owed them something. "Ladies and Gentlemen, I apologize. I know I'm getting worked up, and it's not making it any easier for you to exercise your responsibility to weigh the evidence, but I just can't put aside how terribly wrong it is to level these dastardly charges against a man who can't come into court to clear his name. Only you can do that."

I stole a glance at the wall clock; it was ten minutes to noon. I'd learned a bitter lesson from Baum about time management by the way he finished his direct examination of Captain McGee right at noon allowing the vivid image of the waves shown in the photograph to imbed in their minds like a branding iron over the entire lunch break. I was determined to manage my remaining time to prevent Baum from beginning his rebuttal argument before twelve o'clock, to once again have his words ringing in their ears over the break. One thing remained to be covered.

"A vital question is bound to come up during your deliberations. You will be asking yourselves: how do we go about reconciling the opinions of the expert witnesses when they looked at the same information and came to such different conclusions? Which sides' experts are correct?" The vigorous nods from the jury panel prompted me to try one last rhetorical question.

"In circumstances like these, it might be a good idea to follow a course of action you probably take in your own lives before making any important decision, such as a surgery. You'd get a second opinion from a reliable, independent, source, wouldn't you?" I took a moment to gauge their reaction.

"In this case, with so much conflicting testimony, thankfully there is a reliable, independent, and unbiased source of information available to you." I walked to the clerk's evidence box.

"Ladies and Gentlemen, I want to read something to you. But before I do, I would ask you to consider something. Something all of you know from your own life experience." I took a moment for eye contact. "When someone goes to considerable effort to conceal something from you, they probably have something to hide, don't they?

"Do you recall I asked Captain Seymour a question and, before he even began his answer, both of them leaped out of their seats with a storm of objections? And what was it that they were objecting to so vehemently? It was the Coast Guard's official investigation report . . . despite the fact that the report was moved into evidence by them, through their own witness, Captain Sheppard. But in their determination to keep this report from you, they took the position that its admission had all been a big mistake even though Captain Sheppard repeatedly testified that the report was one of the things he'd based his opinions on.

"Maybe one of these experienced lawyers might make such a mistake, but do you really believe both of them would?" Shaking my head and pointing to their table, I said, "No, Ladies and Gentlemen. What they were trying to do was hide this from you.

"I'm sure you remember the judge didn't waste much time with their objections. Their motion to withdraw the Coast Guard report was denied, and their objections were overruled."

I held the report up. "This is the Coast Guard's official report, the report they don't want you to see. It is an unbiased, impartial and independent 'second opinion' you can rely on.

"Ladies and Gentlemen, I implore you, in fact I beg you, please read this report for yourselves in the jury room." I began reading from the report, squeezing the words out, one drop at a time. "There is no evidence of actionable . . . misconduct . . . incompetence . . . or negligence. . . ."

I looked at the clock. The minute hand was close to twelve. I could finish without worrying about Baum beginning his rebuttal before the noon break. It was time to sum up.

"No one will ever know for certain what happened that morning, but I know what didn't happen, and I believe you know it too." I picked up the photograph, which they had reacted to so vividly, and walked it down the jury box one last time, pointing to the mass of angry waves filling the Channel.

"Ladies and Gentlemen, *you know Francis Dowd . . . would not . . . do . . . this.*"

It was exactly noon.

Walking back to my table, I saw Marsha getting up to leave. Her eyes held mine softly, giving me an encouraging smile, as she mouthed, 'I have to leave.'

As I dropped into my chair, Janet squeezed my forearm, whispering that she thought the closing had gone in well. For the first time I became aware of my shirt clinging to my chest, soaked with sweat. The judge declared the noon recess, once again admonishing the jury not to discuss the case.

Janet looked at me, waiting for me to speak. I had worked over the lunch break every day, downing sandwiches and coffee, but now there was nothing to prepare. On impulse, I asked if she would like to join me for lunch. She quickly accepted. We walked the few blocks to Teske's Germania, an old style German restaurant bedecked with antlered game heads and Bavarian mountain scenes. Flatulent German band music was coming through the sound system. After ordering, we made a few desultory attempts at conversation and then lapsed into silence. The laughter and conversations from the surrounding tables seemed surreal, a part of life we had not engaged in for the last three weeks.

I began running the trial testimony through my head, finding too many holes in my case. By the time the food arrived, my appetite had slipped away.

My thoughts turned to my closing argument. It was longer than thirty minutes, but there was no overt squirming or fidgeting, the dead giveaways that a jury has lost interest. I had made eye contact with all of the jurors, paying considerable attention to the three or four I felt would be leaders during the deliberations. But just as they had done throughout the trial, the twelve silent Sphinxes in the jury box were very circumspect with their reactions.

It suddenly struck me: I had not argued damages to the jury. This was an invitation for disaster. Every lawyer knows that no matter how strong the relative strength or weakness of your case, it is practically written in stone, you must always give the jury some input on assessing damages. I had forgotten to give them any guidance whatsoever on the amount of damages to give the plaintiffs if they disagreed with my arguments and found Fran Dowd was negligent. Their only direction on that subject would be from Baum. I had damage control to think about.

Telling Judge Leahy I had forgotten to argue damages would hardly be grounds for him to allow me to reopen my closing argument and discuss them now. Any such request would be objected to by Baum and sustained by the judge. I had made my closing argument, and that was that. I could think of only one thing to say to the judge. Waiting until Janet finished her lunch, we walked hurriedly back to the courthouse.

I alerted the clerk that I needed to speak with the judge and counsel in chambers. A few minutes before we would be back in session, the clerk sent us in. The judge looked at me inquiringly.

"Your Honor, I did not discuss the amount the jury should award in damages if they find Mr. Dowd was negligent. Since I did not raise the issue, there is nothing to rebut, and I request an order that counsel refrain from mentioning the subject of damages in his rebuttal."

For an uncomfortably long time the judge stared at me before speaking. "I noticed that you didn't argue damages."

He looked at Baum. "Do you wish to be heard?"

"Yes, Your Honor. I do not intend to mention a specific figure to the jury, but I did plan on summing up my damages argument the same way I did this morning."

The judge said that would be acceptable, and asked if there was anything else. When we said No, he stated he would be back on the bench shortly, and we left chambers.

In a few minutes the jury was summoned. Taking their places quickly, they studiously avoided eye contact with anyone.

The judge took his seat as the clerk was completing her cry to come to order. Baum acknowledged his instruction to proceed, and walked to the lectern.

Like a soloist, Baum waited until the courtroom was completely silent before beginning to speak. "We have been here for three weeks and heard from many witnesses. In all that time, and with all these witnesses, only one piece of evidence stands uncontroverted: as many as twenty boats went out that morning, fished all day, and all of them returned safely . . . except one, the *Aloha*."

He looked at them contemplatively. "Doesn't it seem odd to you that the defense made no attempt to explain how this could have happened without someone hearing a call for help on their two-way radios, seeing distress flares, if either had been replaced . . . or even seeing the *Aloha*?"

Shaking his head, he continued. "Counsel made no mention of these critically important facts, and instead has asked you to believe the unbelievable; a set of unlikely possibilities even their experts didn't believe." His tone communicated that he was almost embarrassed they had to sit through my arguments which he all but said were not only erroneous, but disingenuously made by me as well. I noted a few of the jurors scrutinizing me questioningly.

He summarized our evidence in the same disbelieving tone.

"First, the *Aloha* hit a large log and sank, but under cross-examination their expert admitted this was unlikely in the extreme, virtually never happening. Even if such an unlikely event actually occurred, do you believe the boat would have sunk so quickly that there was no time to send up flares, use the radio, or put on life jackets, if any of those required safety items were onboard? No, Ladies and Gentlemen, even though the dead head theory was more fantasy than reality, something even the defense expert himself doubted was the cause," directing a long finger toward me, ". . . counsel has asked you to accept it as a valid explanation."

"In case you didn't believe the dead head theory, they had another equally implausible explanation to offer: the *Aloha* was somehow run over by the one big ship that just happened to be in the area that morning. If a run down actually occurred, someone on the ship, or the dozens of people on the fifteen other fishing boats, would have seen or heard something and reported it, wouldn't they?"

Shaking his head, "No one came forward, for one simple reason—it didn't happen . . . that's why."

Those two theories had deprived Baum of the Res Ipsa instruction he fought so hard to persuade Judge Leahy to give. He was making me pay for it now with a vengeance in front of the jury, implying I was insulting their intelligence by presuming they were gullible enough to believe the run down and deadhead theories, all but saying that I knew they were spurious. And he waited until his rebuttal argument to do so, when I would have no opportunity to respond.

My credibility was very adroitly being put at issue, subliminally telling the jury . . . if you can't trust the messenger, how can you trust his message?

"Still another explanation was thrown out by the defense in a desperate attempt to get you to believe that something, anything other than operator negligence, was the cause of this tragedy: a big wave supposedly appeared out of nowhere and sank the boat."

He hesitated a moment, pulling the jury in closer. "Ladies and Gentlemen, if a wave, which according to the defense was the size of a three-story building, actually occurred, it would have been an event no one would forget. But despite all of the publicity, and the countless hours spent searching for witnesses these past two and a half years, not one person has come forward saying they saw this huge wave which materialized out of nowhere, and then conveniently vanished as fast as it had appeared."

Baum nimbly finessed the time issue.

"This issue has come up because of the conflicting statements made by the defense about when the *Aloha* sailed." Pointing at me, he continued. "If there is confusion on this point, they created it. If the *Aloha* left the marina at six o'clock, which the defense *now* claims, then there is no plausible explanation why the *Aloha* would not have returned safely, just like Captain McGee and the fifteen to twenty other boats that *did* leave at six."

Looking at them gravely, "Ladies and Gentlemen, you have to decide the case based on the facts, not unsubstantiated theories or mere possibilities."

Stepping forward to position himself more intimately with the jury Baum returned to the subject of damages. "The damages suffered by Mrs. Ang and her children for the loss of a loving husband and father are obvious." He then summarized how they should calculate the income lost by Mr. Ang's death, and the additional amount they should award Mrs. Ang and her five children for the loss of care, comfort and society of Mr. Ang.

Before beginning his final summary he provided a long pause, focusing the jurors' attention. "The only explanation supported by all the *credible* evidence is this: for whatever reason, Mr. Dowd went into Bonita Channel when it was unsafe to do so." I listened with concern. This was the fourth or fifth repetition of his central theme, and statements repeated often enough end up being accepted uncritically. I searched the jury box, but just as they had done throughout the trial, their faces revealed little.

Baum turned to one of the most important jury instructions.

"My clients have the burden of proving that the legal cause of Mr. Ang's death was Francis Dowd's negligence, but this is not a criminal case where the burden of proof must be beyond a reasonable doubt. In this civil matter, the burden of the Ang family is to prove their case only by a preponderance of the evidence. If the scales tip just slightly in favor of my clients," Baum began pantomiming with his hands, ". . . this is sufficient proof to render a verdict in their favor. I believe the evidence has been substantially more than that, but as the judge will tell you, all the law requires in order for you to find for the Angs is a slight preponderance of the evidence in their favor," his tone plainly implying that justice demanded that they do so. He thanked them again on behalf of the Angs, and nodded to the judge.

Like his suits, Baum's rebuttal was custom tailored to counter every point I made in my argument.

The judge read carefully the concluding instructions about the law they were to apply, and then looked at them intently. "Ladies and Gentlemen, you will now retire to the jury room, select a foreman, begin your deliberations and reach a verdict."

His final charge had plainly instilled a sense of duty in them. They filed silently from the courtroom with the same solemnity as a processional of priests and nuns going to vespers, the weight of their responsibilities heavy in their faces.

# 27

The most agonizing part of any trial is waiting for the jury to return with its verdict. The gut churning angst of a client on the stand, undergoing cross-examination, pales in comparison to the mounting anxiety, as the minutes drag into hours, frequently stretching for days, with no word from the jury. The waiting consumes you.

I envied opponents who calmly worked on another file, or chatted with their clients and spectators as the time ticked by. My wont is to run the trial through my mind, critiquing each witness's testimony.

Janet and I sat at the table in silence. She finally turned to me. As good as she was at internalizing her worries, her face gave her away. Even with her strength, I wondered if she could withstand it if the jury held Fran responsible. I felt compelled to abate her concerns, not as a friend trying to console her, but as her lawyer.

"Janet, there is no telling how long the jury will be out. Before reaching a verdict they will most likely send a note out requesting that a piece of testimony be read to them, or have the judge explain one of the jury instructions in greater detail. The notes have to be signed, and we will at least learn who the foreman is." She continued looking at me, expectantly.

Making my voice as positive as I could make it, I continued. "I think our case went in well, and now we have to wait."

She gave me a smile that quickly faded, the despairing face of someone whose entire life had been held captive from the day the lawsuit was filed.

After thirty years of marriage and raising five children, Janet knew how to read a face. During lunch, I noticed her looking at me appraisingly. She must have sensed my feeling that we had about an even chance of prevailing.

I needed some caffeine, and said I was going downstairs for a coffee, asking if I could bring one to her. She shook her head.

Taking my coffee outside, I plodded around the block deep in thought. The wind, more than the cold, made me button my coat and lift my collar around my neck. In our many meetings, Janet never succumbed to the temptation so many widows indulge in of practically deifying their late husbands. The words she said in our first private meeting, that I had reflected on so many times, returned: "My husband was not a perfect man, but he was never careless . . . and never negligent . . . ever." Janet had not been eulogizing him, or verbalizing some sort of comforting memory; she meant every word literally. That statement, or pronouncement, or edict, I was never sure what it was, ultimately led to the decision to try this case. And now, here we were in Department Six waiting for the jury's verdict, a judgment on all of us: Fran, Janet, and me as well.

Jane Ang had lost her husband too, but there was a critical difference between them . . . Jane Ang's husband was not the one accused of being responsible for the loss of five lives, causing three women to be widowed, and leaving eleven children without fathers. How different it would have been if only Fran had died. He was a grown man who had come a long way from Irish Hill, accomplished much in life, and died doing something he loved. But a mother can suffer no greater grief than the death of a child, and if the jury ascribed her son's death to her husband, how could Janet live with such heartbreaking torment.

In the three weeks since the trial began, I had been in constant turmoil about not settling. Janet seemed so convinced that settlement was an unacceptable admission that Fran was responsible for this terrible tragedy. Now, I was questioning the wisdom of my conclusion that only an exonerating verdict would protect her. If the jury came back with a verdict for plaintiffs, the effect was going to be far worse for Janet than a settlement would ever have been.

Arriving back in the courtroom, I looked questioningly at the clerk. She shook her head. I noted the time on the wall clock. It seemed the hands had hardly moved.

Janet was sitting with a group of her friends who came to support her on this most important day of the trial. I noticed her daughter there as well. One of the ladies asked how long the jury would be out. My response, that there was no way of knowing, was not very reassuring. I wasn't feeling assured myself.

I sat down at the table, thinking. I'd kept the Res Ipsa instruction out, but at what cost. To do it I had to push the run down and dead head theories which I knew the jury wouldn't believe. Had I lost their trust? I'd seen a lot of folded arms, a vivid reminder that jurors hear evidence inductively but reach their verdict deductively, two very different processes; the former with the left side, the latter with the right side of their brains.

In a few minutes, the door to the jury room hallway opened. Every head swiveled toward the door. It was the bailiff.

My eyes reflexively flashed to her hands; there was no folded sheet of paper. Walking quickly through the courtroom, she went to the clerk's office returning a few moments later with a cup of coffee, departing back through the door. My thoughts followed her as she returned to her post outside the jury room. I resumed critiquing our closing arguments. We each had our theories, but had either of us proved them? A jury has great discretion in sorting through the testimony, weighing and balancing the evidence. Whether they do so consciously or subconsciously, jurors seem to relax the degree of proof they demand in wrongful death cases.

I recalled how effectively Baum pantomimed 'balancing the scales of justice' with his hands during his argument. I wondered which side of the scale the jurors' interpretations of the evidence were coming down on. The plaintiffs did not need to prove their case by direct evidence; it would be enough for the jury to render their verdict on circumstantial evidence alone, which gave them incredible latitude in determining what happened. I reminded myself that fortunes have been lost, and people sent to the gas chamber entirely on circumstantial evidence.

I looked at the jury box and, one by one, began putting faces into the empty chairs. Should I have kept this one? Had I paid enough attention to that one? Had I framed some part of my argument pertinent to something in the background of the others? When I concluded my critique of the panel, there was only one person I was certain about. It was the lady who responded to one of the questions the judge put to the panel during voir dire, "Is anyone familiar with the incident that is the subject of this lawsuit?" She had commented, "I remember thinking at the time, 'that poor woman . . . to have lost her husband and her son too.'"

Throughout the trial she had been attentive to the testimony but, like the other jurors, she gave little away about her feelings. It was not until Baum said in his closing, "All the defense witnesses lied," that I knew she was for me. She reacted to that remark by lifting her hands from her lap, where they had been resting, and tightly folded her arms across her chest. Baum quickly amended his remark, saying, "Except Mrs. Dowd." This quasi apology seemed to mollify the panel, and I was disappointed to see this lady unfold her arms and place her hands back in her lap; apparently accepting Baum's statement as nothing more than a slip of the tongue. This lasted for a few moments, and she then picked her purse up off the floor planting it firmly in her lap. To my great relief she refolded her arms even more tightly across her chest. Unless I completely misread her body language, the trial was over as far as she was concerned.

My mind returned to the witnesses' testimony. How had the jury reacted to Captain McGee and Captain Phelan? They did not have the polish of some of the other witnesses, but they were believable, and their personalities had taken over the courtroom. I hoped the uproar over Phelan's surprise appearance on the stand had not distracted the jury from his testimony. I felt the jurors believed the testimony of both men about when they arrived at Point Bonita, what they observed in the Channel, and taken different routes to Duxbury.

I hoped the jury members reached the same conclusion I did: that the poison pen game had been run on Captain McGee about Francis Dowd.

It never occurred to me the case would turn on the testimony of Noble and Strange, the two wave experts. Rae Strange was supposed to provide foundational evidence for Captain Seymour, but I ended up basing our case on Strange's testimony. Despite the anxiety I was feeling with the jury out deliberating, I couldn't help but smile at the image of Strange in his shiny polyester suit.

I was still puzzled by his nervousness. He hadn't been on the stand ten minutes before perspiration marks began showing under his armpits, which quickly grew into six inch stains. Mercifully, he had been unaware of them. If he had, Strange would have become even more anxious on the witness stand, if that were possible. I was concerned the jury would interpret his nervousness as uncertainty on his part about the opinions he was giving. But the self-effacing way Strange handled himself proved to be the perfect foil to Blake's aggressive cross-examination. The idea never seemed to dawn on Strange that Blake might have a secondary motive in mind with his questioning.

In football and baseball, it's so clear when points are made, but from the first day the twelve stone faces, who were now deliberating Janet's fate, gave little indication about what evidence they found convincing. Even more vexing, it seemed that points made by a witness one day would be undermined by another the following day. It is the nature of trials that the strategies and plans which seem so brilliant back in the office fall short in the heat of battle in the courtroom. In this trial, the ebb and flow of which side was ahead seemed to change every day, almost witness by witness. If the truth was easy to find, and justice was done in every trial, the number of lawyers could be halved.

I looked at the clock. The jury had been out more than an hour. This was a major disappointment. When a verdict is reached in an hour or less, it is almost always for the defense. After an hour, the decision can go either way. The panel had been out long enough to have made their decision on liability and be discussing damages. The calculation of monetary damages would involve nothing more than multiplying the thirteen years Mr. Ang intended to keep working, times the amount he would have earned under the new contract. In calculating the loss of care, comfort and society in a wrongful death case, it is common for jurors to double the amount of lost income. If the jury came back with a verdict between three and four million dollars, it would not be a surprise. Every minute they spent deliberating beyond one hour increased the chances that they would. This was going to be either my first, or maybe my last big trial.

The anxiety was eating me up. I went downstairs for another coffee and a walk around the block before returning to Department Six.

I had barely sat down before the door to the jury room hallway opened again. Every conversation in the courtroom ceased in mid-sentence. The bailiff emerged, walking directly to the clerk and leaned over to whisper. I strained to hear any scrap of conversation, but they were practiced in keeping their voices inaudible. I looked at her hands. There was no slip of paper. The clerk walked toward chambers, knocked and went inside, closing the door behind her. The bailiff stared at the closed door, refusing eye contact with anyone. The clerk came out shortly, asking that all parties and counsel return to the courtroom. It was close to four o'clock.

Did the jury have a question? Was it a verdict?

Baum and the Angs returned quickly. I looked at Janet and nodded; she managed a hopeful look.

In a few minutes, the jurors filed in taking their seats, staring steadfastly straight ahead. The clerk knocked on the door to chambers, and returned to her desk. The door opened and Judge Leahy walked quickly to the bench as the clerk intoned, "Department Six of the Superior Court of California, the Honorable David Leahy, judge presiding, is in session. Remain seated and come to order."

Solemnly, the judge turned toward the jury.

"Ladies and Gentlemen, have you reached a verdict?"

"We have, Your Honor."

A man had spoken, but I couldn't tell who. After a moment the speaker stood. My heart sank; it was one of the engineers. My mind flashed to past experiences with technically trained people on juries, and the very precise manner they applied the jury instructions, particularly instructions involving inferences to be drawn from circumstantial evidence. I had pegged this man as a leader, but not likely to be the foreman. How wrong I was!

He held up the verdict form which had been folded in half, the written part carefully turned inside. The bailiff retrieved the form and walked it over to the clerk who, in turn, handed it up to the judge. He studied the form carefully, assuring himself it had been filled out correctly, and signed and dated by the foreman.

This ordinarily takes a few moments, but Judge Leahy was examining the form an inordinately long time. No hint of what might be troubling him manifested itself on his face. Finally, he handed the form back to the clerk. We were at the moment of truth.

"The clerk will now read the verdict."

She drew herself up, her voice easily carrying to the back of the courtroom, "In the Superior Court of the State of California, in and for the County of Santa Clara, in the matter of Ong Le Chin Ang, et al., versus Janet B. Dowd, et al. We the jury in the above entitled action," she paused, clearing her throat, ". . . find for the Defendant and against the Plaintiffs, and that Plaintiffs take nothing by their action."

Behind me muffled gasps came from the spectator section. My heart was pounding. I had not been breathing while the clerk was reading, and I let my breath out slowly, wonderfully. From the corner of my eye, I noticed Baum. His jaw went slack; a pallid expression of shock running over his face. Then in a kaleidoscope click, his look of shock changed to one of bile driven anger.

The clerk was addressing the jury,

"Ladies and Gentlemen of the jury, is this your verdict as just read?"

There was a muted response of "Yes," and a few "It is."

Janet turned toward me, about to speak. I put my hand up, shaking my head sharply. She froze.

Something important might happen next that could send them back to the jury room for further deliberations. The judge was already speaking in an inquiring tone.

"Do you wish to poll the jury?"

The legal term, 'poll the jury,' meant that the clerk would call the jurors' names, one by one, asking them to state 'yes' or 'no' if the verdict that had just been read was correct. Nine of the twelve jurors would have to respond 'yes' to confirm the verdict.

Polling the jury can turn into a nightmare for the party who apparently won if the vote in the jury room was close, and one of the jurors has a change of heart, stating something different in the courtroom during the poll from the way they voted in the jury room. This can happen if that person's vote was the last one necessary to obtain a verdict, and they had been pressured into voting in a way they didn't want. Then, when they are in the courtroom with the judge present to prevent them from being pushed around, they change their vote.

The winning party never asks for the jury to be polled; to do so would risk having the result changed. I was on my feet instantly, emphatically stating, "No."

The judge had not directed his question to me. Ignoring my response, he focused his attention on Baum.

His face still flushed, Baum immediately said, "Yes."

The judge nodded to the clerk to begin the poll. She picked up her list. Beginning with juror number one, called his name, asking, "Is this your verdict?"

His answer was a blunt "No."

We were off to a bad start—a "No" vote from the very first juror polled. If the vote was nine to three in favor of the verdict, it would take only one person changing their vote from 'yes' to 'no,' and they would be sent back to the jury room. I watched their faces, straining to see signs of potential vote switchers.

The clerk moved to juror number two, the foreman. He responded, "Yes." The clerk continued down the back row, each person responding, "Yes." As I expected, the lady who was my one sure vote responded, "Yes."

The clerk was now polling the front row. I kept track of their responses on my list as she moved along.

Juror number ten responded, "No." This was the second 'no' vote. There were two more to go. Juror number eleven was a "Yes," quickly followed by number twelve, another "Yes."

The clerk turned to the judge, "The vote of the jury is ten in favor of the verdict, Your Honor, and two opposed."

The verdict was confirmed. During the polling, my breathing had been sporadic. I felt lightheaded, and drew in a lung full of air to restore my system.

The judge turned to the jury. "Ladies and Gentlemen, your service as jurors in this matter is now concluded. You are free to leave at this time."

He cleared his throat, and continued. "I also release you from the admonition not to discuss the case. You may do so now with anyone, if you desire. The lawyers may want to speak with you about the case which will assist them in representing their clients, but this is entirely up to you. You are under no obligation to speak to the lawyers, or anyone else, if you choose not to do so."

His tone became more reflective, commenting, "It is the service of citizens such as you that makes the justice system work. I wish to thank each of you for your service in this trial. It has been a pleasure to have you serve as jurors in this case."

He then spoke in a heartfelt tone he had not previously used. "I hope your service has been a positive experience, giving you a sense of confidence in the legal system. I'll be in chambers with my door open, and be happy to answer any questions you may have. I will welcome your suggestions on how I might improve the performance of my duties."

Not many judges do this, and the jury seemed pleased he was willing to have his performance critiqued.

He finished, "Merry Christmas and a very Happy Holiday Season to you all."

This was the cue to the clerk, who quickly stated, "We are now in adjournment."

The courtroom stood as Judge Leahy left the bench for the last time, his robe flowing in and out as he strode toward chambers.

The moment he was in chambers, the courtroom burst into an excited cacophony of voices and activity.

Into the mayhem, the bailiff was trying to make herself heard, reminding the jurors to take all of their personal belongings with them, and report one last time to the jury assembly room. While she was speaking, waves of emotion rolled over me, incredibly relieved that the jury rejected the allegations that Francis Dowd negligently caused the loss of five lives, and instead concluded the untimely deaths to have been a freakish anomaly of nature.

Janet and I stood as the judge left the bench, and were facing each other. While the verdict was being read, she sat bolt upright, probably terrified, waiting for the result. Only when the clerk said—"We find for the defendant . . ."—did the grip she had imposed on herself from the beginning start to unwind.

I struggled to find some words, but nothing would come . . . there was no need. We simultaneously closed the distance, and for the first time embraced. She gave me an unexpectedly strong hug which I returned. Lifting her head, she whispered in an almost childlike voice, "Thank you . . . thank you so very much, you don't know how important this is to me," tightening her embrace. She was shaking so much I thought she might fall.

There was too much activity whirling around her just now for Janet to think, but recognition would come, and soon, that her life which had been held in captivity from the day the lawsuit was filed, could now get back on track. In a moment, she was surrounded by her friends.

I felt a tug at my arm; it was Tracy, Janet's daughter. She wrapped her arms around me stammering, "Thank you. You don't know what this means to Mother. Bless you." She was trembling.

She pulled back giving me one of her mother's tiny, warm smiles. Like her mother's, Tracy's eyes were shimmering too. Tracy was young, not quite a woman yet, but she was a Dowd, and there were to be no tears in a public place. She turned away quickly.

My glance went to the file of jurors preparing to leave. I wanted to thank each of them for their verdict and learn what evidence and arguments were important to them, and their reactions to my role in the trial.

The foreman came right up, offering his hand. "I thought you did a good job. We thought all of you did a good job."

I thanked the foreman, and the two or three others who gathered around him, and asked, "What evidence convinced you the most?"

The foreman said, "We agreed fairly quickly that a run down or a dead head were not the causes." He added, "There was an equally quick consensus that plaintiffs' theories about the *Aloha* leaving late, or not having the proper safety gear, weren't viable either. The real deliberations centered on your big wave theory and plaintiffs' theory that Mr. Dowd headed into Bonita Channel when it wasn't safe."

Before continuing, the foreman reflected for a moment. "The feeling in the jury room was about equally divided on those two points, and there was a wide difference of opinion about which theory was correct. The points people brought up were thoroughly discussed, particularly as we tried to make sense of the experts' testimony. In the end, there was a general consensus that we would never know for sure what happened."

The man standing next to the foreman added, "That's when we began doing what the judge told us to do, weighing and balancing what most likely occurred."

The foreman said, "About the only thing we could all agree on was like you said, 'nobody knows what really happened.'" One of the other men added, "But, in the end we didn't believe Mr. Dowd would take his boat into waters that looked like that photograph, particularly with his son onboard." They shook my hand and moved toward the door.

Some of the women who had been speaking with Janet came up. I inquired, "Ladies, can you tell me what convinced you." As a group they replied, "The testimony of the two wave experts was the most important evidence."

I asked, "Which expert did you find most convincing?"

One of them spoke up. "Since the other fellow used Mr. Strange's data, he agreed with him." There was an immediate chorus of agreement that

Noble's use of Strange's summary of the buoy data somehow meant he agreed with Strange's interpretations.

I was dumbfounded. The fact that Noble had used Strange's data hardly meant he agreed with his opinions, particularly since they had come to such completely different conclusions in their testimony. It was like concluding that if someone read the morning paper, it meant he agreed with the opinions expressed on the editorial page.

I tried to move the conversation to another area, but the ladies were not finished.

"Oh, that nice Mr. Strange," one of them cooed, ". . . the poor thing, he was so nervous. I felt so sorry for him." A chorus of empathy flowed from the others, practically doting on him as if he were a favorite nephew. If Strange were still there, they would have taken him out for a nice cup of hot tea.

The ladies began conversing among themselves, and I excused myself.

Juror number one, who had been the first 'No' vote, had been speaking with Baum and Blake. When he broke free, I asked for his thoughts. He did not want to talk, brusquely saying, "You just don't have a boat go out and disappear, and not have something happen. You know something happened out there, and I don't believe it was some sort of big wave that nobody else saw."

He wouldn't wait for another question and moved away quickly. I spied the young woman who had also voted 'No.' She was about to leave and I approached her. She was impatient to get away, and I quickly asked, "Would you tell me the one thing that you found to be the most convincing?"

Without hesitating, she responded. "Something happened out there. Accidents don't happen without someone causing them. I'm not sure what happened, but something did," and would not be drawn out further. I nodded a thank you as she left.

I caught a glimpse of Baum speaking with Mrs. Ang. It didn't appear she comprehended what happened, and Baum was trying to explain. Dwight Ang was standing next to his mother, his face contorted in disbelief; it was clear that he understood.

At the end of every case, a ritual is followed among trial lawyers. After the verdict is read, losing counsel comes over and shakes the winner's hand. No matter how acrimonious the trial has been, or the dislike the clients have for each other, the ritual had always taken place in every case I'd tried. Losing counsel mumbles congratulations to the winner on his victory, and the winner salutes his opponent's efforts in a hard fought contest. There had been a few times I had to force myself to shake hands, and exchange a few obligatory comments, and I was prepared to do it again now.

Baum began escorting the Angs out of the courtroom. He walked right past me without a look my way, his face still flushed with anger. I was prepared to shake hands and say something complimentary, but he passed by without even acknowledging my presence. Bitter defeat that it must have been for him, I was surprised he chose to disregard the ritual.

I turned to the jurors waiting to speak with me. Before I could, Janet broke from her group of friends and asked whether it would be all right to speak with the judge whose door was still open. I said it would be fine and she headed for chambers. I resumed speaking with the remaining jurors.

They were kind with their congratulations, and while they did not echo the same sentiments as the group of ladies about Strange, they said he was the most convincing expert witness.

Janet came out of chambers looking distressed, and wanted to speak with me. I asked if it could wait a few minutes, explaining it was important that I speak to all of the jurors before they left. She seemed anxious to leave, and I asked if I could drop by her house on my way home. She readily agreed, and I returned to the final group of jurors. They had lots of questions and were willing to discuss the witnesses and the parts of the testimony they found convincing in greater depth.

While I was conversing with this group, I stood at the end of my table to avoid making the ritual any more difficult than necessary for Blake. I presumed the task of exchanging a few words had been relegated to him by Baum. But when Blake finished loading the cart, he, like Baum, passed within a few feet. A quick look at his contorted face told me there would be no ritual observance from him either as he moved stiffly toward the door.

After finishing speaking with the last group of jurors, I noticed the door to chambers was still open. The judge was seated behind his desk reading some papers in his shirt sleeves, his robe hanging from the coat rack in the corner. I knocked. He shifted his weight in the chair and looked up.

I asked if I might have a word with him. He nodded. "I want to thank you, Your Honor. It was a pleasure to appear before you."

He said, "Thank you," and we said good night.

Back in the courtroom, I said goodbye to the clerk, the court reporter and the bailiff, thanking them for their many courtesies throughout the trial.

After loading everything on the cart I headed for the door, the last person there. The door to chambers was closed, the judge and the courtroom staff gone for the day. I stood the cart upright and looked back over the room. It did not seem so austere as it had the first day; the last bit of daylight coming through the small windows was almost gone. In the silence, I could hear the faint sound of the bell being rung by the Salvation Army Santa Claus on the street below.

I gave one last look around the cave-like courtroom which had been our battleground for the past three weeks. As I stood there I sensed Francis Dowd's presence, a sensation I experienced more than once during the trial, and wondered if I had vindicated myself with him. The thought reminded me Janet wanted to see me, and I hurried to my car.

I pulled off the freeway at her exit, and in a few minutes was at her door. A few of her friends were there. I was offered coffee brought by her daughter, and received another round of congratulations from her assembled friends. Janet said she had something to ask me.

Speaking to her in the presence of the others risked breaking the attorney client privilege, and I was reluctant to say anything. Her friends must have picked up on my hesitation and promptly excused themselves. After another round of hugs for Janet, they said their goodbyes and were off. Even her daughter, who had never been shy about staying within earshot, absented herself to another part of the house.

When we were alone, Janet refreshed my coffee and poured a cup for herself. She looked at me appraisingly. I was puzzled, but devoted myself to the coffee, waiting.

She put her cup aside, "Jay, the judge said something very unusual to me just now." I sipped my coffee uneasily. "I told him I thought he had been fair with everyone and wanted him to know that, and thanked him." There was another pause as she considered her next words.

"He then said something very confusing. I don't understand what he meant, and it has upset me." She paused again. "Just as I turned to leave the judge said, 'This case should never have been tried.' I don't know what he meant by that. I didn't ask. He didn't say anything else, and I left." She looked at me inquiringly.

The lack of sleep, and the anxiety I'd carried from the first day of trial crashed down on me. I was dead tired, but Janet was plainly upset and deserved a meaningful response. It took a long moment to think through what I wanted to say, and how to say it.

"Janet, during our first meeting in my office, I explained to you the company would not pay the Angs' claim unless there was some indication that Fran was negligent, and you said: 'My husband was not a perfect man,' and you let that thought sink in for a moment before you continued, '. . . but he was never careless . . . and never negligent . . . ever.'"

She said nothing, staring at me steadily. "Those words were very significant to me." I paused, forcing my mind to continue the train of thought. "You said something else very important. When I explained that a settlement *was not* an admission of liability, and the release would say so, your reaction seemed to me that a settlement *would* be an admission that he was in the wrong, and be a betrayal of Fran." She remained silent.

"You said those things in our first private meeting two years ago. I can't tell you how many times I've thought about those statements since then. Over time, they became the basis for my decision to try this case, to prove that Fran was 'not careless . . . and not negligent.'"

"What Judge Leahy said to you in chambers, 'this case should never have been tried,' is correct."

The transformation in her face was astonishing; her eyebrows shot up like window shades. I explained. "An important duty of every trial court judge is to get cases settled. Judge Leahy has been on the bench a long time, and is fully aware that ninety-five percent of all cases filed are settled out of court."

She remained silent. I continued. "If it hadn't been for your determination, which I drew from our many meetings, that you wanted to clear Fran's name, this case would have been one of the ninety-five percent that settle. Your resolve didn't seem to waver even after I explained that you did not have a lot of insurance coverage for a wrongful death case, and if there was an excess verdict there was a chance, albeit a small one, that the Estate would have to pay it, putting you at financial risk. Despite the potential personal exposure, and the fear most clients have about going to court, you never seemed to waver. And over time, I decided if you were apparently willing to accept the risks of going to trial to have Fran's name cleared, I would try the case."

After a long, yet somehow comfortable silence, she nodded, thanking me for explaining, and walked me to the car. The night air was chilly, and Janet was not wearing a jacket, but she made no move to say goodbye. Her eyes were swimming again as she composed her thoughts. She obviously had something to say. I waited.

After a considerable silence, she spoke. "Jay, I want to thank you for all your work, and how kind you have been to me." She paused a moment. "I've felt all along you have taken a personal interest in the case and me, and I will never be able to thank you enough." She stepped forward and embraced me.

It was the nicest compliment I'd ever received from a client. Overwhelmed, all I could manage in response was, "Janet, it has been an honor to represent you. I can't tell you how pleased I am with the result."

While driving on the freeway to San Francisco and home, the thought came to me of a brief exchange with Janet months earlier. I had mentioned to her, "I wish I'd met Fran; I think I would have liked him." She replied, "I think he would have liked you too." How many times I felt his presence viscerally, looking over my shoulder, observing my work, critiquing my plans. I wondered what he would say to Janet when they talked tonight about the verdict before she fell asleep.

As I came up the steps, Marsha was waiting, her face anxious. At the top of the staircase, I said, "We won!"

Marsha gave me a long hug. She was trembling too.

"You look so tired," she said. "Let's sit down for supper."

Afterwards, I built a fire in the living room, and we sat together on the sofa while I related the jurors' comments. Finally talked out, we went to bed. Marsha pulled me into her arms and I was soon asleep.

Well after midnight, I awoke abruptly with the thought that I needed to make a note on my yellow pad for the next day. Recognition came quickly ... there was no next day. I lay back down. The bedroom was dimly lit by lights from the Bay Bridge and the downtown skyline. My thoughts turned to what awakened me: Janet. I sensed she was awake as well, and probably had been most of the night, talking with Fran. I imagined their conversation, feeling as if I had been invited to listen.

He was saying, "I'm so proud of you. You didn't have to do this, you know."

She replied, "I didn't have much choice."

Not fully understanding, he responded, "What do you mean?"

Smiling softly, she answered him, "I love you, that's why."

The fact that it was a defense verdict would give Janet no sense of elation. For her the jury's verdict was nothing more than an affirmation of what she had known all along: "He was not a perfect man, but he was never careless ... and never negligent ... ever." There was no feeling of elation on my part either. I felt a sense of unburdening. A case that might very well have been lost, I had won for my clients, both of them: Janet and Francis Dowd.

I drifted back to sleep, content that Janet would at long last be at peace, comforted by memories of their lives together, able to look forward to whatever life would bring ... secure in the knowledge that no cloud hung over his good name.

There was no need to worry about Janet anymore. She wasn't alone. Fran hadn't gone anywhere, he was where he'd always been ... in her heart.

# Epilogue

A month after the case was over, the results of the trial were published in *Jury Verdicts Weekly*. A full page was devoted to the case. The very favorable write-up would ordinarily have been very heady stuff to read. It was not.

By then enough time had passed to reflect on the significant gap between my pre-trial strategy and what actually happened in the courtroom. The cold reality was . . . the pieces of evidence that turned the case in our favor had come in more through chance than any planning on my part.

The list was long:

There was the photograph of the waves in Bonita Channel that I tried so hard to keep from being admitted into evidence, and how it turned out to be my most effective weapon in closing argument.

There was also Captain McGee's totally unanticipated testimony that he had *heard* about Dowd. That remark led to his response that only a madman would go through the wave conditions shown in the photo, and his answer to my final question . . . that he didn't think Dowd would have done something so foolish. The jurors told me afterwards that McGee's responses to those two questions were some of the most powerful testimony in the trial.

There was the additional good luck about the Coast Guard report being put into evidence by them. The report salvaged Captain Seymour's testimony as he used it like a club, quoting from it repeatedly during cross-examination to substantiate his opinions. The jury said they used the report just as I hoped they would, as a reliable second opinion.

And finally, Rae Strange. His testimony became the turning point in the trial. In the midst of examining him on an entirely different topic, he mentioned wave refraction. The instant he did, the realization came how I had misinterpreted the evidence. Dowd had not been over by the buoy line, similar to the incident mentioned in the "Graveyard" article where three men had been washed overboard a year earlier. What caused the *Aloha* to go down were two 'in phase' waves refracting around the Bar, and then coinciding in Bonita Channel. Tragically, the *Aloha* happened to be there when those two waves met. In that terrifying moment, tons of green water capsized the boat, instantly sending her to the bottom.

Strange was the most nervous, ill at ease, witness I had ever put on the stand, but he came across stunningly as I peppered him with question after question we had not prepared. Asking unrehearsed questions is ordinarily a recipe for disaster, but Strange metamorphosed into an enormously effective witness during my direct examination. During cross-examination, Strange was even more effective, taking Blake's aggressive questioning and turning it around, almost becoming the kindly professor patiently explaining to an erring student the mistakes in his questions.

The Dowd case became the turning point in my career. The victory ostensibly stated I had successfully defended a million dollar case, gaining entry into the upper echelon of the trial bar. Winning an important case always draws accolades, particularly trials which have the potential to become a precedent if they are lost, but winning against someone in the inner circle like Baum made this case different, a real accomplishment. As much as I wanted to bask in the praise of my colleagues, I knew I had not yet achieved that status. Too much luck and serendipity had been involved in the victory. In the next few years I redoubled my efforts, trying every case I could, obtaining the skills and abilities the victory in the Dowd case implied I already possessed.

About a year after the trial, I saw Baum again. I was standing in a check-in line at the airport and noticed him a short distance away. I recognized him instantly, dressed as always in one of his handsomely tailored suits. He was watching me. We were too far apart to speak. He continued looking my way, and after a moment an unspoken 'you beat me' look crossed his face. I nodded in response.

I had no disagreement with him personally. By then I had drawn what I felt was the correct conclusion that using Blake to communicate with me, instead of speaking directly to me throughout the trial, was a clever tactic on his part. I had reacted just as Baum probably anticipated I would, becoming upset at not being treated as an equal. It crossed my mind to speak to him. The line moved forward, and I pushed my bag ahead. I looked back to where he had been standing. He was gone.

For Janet, the jurors' verdict removed the cloud that hung over Fran's name. Just as she had overcome the adversity of polio earlier in life, she did not allow the loss of her husband and son to overwhelm her. She devoted her life to her family and the community at large. A woman of faith, she taught Sunday school at her church and served in the local hospital's Chaplaincy.

Janet never remarried. Fran was the one and only love of her life. Her grace and strength of character carried her through to the end. She died in 2012 surrounded by family, friends, and ten grandchildren who were her special joy.

After coming to know Janet and defending her in this trial, the words love, honor, loyalty and courage came to have new meaning. For Janet, nothing was more sacred than honor or more faithful than love. It was a privilege to know her.

# Acknowledgments

This book would not have been possible without the insights and assistance of many people.

Captain David J. Seymour. Master Mariner and Navigation Expert. Salt water was in his veins.

Rae Strange. Expert Oceanographer and Climatologist extraordinaire with a gift for translating complex scientific evidence into language the jury could understand.

Captain James Phelan. His coolness under fire on the witness stand was superb.

Francis Michael Dowd. Although we never met, his life was an inspiration to me.

Janet Dowd. A woman of great character who put honor above everything else.

My father, Wyatt Jacobs. The best lawyer I've ever known. He taught me so much. Fathers are good teachers, although not always easy ones.

I am very grateful for the love, understanding and infinite patience of my wife Marsha. She was the faithful reader and grammarian throughout the manuscript's many drafts.

J.W.J.
August 2014

Visit us at *www.quidprobooks.com.*

9/5-3
12/15-4
10/23-4

∅ PLC

**OYSTER BAY-E NORWICH PUB LIBY**
**89 EAST MAIN ST**
**OYSTER BAY, NY 11771**
**(516) 922-1212**

only 1 Nam

**BAKER & TAYLOR**

AUG 2 5 2015

Made in the USA
San Bernardino, CA
17 August 2015